SIKH SOLDIER

VOLUME ONE

Battle Honours

Shaheed Baba Deep Singh Ji (1684-1757).

NARINDAR SINGH DHESI

With the assistance of:
GRAHAM WATKINS B.Sc. (Hons)

Published by

The Naval & Military Press Ltd
Unit 10 Ridgewood Industrial Park,
Uckfield, East Sussex,
TN22 5QE England

Tel: +44 (0) 1825 749494
Fax: +44 (0) 1825 765701

www.naval-military-press.com
www.military-genealogy.com
www.militarymaproom.com

ACKNOWLEDGEMENTS

The sources of the research have included the British Library, the National Army Museum and the Ministry of Defence Library, London. Books I found particularly useful were:

- *Battle Honours of The Indian Army* by Major Sarbans Singh
- *The Battle Honours of the British and Indian Armies* by Colonel H. C. B. Cook

My warmest thanks to darling daughter Surindar for her encouragement and bearing the brunt of daddy's "Sikh Attacks".

In closing, this book would not have seen the light of the day without the contributions of the long-suffering Hon. Prof. Graham Watkins, who helped not only to edit and proof-read most of the manuscript but also made it ready for publication.

FOREWORD

Battle honours are a military tradition. They are an official acknowledgement to military units for their achievements in specific wars or operations of a military campaign. They are usually presented in the form of a name of a country, a region or a city where the regiment's distinguished act took place, together with the year when it occurred. Originally, a regiment's colours (standards) were practical tools for rallying troops in the battlefield. Since 1784 regiments have been authorized to bear battle honours on their colours for displaying the unit's past distinctions and thus represent the regiment's history and commemorate its dead. Presented by the head of state, they are treated with great reverence. Battle honours can normally be found engraved, painted or embroidered on the Regimental Colours (for infantry units) or the Regimental Guidon (for cavalry regiments).

As a result of the Partition in 1947, the Indian Army was split between India and Pakistan. The bulk of the regiments in which the Sikh soldier had served went to Pakistan. This book records all the Battle Honours earned by the Sikh soldier in the regiments of pre-partition India, including the ones that have been declared 'repugnant' to the modern Indian sentiment.

Special mention is made of the Sikh Princely States forces. All the Sikh Princely States acceded to the union of India in 1948. The bulk of the State Forces were absorbed into the Indian Army, thus losing their distinct Sikh identity.

In the early days of British colonial warfare, Sikhs were especially asked for and recruited in the colonial forces. They took part in many minor and major expeditions, sometimes involving heavy fighting and always involving considerable hardship, for which medals but no battle honours were awarded.

The chapters on Chronology give a brief account of each campaign-battle and the units awarded the battle honours.

In this remarkable book, Narindar Singh Dhesi pays tribute to the courage and self-sacrifice of the gallant Sikh soldiers who, over the ages, earned the multitude of worldwide battle honours documented within its pages.

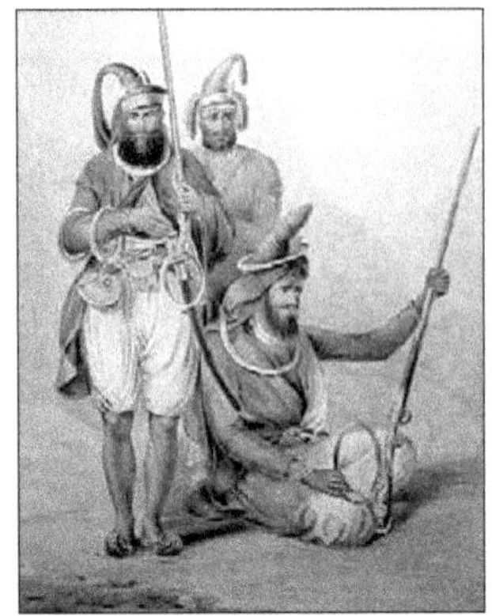

Akali Warriors

DEDICATION

This book is dedicated to the Sikh soldier for his unflinching courage on the field of battle, with his battle cry:

Jo Bole So Nihal, Sat Sri Akal.

Order of the Khalsa

'Guru Gobind appeared in the world as the tenth incarnation.

He recited the name of the Creator who is unseen, eternal and stainless.

He established the Khalsa, a sect of his own, and gave it great glory.

Wearing long hair he grasped the sword and smothered his enemies.

He put the breaches of self-restraint and practiced arms.

He established the Sikh war cry and was victorious in mighty battles.

Thus arose the race of Singhs who wore blue clothes.

Gobind Singh! You were both Guru and disciple!'

(Max Arthur Macauliffe: *The Sikh Religion*)

Guru Gobind Singh set out to:

'... Teach the sparrow how to hunt the hawk and one man to have the courage to fight a legion.'

(Sardar Khushwant Singh: *History of the Sikhs*)

CONTENTS

Nihangs in battle.

INTRODUCTION

Fear is an animal unknown to the Sikh. The valiant Sikh warrior lives in the pages of history, written by him with his own blood. His portrait of courage bears the mark of the blood of his ancestors. A proud heritage pulsates in his blood, and this formidable warrior has added to the glorious traditions of supreme heroism and matchless bravery by his outstanding performance in all the opportunities that have come his way. The historians have paid glowing tribute to this intrepid warrior and torch bearer of liberty, whose religion is universal brotherhood, whose faith is toleration of all other beliefs, whose longing is to fight tyranny and oppression and preserve dignity, honour and freedom of man. The inspiring and elevating history of his battles and campaigns pertain to the bloodstained Mughal period, the tyrannical Afghan period, the feat of arms and the glorious period of the Sikh Empire, the revolutionary British period and the post-Independence National Solidarity period.

This book is a celebration of his unparalleled and matchless courage in virtually every field of battle from the jungles and mountains of Africa, from the deserts of Middle East and Mesopotamia to the steaming jungles of Burma and cold tundra of China. He now stands tall as a Sentinel for his Motherland.

If this book inspires someone to take up an exhaustive study and record the martial history of the Sikh soldier, I shall consider the effort well rewarded.

Old Regimental Colours of the Ludhiana Sikh Regiment showing Battle Honours For China 60-62, Ahmad Khel, Kandahar 80, and Afghanistan 1878-80.

NISHAN SAHIB

The origin of the Nishan Sahib is traced to the time of Guru Hargobind Singh the tenth Master, who hoisted it over the Akal Takhat at Amritsar in 1606.Nishan Sahib in the Sikh tradition means the holy flag or exalted ensign - a symbol representing the values of the Sikh faith, as it is, indeed, the symbol of the freedom of the Khalsa. The Sikhs ask in their prayers everyday to forever keep the Nishan Sahib fluttering high; representing their sovereignty, and the principles of fighting against injustice.

THE KHANDA

The Khanda is one of most important symbols of Sikhism and is emphasized by the fact that all the Sikh flags have the Khanda on them. It is a collection of four weapons commonly used by Sikhs at the time of Guru Gobind Singh.

The weapons are a double-edged sword, called a Khanda, which sits in the middle. A Chakkar is a circular weapon that surrounds the Khanda and indicates that God and eternal life is without end and is perfect. Two single-edged swords, or Kirpans, are crossed at the bottom and sit on either side of the Khanda and Chakkar. They represent the dual nature and duties of the Gurus, Miri and Piri.

The weapons have symbolic meanings. The Khanda symbolises knowledge of God, the Chakkar symbolizes the oneness of God, Miri means political sovereignty and Piri means spiritual sovereignty.

ANTECEDENTS

The Sikh homeland, the Punjab, is a very fertile region in northwest India; the words *panj* (five) and *āb* (water) meaning the land of the five waters. The rivers are the Jhelum, the Chenab, the Ravi, the Beas and the Satluj. In 1947, the Punjab was partitioned between British India's successor states, India and Pakistan. The Pakistani Punjab now comprises the majority of the region. The Indian Punjab has been further sub-divided into the modern states of Punjab, Haryana and Himachal Pradesh. Historically the Punjab embraced the entire plain between the rivers Jamuna and Indus. Beyond the Indus are the Sulaiman and Hindukush Mountains bordering on Afghanistan, which run parallel to the Indus and are generally known as the North West Frontier of India.

Over the centuries many invading armies had poured in great cascades through the mountain passes of the North West Frontier to raid, conquer and rule the fertile plains of the Punjab. As a result the Punjabi people were a mixture of Persians, Greeks, Scythians, and the formidable warriors from central Asia – the Bactrians, the Kushans, and the Huns. They had settled, married local women and were absorbed into the local communities.

Prophet Mohammad (c570-632) established the religion of Islam in the desert wastes of Arabia. His followers, at the point of a sword, furiously and with great enthusiasm carried the Islamic banner to Syria, Egypt, Iran, Sudan, North Africa and southern Spain. In 712 AD, one of his followers, Mohammad Bin Qasim, stormed through the Bolan Pass to Baluchistan, overran Sindh and captured Multan in the Punjab. The Muslims went on to conquer Delhi and establish the Delhi Sultanate, which included the Punjab, and was maintained by different Turco-Afghan clans. This was essentially an armed occupation, sustained by a constant influx of Muslims from across the mountains and Central Asia. At all times during the establishment and consolidation of Muslim rule, there was conflict, chaos, and political upheaval throughout the Punjab.

In 1525, Babbar the Chaghatai Turk, the Mongol descendent of Genghis Khan and Tamerlane, invaded the Punjab. He plundered Lahore and defeated the Sultan's army with great slaughter. As he advanced on Delhi, Sultan Ibrahim Lodhi offered him battle at Panipat. With his seasoned soldiers and strong artillery, Babbar defeated and killed Ibrahim Lodhi and went on to lay the foundation of the Mughal Empire.

At the time the Mughals established their rule, the people of the Punjab were sharply divided into separate religious societies. One, the Muslim, was an occupational army constantly sustained by fresh influx of Turkic and Afghan tribes, which practiced fanaticism and intolerance. The other, the Hindu, was rooted in idol worship, meaningless rituals and the degradation of caste.

Meantime a remarkable people had emerged in the Punjab. They believed in the faith of Guru Nanak (Guru means a spiritual teacher and a guide). The chief doctrines preached by Guru Nanak were 'The Unity of God, Brotherhood of Man, Rejection of Caste and the futility of Idol Worship'. His followers became known as Sikhs.

Antecedents (cont.)

The word Sikh means a disciple and comes from the word shishya, which translates as a seeker of truth. The succeeding gurus nurtured Nanak's mission with great organising ability, energy and devotion. They moulded the Sikhs into a distinct community with their own language, literature, religious beliefs and institutions, culminating in the Order of the Khalsa.

As the people flocked to the new faith in large numbers, it threatened the established religion of the Mughal state, Islam. The Mughal Emperor Jahangir wrote in the *Tuzuk-i-Jahangiri*, which translates as 'Memoirs of Jahangir':

"In Goindwal, which is on the River Biyãh (Beas), there was a Hindu named Arjan, in the garments of sainthood and sanctity, so much so that he had captured many of the simple-hearted of the Hindus, and even of the ignorant and foolish followers of Islam, by his ways and manners, and they had loudly sounded the drum of his holiness. They called him Guru, and from all sides stupid people crowded to worship and manifest complete faith in him. For three or four generations (of spiritual successors) they had kept this shop warm. *Many times it occurred to me to put a stop to this vain affair or to bring him into the assembly of the people of Islam*...I ordered them to produce him and handed over his houses, dwelling-places, and children to Murtaza Khan, and having confiscated his property commanded that he should be put to death."

Guru Arjan was arrested and subjected to severe torture, which resulted in his death.

Guru Hargobind, who succeeded Guru Arjan, resolved to prepare the Sikhs to defend their faith with force if necessary. This martial apostle ascended the Guruship wearing two swords at his waist, one symbolising temporal power and the other spiritual power. "My rosary shall be the sword-belt and on my turban I shall wear the emblem of royalty," he said (Macauliffe: *The Sikh Religion*). Adopting the life of a soldier, he encouraged his followers to bring offerings of arms and horses and engage in martial exercises. Eventually he came to posses a stable of 800 horses. He built a small fortress near Amritsar and, from some of his sturdy followers; raised 300 troopers on horse and 60 gunners. The armed system of Guru Hargobind had formed the Sikhs into a kind of separate entity within the Mughal Empire. Emperor Jahangir could not tolerate the armed policy of Guru Hargobind and consequently ordered the imperial troops against him. Guru Hargobind was the first Guru to engage in warfare. With his devoted followers he fought the Imperial troops in four major battles and three minor engagements. On each occasion the Imperial attackers were routed and their leaders slain. This was the first time in the history of the Punjab that simple peasants had taken up arms and defeated the organized forces of the state.

" . . . after this, the Sikhs were in little danger of relapsing into the limited merit or utility of monks and mendicants." (Cunningham: *History of the Sikhs*)

Antecedents (cont.)

The Mughal Emperor Aurangzeb's (1658-1707) policy of Islamisation was strongly resisted by the Guru Tegh Bahadur. Early in 1675, a group of Kashmiri Pandits, led by Pandit Kirpa Ram of Matton, visited Guru Tegh Bahadur at Anandpur to seek his assistance against persecution from the Mughal rulers. The Mughal emperor Aurangzeb had ordered the conversion of all Hindus to Islam, and the Mughal General Iftikar Khan had threatened the Brahmins with forced conversion. The Mughals assumed that if the Kashmiri Pandits belonging to the Hindu priestly class converted to Islam, others in the region would follow them. The Kashmiri Pandits had been given six months to convert to Islam, or suffer the consequences. Guru Tegh Bahadur asked them to return to their villages and tell the Mughal authorities that they would convert to Islam only after Guru Tegh Bahadur could be persuaded to do so. In 1675, Guru Tegh Bahadur and three disciples proceeded to the Mughal Court in Delhi, to discuss the Emperor's policy towards the non-Muslims. They were arrested and beheaded on 11TH November 1675 at Chandani Chowk after refusing to convert to Islam.

At the martyrdom of Tegh Bahadur, his son Gobind succeeded to the Guruship and stated that his mission was to uphold right in every place and destroy sin and evil; that right may triumph, the good may live and tyranny be rooted from the land.

To save the faith and the infant community from annihilation, he decided to transform the Sikhs into a fierce military brotherhood. In 1699, he created the Order of the Khalsa (the pure). He summoned the Sikhs to the city of Anandpur and baptised them to the fold of the Khalsa. The Guru administered them *Khande-da–Amrit* (Baptism of the Sword). This symbolised their rebirth in the Order of the Khalsa. Henceforth their profession was to wield the sword in the cause of their faith. They formed the nucleus of a fighting fraternity and were given new names with the surname Singh – Lion. They were to observe five Ks, Kesh (unshorn hair), to carry a Kangha (a comb in the hair), to wear Kacha (military pants), to wear a Kara (a steel bracelet) and always carry a Kirpan (a Sabre). The outward symbols of the Singhs, especially their beards and the turbans, were to set them apart, so they could not deny their faith, and to give them the courage to defend it. The orchard of the Sikh faith needed the thorny hedge of armed men for its protection. The Singhs of the Khalsa were the orchard and the hedge rolled into one, ever willing to wield the sword in righteous cause.

When Guru Gobind Singh created the Order of the Khalsa, he laid the foundations of the Sikh military might by setting up a tradition of reckless valour, which became the distinguishing feature of Sikh soldiery. They came to believe in the triumph of their cause as an article of faith, and like their Guru asked for no nobler end than a death on the battlefield.

Antecedents (cont.)

O Lord, with clasped hands this boon I crave,
Let me never shun the righteous task,
Let me be fearless when I go battle,
Give me faith that victory will be mine,
Give me power to sing Thy praise,
And when time comes to end my life,
Let me fall in mighty strife.

(Sardar Khushwant Singh: *History of the Sikhs)*

Guru Gobind Singh fought many desperate unequal battles against the Mughals. Two of his sons died in the fighting and Nawab Wazir Khan, the Mughal Governor of Sarhind, executed the two younger ones. Guru Gobind Singh himself was stabbed to death by one of his own Muslim retainers. What Guru Gobind Singh had succeeded in doing was to " . . . teach the sparrow to hunt the hawk and one man to have the courage to fight a legion." (Sardar Khushwant Singh: *History of the Sikhs*)
Guru Gobind Singh had given a disciple, Lachman Das, who he renamed Banda Bahadur, the task of leading the campaign in the Punjab against the Mughal administration, and to punish Nawab Wazir Khan and his accomplices for their crimes against the people. Banda Bahadur planted the Guru's standard near Delhi and called the Khalsa to arms. Banda's troops were mostly untrained, raw groups armed with matchlocks, spears, swords and bows and arrows. On November 26TH 1709, Banda fell upon the district town of Samana, the home of the executioners of Guru Tegh Bahadur and Guru Gobind Singh's two sons, and razed it to the ground. Within two years Banda ruled the region bounded on the north by the Shiwalik hills, on the west by the River Tangri, on the east by the River Jamuna, and in the south by a line passing through Samana, Thanesar, Kaithal and Karnal. He minted coins and issued orders under his seal and made Lohgarh (the Fort of Steel) the capital of the first Sikh state. Emperor Bahadur Shah dispatched a great imperial force to exterminate the Sikhs. The force, commanded by Abdul Jaman Khan, surrounded the Khalsa at the village of Gurdas Nangal. The Khalsa resisted the siege for eight months; finally starvation broke their resistance. Three hundred Sikhs were beheaded on the spot, and their heads mounted on spears. The procession of seven hundred prisoners and the mounted heads were lead to Lahore, Sarhind, and on to Delhi. Banda Bahadur and the prisoners were paraded through the streets of Delhi in chains, then brutally tortured and beheaded in June 1716. After the brutal murder of Banda and his followers, the Khalsa faced a desperate struggle for survival. The Khalsa Jathas (bands) left the plains and retreated to the hills and jungles.

"The Sikhs, it was thought had been hammered out of existence. But the hammering did not reduce them to pulp, but hardened the remnants to tempered steel." (V. Smith, *History of India*)

Antecedents (cont.)

Under the guidance of Nawab Kapur Singh, a leading Sikh Sardar (chieftain), the Jathas were reorganized into twelve fighting units (misls). These misls (meaning equals) operated independently of each other in the areas under their control, but facing common danger, merged under the banner of the Dal Khalsa - the Sikh Army. As the hammer blows of Afghan invasions weakened the Mughal power, the Khalsa misls spread across the plains. Their enthusiasm was such that, against overwhelming odds, they overran most of central Punjab, and the misl leaders, known as The Barons of the Horse, started carving out independent principalities in the Punjab.

The Sikh Confederacy (Dal Khalsa) evolved from a collection of small-to-medium sized independent sovereign Sikh states, which were governed by the Barons. They were loosely politically linked but strongly bound in cultural and religious spheres. As the Dal Khalsa grew, new regions were conquered and new Sikh Barons came to the fore.

An ambitious young Baron of the Horse, Ranjit Singh of the Sukkarchakkia Confederacy, had inherited a force of 15,000 Horse and 5,000 Foot, with 6 pieces of artillery. He could also call on five feudal chiefs to supply him fighting contingents. From these humble beginnings, and by welding together the rude Barons of the Sikh Confederacy, he forged a powerful military machine that would not only overpower the outmoded and feudal armies of the petty principalities, but also contain the British, who were relentlessly expanding their frontiers. Ranjit Singh single-mindedly modernized the Khalsa forces on the European lines. He created and consolidated the most awesome military muscle ever seen in India, and became King of an Empire extending from Tibet to the deserts of Sindh, and from the Khyber Pass to the Satluj. His army was one of the most powerful at the time in all Asia. It was the first Indian force in a thousand years to carry invasion into the homelands of the traditional conquerors of India - the Pathans and the Afghans.

At the death of Maharajah Ranjit Singh, in the ensuing bloodletting between various competing factions, many a valiant Sardar had lost his life, and the survivors had bribed and used the Sikh Army for their own needs. Having no confidence in the ruling family and the executive, the Sikh Army assumed control and became the Khalsa, the People's Army, the republican army. They had created the Sikh State and Kingdom. They were the State's defenders and preservers, and became an executive sovereign of the State.

The Khalsa ruled through the congregation of the Panchas (five selected members from each unit). They controlled the affairs of the State but had to co-operate with a corrupt Government, and Sardars and the Sovereign, who were seeking British interference to safeguard their estates and privileges. The Khalsa vigorously resisted any foreign intervention in the State and proceeded to punish the traitors. The Sovereign and the leading Sardars frantically sought British intervention.

Antecedents (cont.)

The British had been farsighted in their expansion of India. They wanted to extend their power to the continent's natural border, the North West Frontier. After the fall of Delhi, the British had a standoff against Maharajah Ranjit Singh, who was seeking to expand the Sikh State. The British checked this by taking the Cis Satluj territories under their protection. They also checked the Sikh State's expansion towards Sindh and the sea by taking the Amirs of Sindh under their protection. Additionally, the Anglo-Sikh treaty blocked the State's expansion towards Afghanistan. The British had made no secret of their intention to destroy the Sikh Kingdom and annex the Punjab to the British Empire.

With the turmoil in the Punjab, and their under-estimation of the fighting qualities of the Sikh soldier, the British started massing their armies; the largest force ever assembled in India, on the Kingdom's borders. The British also had an understanding of co-operation with Punjab Government Minister Gulab Singh Dogra, Chief Minister Lal Singh and the Commander-in-Chief Tej Singh, whose intention was to shatter the Khalsa on the British bayonets. As the British advanced on the Punjab, the Khalsa prepared for war.

The morale of the Khalsa was extremely high. The Sikh soldier was extremely brave and had always carried everything before him. The weakness lay in the officer corps, who merely became the figureheads, as the Panchas made all the decisions. The Sikh regimental officers were mostly illiterate and, brave that they might be, were not worthy of the men they commanded. Neither of the two principal generals, Lal Singh and Tej Singh, were Sikhs, but were Brahmins, and were not committed to the cause for which they were fighting.

"A powerful, well-trained, and confident Sikh army prepared for war under the leadership of a Commander-in-Chief under orders from a Vizier, and watched from the sidelines by a powerful and clever chieftain. All three men dedicated to the defeat of the army they lead, and secretly informing their British opponents of that fact!" (Donald Featherstone: *At Them With a Bayonet*)

Traitors on the field and traitors at court commanded the Khalsa armies; their main aim was the destruction of the Khalsa. Gulab Singh Dogra was a feudal chieftain of the Sikh government, and commanded two divisions of Dogras and hill-men. Twice he had refused to reinforce the Khalsa during battle with the aim of complete subjugation of the Khalsa by the British, and to be recognized as an independent sovereign of Jammu. He had been in direct communications with the British and had reached a secret understanding that the Durbar (Royal Council) would openly disavow the acts of the army, and that Maharajah Dalip Singh would be allowed to retain his nominal sovereignty, provided the British forces were allowed to occupy the capital of the Sikhs unopposed.

Thus with ignominious treachery and deceit were sold the lives of the valiant soldiers of the Khalsa by their rulers, and thus was fought the First Anglo-Sikh War.

Antecedents (cont.)

The British Generals, although they had had the co-operation of the Sikh commanders, had won the war at enormous cost. They duly paid tribute to the Khalsa soldiery. Governor General Harding wrote:

" . . . the republican army had more vigour and resolution in it than any in which we have yet had to contend" and ". . . the Sikh soldiers are the finest men I have seen in Asia, bold and daring republicans."

Commander in Chief General Gough paid tribute to the gallantry of the Sikhs:

"Policy precluded me publicly recording my sentiments on the splendid gallantry of our fallen foe, or record the acts of heroism displayed, not only individually, but almost collectively, by Sikh Sardars and the army."

The British government became the guardian of the young Maharajah Dalip Singh, and the Punjab became a British protectorate. The Khalsa was restricted to 20,000 infantry and 12,000 cavalry, and was crushed as a military power.
However the Governor General Lord Dalhousie wrote:

"The task before me is the utter destruction and prostration of the Sikh power, the subversion of its dynasty, and the subjection of its people. This must be done promptly, fully and finally."

The district of Multan was a tributary of the Sikh Kingdom, and the revolt of the Hindu governor of Multan provided the excuse for the British annexation of the Punjab. As the remnants of the Khalsa rallied around the city of Multan, the British declared war on the Sikh Nation!

The British were the rulers of the Punjab and the guardians of the young Maharajah. The rebellion at Multan was against the authority of the Maharajah. But the British held him accountable for the rebellion and were set to punish and destroy him, although they were bound to protect him under the treaty of Bhayirowal! Even the commander in chief, Lord Gough, appears to have been in some doubt whether he was carrying out operations to suppress a rebellion on the behalf of the Durbar or whether the Durbar in Lahore was itself to be regarded as an enemy. The British invading forces deployed at various points in the Punjab were a staggering total of 104,666 men, comprising of 61,366 Regular British Army, 5,300 Lahore Army, 38,000 Irregular troops, plus 13,542 Cavalry, 123 Field guns and 22 Heavy guns.

At the conclusion of the First Anglo-Sikh War, the British had methodically destroyed the military power of the Sikhs. The soldiers had been disarmed, disbanded and dispersed. The pride of the Khalsa, the guns, were dismantled and taken away. What remained was but a shadow of the colossal military machine of Maharajah Ranjit Singh.

Antecedents (cont.)

The total force the Sikhs could muster was 23,000; these were the various contingents from Hazara, Peshawar, Tank, Bannu, Kohat and Attock, including 10,000 Irregulars.

The major battle of the Second Sikh War was fought near Chillianwala. When darkness fell the British left the battlefield and fell back on the village of Chillianwala. The British casualties amounted to 2,446 men, with 132 officers killed and 4 guns lost. Chillianwala was the worst defeat the British had suffered in their annals of Indian warfare. However, re-enforced with fresh forces, they turned defeat into victory at the battle of Gujarat.

The observers who watched the Sikh surrender greatly admired the bearing of the Sikh soldiers, who still carried themselves with pride. They were tired and hungry, but their spirit was by no means broken. It was noticed that many of the older men threw down their Tulwars (swords) with a gesture of disgust. On 29TH March 1849, Maharajah Dalip Singh took his seat on the throne for the last time. The Punjab was annexed to British India, the Sikh Kingdom ended, and Dalip Singh was pensioned off to England.

Having annexed the Punjab, the British had to police and guard its frontiers against the turbulent tribes of the North West Frontier Province. The British had the right material at hand: the disbanded soldiers of the Khalsa, who had subdued and ruled the same territories. The Sikhs were considered the finest soldiers in the East. “If I had anything to say to annexation,” Harding had commented “I should enlist whole regiments of Sikhs into our service.” The Sikh soldiers saw the Sikh dominions overrun and their leaders surrendering their swords. They were trained soldiers and knew no other calling and, when the offer came, flocked to the British standards. Sikhs readily volunteered for military service, displaying an enthusiasm for martial adventure, much of it involving lengthy tours of duty overseas. They became a conspicuous element within numerous regiments of infantry, cavalry and artillery battalions. Eventually Sikhs contributed twenty percent of the Indian army, although they only comprised two percent of the population.

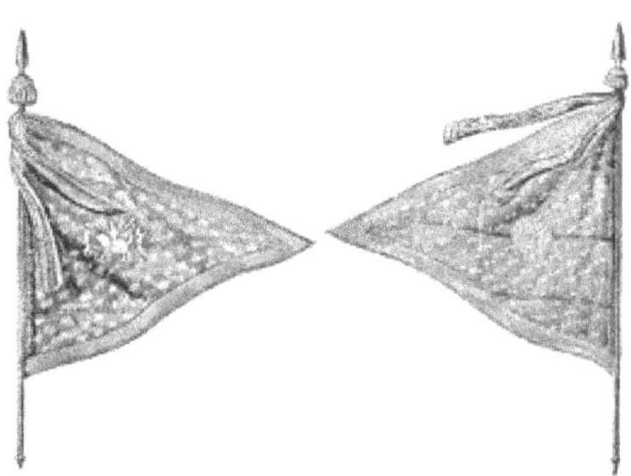

Khalsa Standards 1840

THE KHALSA

Below is the Order of Battle, Khalsa Army, 1845. This shows the composition of the Khalsa Army on the eve of the first Anglo-Sikh War.
(As recorded by J.D.Cunningham in his *History of the Sikhs*)

Order of Battle, 1845.

Commandant	**Forces**	**Class Composition**
Fauj I Khas (Special Brigade)		
Diwan Ajudhia Parshad	4 Infantry Battalions	Sikh
	2 Cavalry Regiments	Sikh and Muslim
	Artillery	Sikh and Muslim
Artillery of General Illahi Baksh (attached to Fauj I Khas)		
Fateh Khan	12 Light Artillery Pieces	Sikh and Muslim
Lahora Singh	22 Heavy Field Guns	Sikh and Muslim
Independent Artillery		
Commandant Bhag Singh	6 Light Artillery Pieces	Sikh and Muslim
Commandant Shev Parshad	8 Light Artillery Pieces	Sikh and Muslim
Missar Lal Singh	10 Light Artillery Pieces	Sikh and Muslim
Sardar Kishan Singh	10 Heavy Field Guns	Sikh and Muslim
General Kishan Singh	22 Light Artillery Pieces	Sikh and Muslim
Sardar Sham S. Attariwala	10 Heavy Field Guns	Sikh and Muslim
Mian Pirthi Singh	56 Heavy Field Guns	Sikh and Muslim
General Mahwa Singh	10 Light Artillery Pieces	Sikh and Muslim
	10 Heavy Field Guns	Sikh and Muslim
Colonel Amir Chand	10 Heavy Field Guns	Chiefly Muslim
Mal Misr	10 Light Artillery Pieces	Hindu
Commandant Sukhu Singh	20 Heavy Field Guns	Sikh and Muslim
	12 Heavy Garrison Cannon	Sikh and Muslim
Commandant Ali Beg	10 Light Artillery Pieces	Muslim
(Miscellaneous Cannon)	50 Heavy Garrison Cannon	Sikh and Muslim

The Khalsa (cont.)

Order of Battle, 1845 (cont.)

Independent Gurkha Battalion

Captain Kuldip Singh	1 Battalion	Gurkha

General Kanh Singh Man's Brigade

	4 Infantry Battalions	Sikh and Muslim
	10 Light Artillery Pieces	Sikh and Muslim

General Gulab Singh Puhunindhia's Brigade

	3 Infantry Battalions	Muslim
	14 Light Artillery Pieces	Sikh and Muslim

General Dhaukhal Singh's Brigade

	2 Infantry Battalions	Sikh and Hindu

General Jawala Singh's Brigade

	2 Infantry Battalions	Sikh
	4 Light Artillery Pieces	Sikh and Muslim

Courtland's Brigade (after Colonel Courtland had been discharged)

	1 Infantry Battalion	Sikh
	1 Infantry Battalion	Hindu
	10 Light Artillery Pieces	Sikh and Muslim

Sardar Lehna Singh Majithia's Brigade

	2 Infantry Battalions	Sikh
	10 Light Artillery Pieces	Sikh
	3 Heavy Field Guns	Sikh
	2 Heavy Garrison Pieces	Sikh

Sardar Nihal Singh Ahluwalia's Brigade

	1 Infantry Battalion	Sikh and Muslim
	4 Light Artillery Pieces	Muslim
	11 Heavy Field Guns	Muslim

Order of Battle, 1845 (Cont.)

General Mehtab Singh Majithia's Brigade

	4 Infantry Battalions	Sikh
	1 Cavalry Regiment	Sikh
	12 Light Artillery Pieces	Sikh and Muslim

General Bishan Singh's Brigade

	2 Infantry Battalions	Sikh and Muslim
	3 Light Artillery Pieces	Sikh and Muslim

Diwan Ajudhia Parshad's Brigade

	4 Infantry Battalions	Sikh
	2 Cavalry Regiments	Sikh
	Artillery	Sikh and Muslim

Raja Suchet Singh's Brigade

DID NOT CO-OPERATE WITH THE KHALSA IN THE ANGLO-SIKH WARS.	2 Infantry Battalions	Dogras
	1 Cavalry Regiment	Dogras
	4 Light Artillery Pieces	Dogras
	10 Heavy Garrison Cannon	Dogras

Raja Hira Singh's Brigade

DID NOT CO-OPERATE WITH THE KHALSA IN THE ANGLO-SIKH WARS.	2 Infantry Battalions	Dogras
	1 Cavalry Regiment	Dogras
	3 Heavy Field Guns	Dogras
	5 Heavy Garrison Cannon	Dogras

Raja Gulab Singh's Brigade

OFFERED HIS TROOPS TO THE BRITISH DURING THE SECOND ANGLO-SIKH WAR.	3 Infantry Battalions	Dogras
	15 Light Artillery Pieces	Dogras
	40 Heavy Garrison Cannon	Dogras

The Khalsa (cont.)
Order of Battle, 1845 (Cont.)

General Pertab Singh's Brigade

	3 Infantry Battalions	Sikh

Diwan Sawan Mal's Brigade

	3 Infantry Battalions	Muslim and Sikh
	6 Light Artillery Pieces	Muslim and Sikh
	40 Heavy Garrison Cannon	Muslim and Sikh

General Gurdit Singh Majithia's Brigade

	4 Infantry Battalions	Sikh
	10 Light Artillery Pieces	Sikh and Muslim

Sheikh Imam-ud-din's Brigade

	3 Infantry Battalions	Muslim
	4 Light Artillery Pieces	Muslim

Sheik Ghulam Muhi-ud-din's Brigade

	1 Infantry Battalion	Sikh
	6 Light Artillery Pieces	Sikh and Muslim
	8 Heavy Field Guns	Sikh and Muslim

Diwan Jodha Ram's Brigade

	4 Infantry Battalions	Sikh, Muslim and Dogras
	1 Cavalry Regiment	
	12 Light Artillery Pieces	
	3 Heavy Field Cannon	

General Tej Singh's Brigade

	4 Infantry Battalions	Sikh
	1 Cavalry Regiment	Sikh
	10 Light Artillery Pieces	Sikh

The Khalsa (cont.)

Order of Battle, 1845 (Cont.)

General Gulab Singh Calcuttawalia's Brigade

	4 Infantry Battalions	Sikh
	1 Cavalry Regiment	Sikh
	10 Light Artillery Pieces	Sikh

The Nihangs - also known as Akalis

The Nihangs were self-appointed guardians of the faith and the state. At times of war or major conflict, they allied themselves to the Khalsa, in four mounted Jathas called *Changri*; a total of 5,000 men. They were a fanatic band of warriors, who formed the suicide squad of the Khalsa. Ranjit Singh owed many of his victories to the desperate valour of these Nihangs.

In 1846, immediately after the First Anglo-Sikh War, the British raised two battalions of Sikh Infantry in the Cis-Satluj territories: The Regiment of Ferozepore and The Regiment of Ludhiana. A special unit, the Corps of Guides, was also raised and was the regiment, part cavalry, part infantry, which in due course would recruit, apart from Sikhs, all classes of desperados of northern India, as well as Gurkhas. A further force was raised out of the disbanded soldiers of the Sikh armies, called the Punjab Irregular Force. The strength of the newly raised forces was five regiments of Punjab Cavalry and five battalions of Punjab Infantry.

At the conclusion of the Second Anglo-Sikh War and the annexation, four battalions of Sikh Infantry and three Mountain Batteries increased the force. The Mountain Batteries were bodily transferred from the Horse Artillery of the Sikh army. The expanded Irregular Force, which in due course would be renamed The Punjab Frontier Force, was transferred to the North West Frontier and became the elite arm of the Indian army.

The Sikh soldier went on to fight on the far-flung corners of the British Empire including Egypt, Sudan, Abyssinia, British Somaliland, Jubaland, Aden, British East Africa, the Persia Gulf, Persia, Afghanistan, the North West Frontier of India, the North East Frontier of India, Tibet, Burma, China, France and Flanders, and Turkey. He went on to fight the Russians in Trans-Caspia and the Germans in Italy. He was the first in the field to fight for Independent India, earning a galaxy of Battle Honours.

After Independence in 1947, with the division of the Indian sub-continent into the States of India and Pakistan, the division of the army followed on the basis of one third for Pakistan and two thirds for India, as shown in the following pages.

The Khalsa (cont.)

Division of the Army after Independence

Cavalry Regiments

Regiment	Class Composition	State
IST Skinner's Horse	Rajputs, Hindustani Muslims, Jats.	India
2ND Lancers	Rajputs, Hindustani Muslims, Jats.	India
3RD Cavalry	Rajputs, Hindustani Muslims, Jats.	India
4TH Hodson's Horse	Sikhs, Punjabi Mussulmans, Dogras.	India
5TH Probyn's Horse	Sikhs, Punjabi Mussulmans, Dogras.	Pakistan
6TH DCO Lancers	Sikhs, Punjabi Mussulmans, Dogras.	Pakistan
7TH Light Cavalry	Sikhs, Punjabi Mussulmans, Jats.	India
8TH Light Cavalry	Sikhs, Punjabi Mussulmans, Jats.	India
9TH Horse	Sikhs, Punjabi Mussulmans, Jats.	India
10TH The Guides	Sikhs, Punjabi Mussulmans, Dogras.	Pakistan
11TH Frontier Force	Sikhs, Punjabi Mussulmans, Dogras.	Pakistan
12TH Frontier Force	Sikhs, Punjabi Mussulmans, Dogras.	Pakistan
13TH DCO Lancers	Sikhs, Pathans, Muslim Rajputs.	Pakistan
14TH Scinde Horse	Sikhs, Pathans, Ranghars.	India
15TH Lacers	Punjabi Mussulmans, Pathans.	Pakistan
16TH Light Cavalry	Kaimkhanis, Rajputs, Jats.	India
17TH Poona Horse	Kaimkhanis, Rajputs, Jats.	India
18TH KEO Cavalry	Sikhs, Jats, Kaimkhanis, Rajputs.	India
19TH KGO Lancers	Sikhs, Punjabi Mussulmans, Jats.	Pakistan
21ST Central India Horse	Sikhs, Punjabi Mussulmans, Jats.	India
20TH Lancers	Jats, Multani Pathans.	India

Infantry Regiments

Regiment	Class Composition	State
1ST Punjab Regiment	Sikhs, Punjabi Mussulmans, Rajputs.	Pakistan
2ND Punjab Regiment	Sikhs, Punjabi Mussulmans, Dogras.	India
8TH Punjab Regiment	Sikhs, Punjabi Mussulmans, Rajputs.	Pakistan
11TH Sikh Regiment	Sikhs, Punjabi Mussulmans.	India
12TH Frontier Force Regiment	Sikhs, Punjabi Mussulmans, Dogras, Pathans.	Pakistan
13TH Frontier Force Rifles	Sikhs, Punjabi Mussulmans, Dogras, Pathans.	Pakistan
14TH Punjab Regiment	Sikhs, Punjabi Mussulmans, Dogras, Pathans.	Pakistan
15TH Punjab Regiment	Sikhs, Punjabi Mussulmans, Jats.	Pakistan
16TH Punjab Regiment	Sikhs, Punjabi Mussulmans Dogras.	Pakistan
The Sikh Light Infantry	Sikhs.	India
The Indian Parachute Regiment	All Indian Classes.	India
The Jammu and Kashmir Light Infantry	All Indian Classes.	India
Jammu and Kashmir Rifles	Sikhs, Dogras, Gurkhas.	India

The Engineers

Partition 1947: Pakistan received 34 Engineer units while India received 61 Engineer units. All the Muslim Sappers opted for Pakistan and the Sikhs for India.

BATTLE HONOURS

The regiments are listed together with their class composition, evolution and Battle Honours (combined where the regiment has changed title over the years).

Cavalry Regiments

SKINNER'S HORSE (1ST DUKE OF YORK'S OWN CAVALRY)

Class composition: Rajputs, Hindustani Muslims and Jats.

The 1ST DYO Lancers and 3RD Skinner's Horse were merged in 1922 to form Skinner's Horse. At the conclusion of the Sepoy Mutiny in 1858, the 2ND Skinner's Horse gained a squadron of Sikhs. In the re-organisation of 1885, the regiment gained another Sikh Squadron. However both Sikh Squadrons were posted out at the re-organisation of 1903. The Sikhs had served in the Squadrons for 35 years.

Changes of Title:

1814 1ST Skinner's Irregular Horse.	1814 2ND Skinner's Irregular Horse.
1903 1ST DYO Lancers (Skinner's Horse).	1903 3RD Skinner's Horse.
1922 1ST Duke of York's Own Skinner's Horse.	1922 1ST Duke of York's Own Skinner's Horse.
1927 Skinner's Horse (1ST Duke of York's Own Cavalry).	1927 Skinner's Horse (1ST Duke of York's Own Cavalry).

Combined Battle Honours of the Squadrons:
Pre First World War: Nepal 1814, Pindari War 1818, Bhurtpore, Ghuznee 1839, Afghanistan 1839, Kandahar 1842, Maharajpore, Moodkee, Ferozeshah, Aliwal, Kandahar 1880, Afghanistan 1879-80, Punjab Frontier, Pekin 1900, and China 1900.

First World War: France and Flanders 1914-16, North West Frontier of India 1915, Baluchistan, and Afghanistan 1919.

Second World War: Agordat, Keren, Amba Alagi, Abyssinia 1940-41, Italian East Africa, Egypt, Sinio Floodbank, and Italy 1942-45.

Partition: The Regiment was allotted to India in 1947 and became the 1ST Horse.

1ST HORSE (POST 1947)

Class composition: Sikhs, Jats and Rajputs.

Battle Honours:
Harar Kalan and Punjab 1971.

2ND ROYAL LANCERS (GARDNER'S HORSE)

Class composition: Rajputs, Hindustani Muslims and Jats.

In 1844 a Sikh Squadron was added to Bengal Irregular Cavalry. At the conclusion of the Sepoy Mutiny in 1858 the 2ND Bengal Cavalry also gained a Sikh Squadron. The 2ND Lancers (Gardner's Horse) and 4TH Cavalry were merged in 1922 to form the 2ND Royal Lancers. This class composition was maintained until the re-organisation of 1937, when the Sikh Squadrons were posted out. The Sikh cavalrymen had served the Regiments with distinction for 93 Years.

Changes of Title:

1809 2ND Bengal Cavalry.	1838 Bengal Irregular Cavalry.
1890 2ND Bengal Lancers.	1903 4TH Lancers.
1904 2ND Lancers (Gardner's Horse).	1904 4TH Cavalry.
1922 2ND Royal Lancers (Gardner's Horse).	1922 2ND Royal Lancers (Gardner's Horse).

Combined Battle Honours of the Squadrons:
Pre First World War: Arracan, Sobraon, Punjab, Mooltan 1857-58, Afghanistan 1879-80, and Egypt 1882.

First World War: La Bassée 1914, Givenchy 1914, Neuve Chapelle, Festubert 1915, Somme 1916, Morval, Cambrai 1917, France and Flanders 1914-18, Egypt 1915, Megiddo, Sharon, Damascus, Palestine 1918, Tigres 1916, Mesopotamia 1915-16, and Afghanistan 1919.

Second World War: El Mechili, Egypt, Syria, and Malaya.

Partition 1947: The Regiment was allotted to India and became the 2ND Lancers.

2ND LANCERS (POST 1947)

Class composition: Jats and Rajputs.

Battle Honours:
Punjab 1965.

Battle Honours (cont.)

Cavalry Regiments (cont.)

3RD CAVALRY

Class composition: Hindustani Mussulmans, Jats and Rajputs.

The 5TH Cavalry and 8TH Cavalry were merged in 1922 to form 3RD Cavalry.

A new class composition was laid down for the 5TH Bengal Cavalry in 1857, consisting of six troops, with one troop of Sikhs and Mohammedan Rajputs, and another of Sikhs and Dogras. In 1875 the Regiment reverted to separate class troops. The six troops became one each of Sikhs, Punjabi Mussulmans, Rajputs, Dogras, Jats and Mohammedans. The class composition changed again in 1889, when the Sikh troop was posted out. At conclusion of the Sepoy Mutiny in 1857, the 8TH Bengal Cavalry had gained a squadron of Sikhs; they served the regiment until the amalgamation of 1922, when they were posted out. The Sikhs had served the Regiments well for 65 years.

Changes of Title:

1841 Bengal Irregular Cavalry.	1846 18TH Bengal Irregular Cavalry.
1861 5TH Bengal Cavalry.	1890 8TH Bengal Lancers.
1906 5TH Cavalry.	1906 8TH Cavalry.
1922 3RD Cavalry.	1922 3RD Cavalry.

Combined Battle Honours of the Squadrons:
Pre First World War: Mooltan, Punjaub, Sepoy Mutiny 1857, and Afghanistan 1878-80.

First World War: Mesopotamia 1917-18, and Palestine.

Second World War: North Malaya, Central Malaya, and Malaya 1941-42.

Partition 1947: The Regiment was allotted to India.

A Sikh Squadron from the 11TH Pavo Cavalry (Frontier Force) destined for Pakistan was posted to the 3RD Cavalry.

3RD CAVALRY (POST 1947)

Class composition: Sikhs, Jats and Rajputs.

Battle Honours:
Asal Uttar, Punjab 1955, Shahjra, and Punjab 1971.

Battle Honours (cont.)

Cavalry Regiments (cont.)

HODSON'S HORSE
(4TH DUKE OF CAMBRIDGE'S OWN LANCERS)

Class composition: one Squadron each of Sikhs, Punjabi Mussulmans and Dogras.

The two regiments, which went to form the 4TH DCO Lancers in 1922, were the 9TH Hodson's Horse and the 10TH DCO Lancers (Hodson's Horse). Hodson's Horse was the first cavalry regiment to be raised during the Sepoy Mutiny and was known as 1ST and 2ND Hodson's Horse. The first troop was raised and commanded by an ex-officer of the Sikh Cavalry, Sardar Man Singh. An ex-Colonel of the Sikh Artillery, Sardar Bal Singh, commanded the second troop. The former Sikh Governor of Kashmir raised the third troop. The Sikh Sandhawalia Sardars raised the fourth troop. The prominent Punjabi Muslim Sardars raised the fifth troop.

Changes of Title:

1857 9TH Bengal Lancers (Hodson's Horse).	1857 10TH Bengal Lancers (Hodson's Horse).
1903 9TH Hodson's Horse.	1903 10TH DCO Lancers (Hodson's Horse).
1922 Hodson's Horse (4^{1H} DCO Lancers).	1922 Hodson's Horse (4^{1H} DCO Lancers).

Combined Battle Honours of the Squadrons:
Pre First World War: Delhi 1857, Lucknow, Abyssinia, Afghanistan 1878-80, Suakin 1885, Chitral, Punjab Frontier, Malta, and Sudan.

First World War: Givenchy, Somme 1916, Bazentin, Flers-Courcelettes, Cambrai 1917, France and Flanders 1914-18, Megiddo, Sharon, Damascus, Palestine 1918, Khan Baghdadi, and Mesopotamia.

Second World War: The Regiment served in Iran, Iraq, Egypt, and Syria, but the Regiment did not have the opportunity to earn any battle honours.

Partition 1947: The Regiment was allotted to India and became the 4TH Horse.

4TH HORSE (POST 1947)
Class composition: two squadrons of Sikhs and one squadron of Dogras.

Battle Honours:
Phillora, Punjab 1965, Basantar River and Punjab 1971.

Battle Honours (cont.)

Cavalry Regiments (cont.)

8TH KING GEORGE V'S OWN LIGHT CAVALRY (5TH KING EDWARD VII'S OWN LANCERS)

Class composition: Sikhs, Punjabi Mussulmans and Dogras.

The two regiments, which went to form the Probyn's Horse, were the 11TH Bengal Lancers and the 12TH Cavalry. The regiments were raised during the Sepoy Mutiny, and were known as 1ST and 2ND Regiments of Sikh Irregular Cavalry. Both regiments were raised from the veterans of the Sikh Army.

Changes of Title:

1857 1ST Sikh Irregular Cavalry.
1861 11TH Bengal Cavalry.
1903 11TH Prince of Wales' Own Lancers.
1922 Probyn's Horse (5TH King Edward V11's Own Lancers).

1857 2ND Sikh Irregular Cavalry.
1861 12TH Bengal Cavalry.
1903 12TH Cavalry.
1922 Probyn's Horse (5TH King Edward V11's Own Lancers).

Combined Battle Honours of the Squadrons:

Pre First World War: Lucknow, Taku Forts, Pekin 1860, Abyssinia 1867, Ali Masjid, Peiwar Kotal, Charasiah, Kabul 1879, Afghanistan 1878-80, Malakand, and Punjab Frontier.

First World War: Mesopotamia 1915-18.

Second World War: Meiktila, Capture of Meiktila, Defence of Meiktila, Taungtha, Rangoon Road, Pwabwe, Pyinmana, Taungoo, Pegu 1945, and Burma 1942-45.

Partition 1947: The Regiment was allotted to Pakistan.

The Sikh Squadron was transferred to The Scinde Horse (India).

Commandant Patiala Lancers

6TH DUKE OF CONNAUGHT'S OWN LANCERS (WATSON'S HORSE)

Class composition: one squadron each of Sikhs, Punjabi Mussulmans and Dogras.

The two regiments, which went to form 6TH DCO Lancers, were 13TH Bengal Lancers and the 16TH Bengal Lancers. At the time of raising they were known as the 4TH Regiment of Sikh Irregular Cavalry and the Rohikhand Horse. The Sikh Irregular Cavalry was entirely composed of Sikh volunteers.

Changes of Title:

1857 Sikh Irregular Cavalry.
1861 13TH Bengal Cavalry.
1903 13TH Bengal Lancers.
1922 6TH DCO's Own Lancers (Watson's Horse).

1862 16TH Bengal Cavalry.
1885 16TH Bengal Lancers.
1922 6TH DCO's Own Lancers (Watson's Horse).

Combined Battle Honours of the Squadrons:
Pre First World War: Sepoy Mutiny, Afghanistan 1878-80, Tel el Kebir, Egypt 1882, Punjab Frontier, and China 1900.

First World War: Kut al Amara 1915-18, Ctesiphon, Tigres 1916, Baghdad, Sharqat, Mesopotamia 1915-18, North West Frontier of India, and Afghanistan 1919.

Second World War: The Trigno, Tuffilo, The Sangro, The Moro, Cassino 11, Pignataro, Liri Valley, The Senio, Santerno Crossing, and Italy 1943-45.

Partition 1947: The Regiment was allotted to Pakistan.

The Sikh Squadron was transferred to the 8TH Cavalry (India).

Commandant Jind Lancers

Battle Honours (cont.)

Cavalry Regiments (cont.)

7TH LIGHT CAVALRY

Class composition: one squadron each of Sikhs, Punjabi Mussulmans and Jats.

Changes of Title:

1788 3RD Madras Lancers.
1903 28TH Light Cavalry.
1922 7TH Light Cavalry.

Combined Battle Honours of the Squadrons:
Pre First World War: Mysore, Seringapatam, and Maheidpoor.

First World War: Merv, Persia 1915-19, and Afghanistan 1919.

Second World War: Mandalay, Meiktila, Rangoon Road, Imphal, Kyaukmymyaung, and Burma 1942-45.

Lt. Govind Singh won a Victoria Cross while serving with 28TH Light Cavalry's detachment, seconded to 2ND Royal Lancers (Gardner's Horse) in France and Flanders, during the First World War.

At the outbreak of the war in 1914, the 28TH Cavalry was sent to East Persia to patrol 350 miles of the Russian border. They made many charges against the Bolshevik forces. In one action thirteen troopers charged 150 Russian cavalry, killing twenty-two. For this action they earned the unusual battle honour 'Merv'.

Partition 1947: The Regiment was allotted to India and became the 7TH Light Cavalry.

7TH LIGHT CAVALRY (POST 1947)

Class composition: Sikhs and Jats.

Battle Honours:
Naushera, Jhangra, Zojila, Jammu and Kashmir 1947-48, Punjab 1971, and East Pakistan 1971.

The Guidon of the 7TH Light Cavalry.

Battle Honours (cont.)

Cavalry Regiments (cont.)

8TH KING GEORGE V'S OWN LIGHT CAVALRY

Class composition: one squadron each of Sikhs, Deccani Muslims and Jats.

The two regiments, which went to form the 8TH KGO V's Light Cavalry in 1937, were the 26TH Light Cavalry and the 30TH Lancers.

Changes of Title:

1788 1ST Madras Lancers. 1903 26TH Light Cavalry. 1937 8TH King George V's Own Light Cavalry.	1788 4TH Madras Lancers. 1903 30TH Lancers. 1937 8TH King George V's Own Light Cavalry.

Combined Battle Honours of the Squadrons:
Pre First World War: Mysore, Seringapatam, Ava, Central India, Afghanistan 1879-80, and Burma 1885-87.

First World War: Givenchy 1914, France and Flanders 1914-18, and Afghanistan 1919.

Second World War: Sittang 1945, and Burma 1942-45.

Partition 1947: The Regiment was allotted to India and became the 8TH Light Cavalry.

8TH LIGHT CAVALRY (POST 1947)

Class composition: Sikhs, Rajputs and Jats.

Battle Honours: Punjab 1965.

Commandant Nabha Lancers

THE ROYAL DECCAN HORSE
(9TH HORSE)

Class composition: one squadron each of Sikhs, Punjabi Mussulmans and Jats.

The 29TH Lancers and the 20TH Royal Deccan Horse were merged in 1922 to form Royal Deccan Horse (9TH Horse).

Changes of Title:

1854 1ST Lancers (Hyderabad Contingent).
1903 20TH Deccan Horse.
1921 20TH Royal Deccan Horse.
1922 Royal Deccan Horse (9TH Horse).

1854 2ND Lancers (Hyderabad Contingent).
1903 29TH Lancers (Deccan Horse).
1921 29TH Lancers (Deccan Horse).
1922 Royal Deccan Horse (9TH Horse).

Combined Battle Honours of the Squadrons:
Pre First World War: Central India 1857.

First World War: Givenchy 1914, Somme 1916, Bazentin, Delville Wood, Flers-Courcelettes, Cambrai 1917, France and Flanders 1914-18, Megiddo, Sharon, Damascus, and Palestine 1918.

Second World War: Meiktila, Capture of Meiktila, Defence of Meiktila, Rangoon Road, Pwabwe, and Burma 1942-45.

Partition 1947: The Regiment was allotted to India in 1947 and became the 9TH Horse.

9TH HORSE (POST 1947)

Class composition: Sikhs, Jats and Dogras.

Battle Honours:

Asal Uttar, and Punjab 1965.

THE GUIDES CAVALRY
(10TH QUEEN VICTORIA'S OWN FRONTIER FORCE)

Class composition: one squadron each of Sikhs, Punjabi Mussulmans, Pathans and Dogras.

Changes of Title:

1846 Guides.
1874 Queen's Own Guides.
1903 Queen's Own Corps of Guides (Frontier Force).
1922 10TH Queen's Own Corps of Guides (Frontier Force).
1927 The Guides Cavalry (10TH Queen Victoria's Own Frontier Force).

Battle Honours:
Pre First World War: Mooltan, Gujarat, Punjaub, Delhi 1857, Ali Masjid, Kabul 1879, Afghanistan 1878-80, Chitral, Malakand, and Punjab Frontier.

First World War: Khan Baghdadi, Sharqat, Mesopotamia 1917-18, and North West Frontier of India 1919.

Second World War: Bir Hacheim, Minqar Qaim, Deir el Shein, and North Africa 1940-43.

Partition 1947: The Regiment was allotted to Pakistan.
The Sikh Squadron was transferred to The Poona Horse (India).

The Amir of Afghanistan signed the treaty of Gandamak in 1879 and agreed to accept a British Envoy. The Envoy proceeded to Kabul with an escort of one officer and 76 men from the Guides Cavalry, and was based at the British Residency in the Bala Hissar. The Afghans attacked the Residency and all of the British officers were killed. The Afghans offered quarter to The Guides but The Guides, under a Sikh Jemadar, Jewand Singh, chose to fight. The Residency finally fell twelve hours later, its defenders dead, surrounded by 600 dead Afghans. A national memorial was raised at Mardan to these heroes, and on it is written:

'The annals of no army and no regiment can show a brighter record of devoted bravery than has been achieved by this small band of Guides.'

Battle Honours (cont.)

Cavalry Regiments (cont.)

PRINCE ALBERT VICTOR'S OWN CAVALRY (11TH FRONTIER FORCE)

Class composition: one squadron each of Sikhs, Punjabi Mussulmans and Dogras.
The two regiments, which went to form the PAVO Cavalry in 1922, were the 1ST Punjab Cavalry and the 3RD Punjab Cavalry. Both regiments were raised from the disbanded veterans of the Sikh Army.

Changes of Title:

1849 1ST Punjab Cavalry. 1903 21ST Albert Victor's Own Cavalry (Frontier Force). 1922 PAVO Cavalry (11TH Frontier Force).	1849 3RD Punjab Cavalry. 1903 23RD Cavalry. 1922 PAVO Cavalry (11TH Frontier Force).

Combined Battle Honours of the Squadrons:
Pre First World War: Delhi 1857, Lucknow, Ahmed Khel, Kandahar 1880, and Afghanistan 1878-80.

First World War: Kut al Amara 1917, Baghdad, Khan Baghdadi, Sharqat, Mesopotamia 1915-18, and Afghanistan 1919.

Second World War: El Mechili, Halfaya 1941, Bir Hacheim, North Africa 1940-43, Relief of Kohima, Monywa 1945, Mandalay, Myinmu Bridgehead, Capture of Meiktila, The Irraawaddy, Rangoon Road, and Burma 1942-45.

Partition 1947: The Regiment was allotted to Pakistan.
The Sikh Squadron was transferred to the 18TH Cavalry (India).

Risaldar Kapurthala Lancers

SAM BROWN'S CAVALRY (12TH FRONTIER FORCE)

Class composition: one squadron each of Sikhs, Punjabi Mussulmans and Dogras.

The two regiments, which went to form Sam Brown's Cavalry in 1922, were the 2ND Punjab Cavalry and the 5TH Punjab Cavalry. The regiments were raised in 1849 from the disbanded veterans of the Sikh Army.

Changes of Title:

1849 2ND Punjab Cavalry.	1849 5TH Punjab Cavalry.
1922 Sam Brown's Cavalry (12TH Frontier Force).	1922 Sam Brown's Cavalry (12TH Frontier Force).

In 1937 the Regiment became a permanent training regiment.

Combined Battle Honours of the Squadrons:
Pre First World War: Delhi 1857, Lucknow, Charasiah, Kabul 1879, Ahmed Khel, and Afghanistan 1878–80.

First World War: Kut al Amara 1917, Baghdad, Mesopotamia 1916-18, North West Frontier of India, East Africa 1917, and Afghanistan 1919.

The regiment dropped out of the Order of Battle in 1937 when they were made a permanent training regiment.

Partition 1947: The Regiment was allotted to Pakistan.

The Sikh Troopers were absorbed into the Indian Cavalry Regiments.

Sikh Lancers 1879

Battle Honours (cont.)

Cavalry Regiments (cont.)

13TH DUKE OF CONNAUGHT'S OWN LANCERS

Class composition: one squadron each of Sikhs, Pathans and Muslim Rajputs.

The two regiments that went to form 13TH DCO Lancers in 1922 were 31ST DCO Lancers and the 32ND Lancers.

Changes of Title:

1817 1ST DCO Bombay Lancers.	1817 2ND Bombay Lancers.
1903 31ST DCO Lancers.	1903 32ND Lancers.
1922 13TH DCO Lancers.	1922 13TH DCO Lancers.

Combined Battle Honours of the Squadrons:

Pre First World War: Ghuznee, Afghanistan 1839, Mooltan, Punjaub, Central India, Afghanistan 1878-80, and Burma 1885-87.

First World War: Kut al Amara 1917, Baghdad, Sharqat, Mesopotamia 1916-18, North West Frontier of India, Afghanistan 1919, and North West Frontier of India.

Second World War: Damascus, Deir ez Zor, Raqqa, Syria 1941, Gazala, Bir Hacheim, El Edem, Gambut, Sidi Razegh 1942, Tobruk 1942, and North Africa 1940-43.

Partition 1947: The Regiment was allotted to Pakistan.

The Sikh Squadron was posted to India.

Sikh Daffadar 1880

SCINDE HORSE
(14TH PRINCE OF WALES' OWN CAVALRY)

Class composition: one squadron each of Sikhs, Pathans and Ranghars.

The two regiments that went to form 14TH Scinde Horse in 1922 were 35TH Scinde Horse and the 36TH Jacob's Horse.

Changes of Title:

1846 5TH Bombay Cavalry. 1903 35TH Scinde Horse. 1927 Scinde Horse (14TH Prince of Wales' Own Cavalry).	1846 6TH Bombay Cavalry. 1903 36TH Jacob's Horse. 1927 Scinde Horse (14TH Prince of Wales' Own Cavalry).

Combined Battle Honours of the Squadrons:

Pre First World War: Meenee, Hyderabad, Cutchee, Mooltan, Punjaub, Persia, Central India, and Afghanistan 1878-80.

First World War: Somme 1916, Morval, Cambrai 1917, France and Flanders 1914-18, Megiddo, Sharon, Palestine 1918, and North West Frontier of India.

Second World War: The Regiment served as a Frontier Force Regiment for two years, before going to serve in Egypt and Syria. Unfortunately they received no battle honours for the Second World War.

Partition 1947: The Regiment was allotted to India and became the 14TH Horse.

14TH HORSE (POST 1947)

Class composition: two Squadrons of Sikhs and one of Dogras.

Battle Honours:

Dograi, Punjab 1965, Malakpur, and Punjab 1971.

POONA HORSE
(17TH QUEEN VICTORIA'S OWN CAVALRY)

Class composition: one squadron each of Jats, Kaimkhanis and Rajputs.

The two regiments that went to form the 17TH Queen Victoria's Own Poona Horse in 1922 were the 33RD Queen's Own Light Cavalry and the 34TH Prince Albert Victor's Own Poona Horse.

Changes of Title:

1820 3RD Bombay Light Cavalry.
1847 3RD Poona Irregular Horse.
1903 33RD Queen's Own Light Cavalry.
1922 Poona Horse (17TH Queen Victoria's Own Cavalry).

1820 4TH Bombay Cavalry.
1847 4TH Poona Irregular Horse.
1903 34TH Prince Albert Victor's Own Poona Horse.
1922 Poona Horse (17TH Queen Victoria's Own Cavalry).

Combined Battle Honours of the Squadrons:

Pre First World War: Corygaum, Ghuznee 1839, Afghanistan 1839, Candahar 1842, Ghuznee 1842, Meenee, Hyderabad, Reshire, Bushier, Koosh Ab, Persia, Central India, Abyssinia, Kandahar 1880, Afghanistan 1878-80, and China 1900.

First World War: La Bassée 1914, Armentieres, Somme 1916, Bazentin, Flers-Courcelettes, Cambrai 1917, France and Flanders 1914-18, Megiddo, Sharon, Damascus, Palestine 1918, Shaiba, Ctesiphon, Tigres 1916, Mesopotamia 1914-16, and Afghanistan 1919.

Second World War: North Africa 1940-43.

Partition 1947: The Regiment was allotted to India and became the 17TH Horse.

17TH HORSE (POST 1947)

Class composition: Sikhs, Jats and Rajputs.

Battle Honours:

Phillora 1965, Buttal Dugandi 1965, Basantar River 1971, and Punjab 1971.

Battle Honours (cont.)

Cavalry Regiments (cont.)

18TH KING EDWARD V11'S OWN CAVALRY

The two regiments that went to form 18TH King Edward V11's Own Cavalry in 1922 were the 6TH Prince of Wales' Own Cavalry and the 7TH Hariana Lancers.

Class composition:

6TH Prince of Wales' Own Cavalry	**7TH Hariana Lancers**
A Squadron: Ranghars.	A Squadron: Muslims.
B Squadron: Sikhs.	B Squadron: Jats.
C Squadron: Jats.	C Squadron: Sikhs.
D Squadron: Sikhs.	D Squadron: Dogras.

Changes of Title:

1842 8TH Bengal Irregular Cavalry.	1903 7TH Bengal Lancers.
1846 17TH Bengal Irregular Horse.	1905 6TH King Edward's Own Cavalry.
1903 6TH Prince of Wales' Own Cavalry.	1903 7TH Hariana Lancers.
1922 18TH King Edward V11's Own Cavalry.	1922 18TH King Edward V11's Own Cavalry.

Combined Battle Honours of the Squadrons:

Pre First World War: Punniar, Moodkee, Ferozeshah, Sobraon, Punjaub, Tel el Kebir, Egypt 1882, Burma 1885-87, and Punjab Frontier.

First World War: Somme 1916, Morval, Cambrai 1917, France and Flanders 1914-18, Megiddo, Sharon, Damascus, Palestine 1918, Shaiba, Kut al Amara 1915, Ctesiphon, Tigres 1916, and Mesopotamia 1915-16.

Second World War: El Mechili, The Kennels, Defence of Tobruk, and North Africa 1940-43.

Partition 1947: The Regiment was allotted to India and called 18TH Cavalry.

18TH CAVALRY (POST 1947)

Battle Honours:

Tilakpur-Mahadipur, Punjab 1965, and Jammu and Kashmir 1965.

Battle Honours (cont.)

Cavalry Regiments (cont.)

19TH KING GEORGE V'S OWN LANCERS

Class composition: one squadron each of Sikhs, Punjabi Mussulmans and Jats.

The two regiments that went on to form 19TH King George V's Own Lancers in 1922 were 18TH Tiwana Lancers and the 19TH Lancers (Fane's Horse). Most of the volunteers for the Fane's Horse were the disbanded veterans of the Sikh Army.

Changes of Title:

1858 18TH Bengal Lancers.
1903 18TH Tiwana Lancers.
1922 19TH King George V's Own Lancers.

1860 19TH Bengal Lancers.
1903 19TH Lancers (Fane's Horse).
1922 19TH King George V's Own Lancers.

Combined Battle Honours of the Squadrons:
Pre First World War: Taku Forts, Pekin 1860, Ahmed Khel, Afghanistan 1878-80, and Punjab Frontier.

First World War: Somme 1916, Bazentin, Flers-Courcelettes, Morval, Cambrai 1917, France and Flanders 1914-18, Sharon, Damascus, and Palestine 1919.

Second World War: Buthidaung, Rangoon Road, Mayu Valley, Myebon, Kangaw, Ru-Ywa, Dalet, Tamandu, and Burma 1942-45.

Partition 1947: The Regiment was allotted to Pakistan.

The Sikh Squadron was transferred to Skinner's Horse (India).

Sikh Lancer 1901

Battle Honours (cont.)

Cavalry Regiments (cont.)

THE CENTRAL INDIA HORSE (21ST KING GEORGE V'S OWN HORSE)

Class composition: one squadron each of Sikhs, Punjabi Mussulmans and Jats.

In 1858 Captain Mayne raised the Irregular Cavalry Regiment, Mayne's Horse. In the same year Captain Meade raised another Irregular Cavalry Regiment, and in Hyderabad Lt. Col. Beatson raised two Irregular Cavalry Regiments, Beatson's Horse.

In 1860, they were amalgamated into two regiments and called IST and 2ND Central India Horse, and in 1927 became The Central India Horse (21ST King George's Own Horse).

Changes of Title:

1858 2 Irregular Cavalry Regiments.	1858 2 Irregular Cavalry Regiments.
1860 1ST Central India Horse.	1860 2ND Central Indian Horse.
1903 38TH Central India Horse.	1903 39TH Central India Horse.
1927 Central India Horse (21ST King George's Own Horse).	1927 Central India Horse (21ST King George's Own Horse).

Combined Battle Honours of the Squadrons:
Pre World War: Kandahar 1880, Afghanistan 1878-80, and Punjab Frontier.

First World War: Somme 1916, Marval, Cambrai, France and Flanders 1914-18, Megiddo, Damascus, and Palestine 1918.

The Sikh Squadron was disaffected and was mustered out in July 1940.

Second World War: Keren, Asmara Road, Abyssinia 1940-41, Relief of Tobruk 1941, North Africa 1940-43, Gothic Line, Italy 1944-43, and Greece 1944-45.

Partition 1947: The Regiment was allotted to India.

CENTRAL INDIA HORSE (POST 1947)

Battle Honours:
Rajauri, Jammu and Kashmir 1947, Burki, and Punjab 1965.

Battle Honours (cont.)

Infantry Regiments

1ST PUNJAB REGIMENT

Class composition: Sikhs, Punjabi Mussulmans and Rajputs.

Changes of Title:

1759 3RD Bn. Coast Sepoys. 1922 1ST Bn. 1ST Punjab Regiment.	1761 7TH Bn. Coast Sepoys. 1922 2ND Bn. 1ST Punjab Regiment.
1861 16TH Madras Native Infantry. 1922 3RD Bn. 1ST Punjab Regiment.	1861 1ST Bengal Native Infantry. 1922 4TH Bn. 1ST Punjab Regiment.
1903 82ND Punjabis. 1922 5TH Bn. 1ST Punjab Regiment.	1903 84TH Punjabis. 1922 10TH Bn. 1ST Punjab Regiment.

Combined Battle Honours of the Battalions:
Pre First World War: Sholinghur, Carnatic, Seringapatam, Mysore, Assaye, Laswarrie, Boiurbon, Nagpore, Arakan, Bhurtpore, China, and Burma 1885-87.

First World War: Suez Canal, Egypt 1915, Aden, Shaiba, Kut al Amara, Defence of Kut al Amara, Ctesiplhon, Tigres 1916, Baghdad, Mesopotamia 1915-18, North West Frontier of India, and Afghanistan 1919.

Second World War: Agordat, Keren, Kissoue, Damascus, Sidi Barrani, Tobruk 1941, Omars, Alam Hams Gazelle, Carmusa, Defence of Alamein, Ruweisat Ridge, El Alamein, Montone, Gothic Line, Lamone Crossing, Ppideura, Singapore Island, Pyuntaza-Shwegyin, Yenaungyaung 1942. Monya 1942. Donbaik, Hitzwe, North Arakan, Razorbill, Mayu Tunnels, Ngakyedauk Pass, Imphal, Litan, Kohima, Defence of Kohima, Kennedy Peak, Meiktila, Taungtha, Rangoon Road, Shwemyo Bluff, Sittang 1945, Arakan Beaches, Ramree, and Burma 1942-45.

Partition 1947: The Regiment was allotted to Pakistan.

The Sikh companies were transferred to the Sikh Regiment (India).

Two 1ST Punjab Regiment Sikh Officers went on to become Indian Army Generals:

Lt General Kalwant Singh.

Major General Atma Singh.

Battle Honours (cont.)

Infantry Regiments (cont.)

2ND PUNJAB REGIMENT

2ND Punjab Regiment was created in 1903 from the original Madras regiments, and the class composition was converted to men from the Punjab.
Class composition: Sikhs, Punjabi Mussulmans and Dogras.

Changes of Title:

1903 67TH Punjabis. 1922 1ST Bn. 2ND Punjab Regiment.	1903 69TH Punjabis. 1922 2ND Bn. 2ND Punjab Regiment.
1903 72ND Punjabis. 1922 3RD Bn. 2ND Punjab Regiment.	1903 74TH Punjabis. 1922 4TH Bn. 2ND Punjab Regiment.
1903 87TH Punjabis. 1922 5TH Bn. 2ND Punjab Regiment.	1903 2/67TH Punjabis. 1922 10TH (Training) Bn. 2ND Punjab Regiment.

Combined Battle Honours of the Battalions:
Pre First World War: Sholinghur, Carnatic, Mysore, Maheidpoor, Ava, China, Pegu, Lucknow, and Burma 1885-87.

First World War: Loos, France and Flanders 1915, Helles. Krithia, Gallipoli 1915, Suez Canal, Egypt 1915, Megiddo, Sharon, Nablus, Palestine 1918, Aden, Defence of Kut al Amara, Kut al Amara 1917, Baghdad, Mesopotamia 1915-18, North West Frontier of India 1915-17, and Afghanistan 1919.

Second World War: Gogni, Agordat, Keren, Ad Teclesan, Berbera, Amba Alagi, Abyssinia 1940-41, British Somaliland 1940, North Africa 1940-43, Patelle Pass, San Marino, Sogliano, Casa Bettini, Idice Bridgehead, Italy 1943-45, Central Malaya, Ipoh, Singapore Island, Malaya 1941-42, Buthidaung, Point 551, Ngakyedauk Pass, Imphal, Litan, Kanglatonbi, Tengnoupal, Kennedy Peak, Tongzang, Kangaw, Defence of Meiktila, Pyinmana, and Burma 1942-45.

Partition 1947: The 2ND Punjab Regiment was the only Punjab regiment allotted to India and became The Punjab Regiment.

The Punjab Regiment (Post 1947) is listed separately.

Battle Honours (cont.)

Infantry Regiments (cont.)

8TH PUNJAB REGIMENT

8TH Punjab Regiment was created in 1903 from the original Madras regiments. Class composition: Sikhs, Punjabi Mussulmans and Rajputana Hindus.

Changes of Title:

1903 89TH Punjabis. 1922 1ST Bn. 8TH Punjab Regiment.	1903 90TH Punjabis. 1922 2ND Bn. 8TH Punjab Regiment.
1903 91ST Punjabis. 1922 3RD Bn. 8TH Punjab Regiment.	1903 92ND Punjabis. 1922 4TH Bn. 8TH Punjab Regiment.
1903 93RD Burma Infantry. 1922 5TH Bn. 8TH Punjab Regiment.	1903 2/89TH Punjabis. 1922 10TH (Training.) Bn. 8TH Punjab Regiment

Combined Battle Honours of the Battalions:
Pre First World War: Burma 1885-87, and China 1900.

First World War: France and Flanders 1915, Macedonia 1918, Helles, Krithia, Gallipoli 1915, Meggido, Sharon, Palestine 1918, Tigres 1916, Kut al Amara 1917, Baghdad, Khan Baghdadi, Mesopotamia 1915-18, and Afghanistan 1919.

Second World War: North Malaya, Jitra, Malaya 1941-42, The Trigno, Perano, The Sangro, Villa Grande, Gustav Line, Monte Grande, The Senio, Italy 1943-45, Donbaik, North Arakan, The Shweli, Myitson, Kama, and Burma 1942-45.

Partition: 1947: The Regiment was allotted to Pakistan.
The Sikh companies were transferred to the Sikh Regiment (India).

Medals of Major Parkash Singh VC - 8TH Punjab Regiment, Indian Army.

Battle Honours (cont.)

Infantry Regiments (cont.)

11TH SIKH REGIMENT

Changes of Title:

1846 The Regiment of Ferozepore (14TH Ferozepore Sikhs). 1922 1ST Bn. 11TH Sikh Regiment.	1846 The Regiment of Ludhiana (15TH Ludhiana Sikhs). 1922 2ND Bn. 11TH Sikh Regiment.
1856 The Bengal Military Police Bn. 1922 3RD Bn. 11TH Sikh Regiment.	1857 Bariely Levy. 1922 4TH Bn. 11TH Sikh Regiment.
1857 Bengal Military Police. 1922 5TH Bn. 11TH Sikh Regiment.	1887 35TH (Sikh) Regt. Bengal. 1922 10TH Bn. 11TH Sikh Regiment.

Combined Battle Honours of the Battalions:
Pre First World War: Defence of Arrah 1857, Lucknow 1857-58, Behar 1857, China 1860-62, Ali Masjid, Ahmed Khel 1878, Kandahar 1880, Afghanistan 1878-80, Tofrek 1885, Suakin 1885, Samana 1890, Defence of Chitral 1894, Chitral 1895, Saragarhi 1897, Tirah 1897, Malakand 1897, Punjab Frontier 1897, China 1900, and North West Frontier of India 1908 and 1914-17.

First World War: La Bassée 1914, Armentieres 1914, Givenchy 1914, St Julien 1914, Aubers 1914, Neuve Chapelle 1914-15, Festubert 1915, France and Flanders 1914-15, Helles, Tsingtao 1914. Krithia 1915, Suvla, Sari Bair, Gallipoli 1915, Suez Canal, Egypt 1915-16, Megiddo 1918, Sharon 1918, Palestine 1918, Tigres 1916, Kut al Amara 1917, Baghdad, Sharqat, Mesopotamia 1916-18, Persia 1918, and Afghanistan 1919.

Second World War: Agordat 1940-41, Keren, Abyssinia 1940-41, Iraq 1941, Omars 1940-43, Mersa Matruh, Deir el Shein 1940-43, North Africa 1940-43, Gothic Line, Monte Calvo, Coriano, Poggio, San Giovanni, San Marino, Italy 1943-45, Greece 1944-45, Kuantan, Niyor, Malaya 1941-42, North Arakan, Buthidaung, Kanglatonbi, Nyaungu Bridgehead, The Irraawaddy 1945, Shandatgyi, Kama, Sittang 1945, and Burma 1942-45.

Partition 1947: The Regiment was allotted to India.

THE SIKH REGIMENT (POST 1947)

Battle Honours:
Srinagar, Tithwal, Jammu and Kashmir 1947, Burki, Punjab 1965, Jammu and Kashmir 1965, Defence of Punch, Siramani, Parbat Ali, Punjab 1971, Sindh 1971, and East Pakistan 1971.

12TH FRONTIER FORCE REGIMENT

Class composition: Sikhs, Punjabi Mussulmans, Rajputs and Pathans.

Changes of Title:

1846 1ST (Hill Regiment). 1922 1ST Bn. 12TH Frontier Force Regiment.	1846 2ND (Hill Regiment). 1922 2ND Bn. 12TH Frontier Force Regiment.
1846 3RD Sikh Local Infantry. 1922 3RD Bn. 12TH Frontier Force Regiment.	4TH Sikh Local Infantry. 1922 4TH Bn. 12TH Frontier Force Regiment.

Combined Battle Honours of the Battalions:
Pre First World War: Pegu, Mooltan, Punjaub, Delhi 1857, Ali Masjid, Kabul 1879, Ahmed Khel, Kandahar 1880, Afghanistan 1878-80, Chitral, Malakand, Punjab Frontier, Tirah, Pekin 1900, and Somaliland 1901-04.

First World War: Suez Canal, Egypt 1915, Megiddo, Sharon, Nablus, Palestine 1918, Aden, Tigres 1916, Kut al Amara 1917, Baghdad, Sharqat, Mesopotamia 1915-18, North West Frontier of India 1914-17, and Afghanistan 1919.

Second World War: Gallabat, Tehamiyam Wells, Agordat, Barentu, Keren, Amba Alagi, Abyssinia 1940-41, Gazala, Bir Hacheim, El Adem, North Africa 1940-43, Landing in Sicily, Sicily 1943, Landing at Reggio, The Sangro, Mozzagrogna, Romagnoli, The Moro, Impossible Bridge, Cassino 11, Pignataro, Advance to Florence, Campriano, Gothic Line, Coriano, The Senio, Santerno Crossing, Italy 1943-45, Athens, Greece 1944-45, North Malaya, Kota Baru, Central Malaya, Kuantan, Machang, Singapore Island, Malaya 1941-42, Moulmein, Sittang 1942-45, Pegu 1942-45, Taukkyan, Shwegyin, North Arakan, Buthidaung, Maungdaw, Ngakyedauk Pass, Imphal, Tamu Road, Shenam Pass, Bishenpur, Kyaukmyaung Bridgehead, Arakan Beaches, Ramree, Taungup, Mandalay, Myinmu, Fort Dkufferin, Kyaukse 1945, Meiktila, Nyaungu Bridgehead, Capture of Meiktila, Defence of Meiktila, The Irrawaddy, Rangoon Road, Pyawbwe, Taungoo, and Burma 1942-45.

Partition 1947: The Regiment was allotted to Pakistan.
The Sikh soldiers were transferred to the Sikh Regiment (India).

Battle Honours (cont.)

Infantry Regiments (cont.)

13TH FRONTIER FORCE RIFLES

Class composition: Sikhs, Punjabi Mussulmans, Dogras and Pathans.

Changes of Title:

1849 1ST Punjab Infantry. 1922 1ST Bn. 13TH Frontier Force Rifles.	1849 2ND Punjab Infantry. 1922 2ND Bn. 13TH Frontier Force Rifles.
1849 4TH Punjab Infantry. 1922 4TH Bn. 13TH Frontier Force Rifles.	1849 5TH Punjab Infantry. 1922 5TH Bn. 13TH Frontier Force Rifles.
1843 The Scinde Camel Corps. 1922 6TH Rifles Bn. 13TH Frontier Force Rifles.	1917 1/2ND Bn 56TH Punjabi Rifles. 1922 10TH Bn. 13TH Frontier Force Rifles.

Combined Battle Honours of the Battalions:

Pre First World War: Delhi 1857, Lucknow, Peiwar Kotal, Kabul 1879, Afghanistan 1878-80, Punjab Frontier, and China 1900.

First World War: Le Bassée 1914, Armentieres, Festubert 1914, Givenchy 1914, Neuve Chapelle, Pyres 1915, Julian, Aubers, Loos, France and Flanders 1914-15, Suez Canal, Egypt 1915-17, Gaza, Al Mughar, Nebi Samwil, Jerusalem, Megiddo, Sharon, Palestine 1917-18, Aden, Tigres 1917, Kut al Amara, Baghdad, Mesopotamia 1916-18, Persia 1918-19, North West Frontier of India, Baluchistan 1918, East Africa 1916-18 and Afghanistan 1919.

Second World War: Gash Delta, Barentu, Keren, Ad Teglesan, Abyssinia 1940-41, Deir ez Zor, Raqqa, Syria 1941, Gazala, Sidi Razegh 1942, Mersa Matruh, North Africa 1940-43, Trigno, Tuffillo, The Sangro, Impossible Bridge, Villa Grande, Cassino 11, Gustav Line, Pignataro, Advance to Florence, Gothic Line, Monte Grande, The Senio, Bologna, Monte Sole, Italy 1943-45, North Malaya, Kota Bharu, Johore, Gemas, The Muar, Singapore Island, Malaya 1941-42, Taukkyan, Monywa 1942, Shegyin, North Arakan, Point 551, Manu Tunnels, Maungdaw, Ngakyedauk Pass, Imphal, Litan, Araran Beaches, Myebon, Ranree, Mandalay, Myinmu, Meiktila, Nyaungu Bridgehead, Capture of Meiktila, Taungha, Myingyan, The Irrawaddy, and Yenangyaung.

In 1947: The Regiment was allotted to Pakistan.
The Sikh companies were absorbed into the Sikh Regiment (India).

Battle Honours (cont.)

Infantry Regiments (cont.)

14TH PUNJAB REGIMENT

Class composition: Sikhs, Punjabi Mussulmans, Dogras and Pathans.

Changes of Title:

1857 7TH Punjab Infantry. 1922 1ST Bn. 14TH Punjab Regiment.	1857 8TH Punjab Infantry. 1922 2ND Bn. 14TH Punjab Regiment.
1857 11TH Punjab Infantry. 1922 3RD Bn. 14TH Punjab Regiment.	1857 16TH Punjab Infantry. 1922 4TH Bn. 14TH Punjab Regiment.
1858 Shahjehanpur Levy. 1922 5TH Bn. 14TH Punjab Regiment.	1857 9TH Punjab Infantry Regiment. 1922 10TH Bn. 14TH Punjab Regiment.

Combined Battle Honours of the Battalions:
Pre First World War: Taku Forts, China 1860-62, Pekin 1860, Abyssinia, Ali Masjid, Ahmed Khel, Kandahar 1880, Afghanistan 1878-80, Tel el Kebir, Egypt 1882, Punjab Frontier, Malakand, Pekin 1900, and China 1900.

First World War: Ypres 1915, St Julien, Aubers, France and Flanders 1915, Macedonia 1918, Suez Canal, Egypt 1915, Meggido, Sharon, Palestine 1918, Basra, Shaiba, Kut al Amara 1915-17, Ctesiphon, Defence of Kut al Amara, Baghdad, Khan Baghdadi, Mesopotamia 1914-18, Merv, Persia 1915-19, North West Frontier of India 1915-17, Narugombe, East Africa 1816-18, and Afghanistan 1919.

Second World War: Agordat, Keren, Abyssinia 1940-41, Alam el Halfa, Defence of Alamein, North Africa 1940-43, Kampar, Singapore Island, Malaya 1941-42, Hong Kong, South East Asia 1941-42, The Yu, North Arakan, Buthidaung, Razabil, Maungdaw, Ngakyedauk Pass, Imphal, Shenam Pass, Nungshigum, Bishenpur, Kanglatongbi, Jessami, Naga Village, Mao Songsang, Monya 1945, Kyaukse 1945, Nyaungu Bridgehead, Letse, Magwe, Rangoon Road, Pegu 1945, Sittang 1945, and Burma 1942-45.

Partition 1947: The Regiment was allotted to Pakistan.
All the Sikh soldiers were transferred to the Sikh Regiment (India).

Battle Honours (cont.)

Infantry Regiments (cont.)

15TH PUNJAB REGIMENT

Class composition: Sikhs, Punjabi Mussulmans and Jats.

Changes of Title:

1857 17TH Punjab Infantry.
1922 1ST Bn. 15TH Punjab Regiment.

1857 18TH Punjab Infantry.
1922 2ND Bn. 15TH Punjab Regiment.

1857 19TH Punjab Infantry.
1922 3RD Bn. 15TH Punjab Regiment.

1857 20TH Punjab Infantry.
1922 4TH Bn. 15TH Punjab Regiment.

1857 21ST Punjab Infantry.
1922 10TH (Training) Bn. 15TH Punjab Regiment.

Combined Battle Honours of the Battalions:
Pre First World War: China 1860-62, Ali Masjid, Peiwar Kotal, Charasiah, Ahmed Khel, Kabul 1879, Kandahar 1880, Afghanistan 1878-80, Burma 1885-87, Chitral, and Somaliland 1901-04.

First World War: Loos, France and Flanders 1915, Suez Canal, Egypt 1915, Megiddo, Sharon, Palestine 1918, Tigres, Kut al Amara 1917, Baghdad, Mesopotamia 1915-18, Persia 1918, North West Frontier of India 1917, Kilimanjaro, and East Africa 1914.

Second World War: Berbera, Abyssinia 1940-41, Tug Argan, British Somaliland 1940, West Borneo 1941-42, South East Asia 1941-42, The Sangro, The Moro, Cassino 11, Gothic Line, The Senio, Italy 1943-45, Rathedaung, North Arakan, Kohima, Jail Hill, Naga Village, Kyaukmyaung Bridgehead, Mandalay, Fort Dufferin, Meiktila, Nyaungu Bridgehead, Taungtha, The Irrwaddy, Yenaungyaung 1945, Kama, Taungoo, Sittang 1945, and Burma 1942-45.

Partition 1947: The Regiment was allotted to Pakistan.
The Sikh soldiers were posted to India.

Battle Honours (cont.)

Infantry Regiments (cont.)

16TH PUNJAB REGIMENT

Class composition: Sikhs, Punjabi Mussulmans and Dogras.

Changes of Title:

1857 22ND Punjab Infantry. 1922 1ST Bn. 16TH Punjab Regiment.	1857 23RD Punjab Infantry. 1922 2ND Bn. 16TH Punjab Regiment.
The Allahabad Levy. 1922 3RD Bn. 16TH Punjab Regiment.	The Bhopal Levy. 1922 4TH Bn. 16TH Punjab Regiment.

Combined Battle Honours of the Battalions:

Pre First World War: Afghanistan 1878-80, Burma 1885-87, Chitral, Tirah, Punjab Frontier, and Malakand.

First World War: La Bassée 1914, Messines 1914, Armentieres 1914, Festubert 1914, Givenchy 1914, Ypres 1915, St Julien, Aubers, Loos, France and Flanders 1914-15, Macedonia 1918, Suez Canal, Egypt 1915-16, Meggido, Nablus, Palestine 1918, Aden, Tigres 1916, Kut al Amara 1917, Baghdad, Mesopotamia 1915-18, North West Frontier of India 1915, Beho Beho, Narugombe, East Africa 1917-18, and Afghanistan 1919.

Second World War: Mescelit Pass, Mt Engiahat, Massawa, Abyssinia 1940-41, Jitra, Ipoh, Kampar, The Mauar, Singapore Island, Malaya 1941-42, Sidi Barrani, Omars, Benghazi, El Alamein, Mareth, Akarit, Djebel Garci, Tunis, North Africa 1940-43, Cassino 11, Kaladan, Imphal, Tamu Road, Litan, Arakan Beaches, and Burma 1942-45.

Partition 1947: The Regiment was allotted to Pakistan.
The Sikh soldiers were transferred to the Sikh Regiment (India).

Sikh Sepoy 1897

Infantry Regiments (cont.)

THE PUNJAB REGIMENT

Class composition: Sikhs and Dogras.
This was the only Punjab Regiment allotted to India in 1947.

To bring the regiment to full strength and expand, four battle-experienced regiments of the former Sikh Princely States were absorbed into the regiment. These were a regiment each from the Jind and Nabha State Forces, and 1ST and 2ND Regiments of the Patiala Infantry.

Changes of Title:

1750 The Suraj Mukhi and Kartar Mukhi Regiments.
1923 Jind Infantry.
1954 13TH (Jind) Bn. The Punjab Regiment.

1760 Nabha Infantry.
1924 Nabha Akal Infantry.
1954 14TH (Nabha) Bn. The Punjab Regiment.

1710 Patiala Dehra.
1783 1ST Patiala Infantry.
1922 1ST Patiala Infantry (Rajindra Sikhs).
1954 15TH (Patiala) Bn. The Punjab Regiment.

1710 Patiala Dehra.
1783 2ND Patiala Infantry.
1922 2ND Patiala Yadavindra Infantry.
1954 16TH (Patiala) Bn. The Punjab Regiment.

Battle Honours (Post 1947):
Naushera, Jhangar, Zoji La, Punch, Jammu and Kashmir 1947-48, Dograi, Tilakpur-Mahadipur, Burki, Haji Pir, Kalidhar, Punjab 1965, Jammu and Kashmir 1965, Longanwala, Nanga Tekri, Brachil Pass, Wali Malik, Punjab 1971, Sindh 1971, and East Pakistan 1971.

Sikh Sepoy 1944

Battle Honours (cont.)

Infantry Regiments (cont.)

THE SIKH LIGHT INFANTRY

Class composition: The Mazhbi and Ramdassia Sikhs.

The regiment was created in 1941 and was accorded the traditions and honours of the Sikh Pioneer battalions, which were raised during the Sepoy Mutiny in 1857 and disbanded in 1933. The battle honours of the Sikh Pioneers are listed separately.

The Mazhbi and Ramdassia Sikh Regiment.

1ST Battalion raised in 1941.

2ND Battalion raised in 1942.

3RD Battalion raised in 1942.

Changes of Title:

1944 The Sikh Light Infantry.

Battle Honours:
Burma 1941, Meiktila, Pyawbwe, Rangoon, Operations in southern Shan States 1947, Deir ez Zor, Lattakia, Syria 1946, Azzubeir, Shaibah, and Iraq 1946.

Partition 1947: Being all Sikh in composition the Regiment was allotted to India and retained its distinct Sikh identity. Since 1947 a dozen more battalions have been added to the Regiment.

Battle Honours (Post 1947):

Op Hill, Punjab 1965, Jammu and Kashmir 1965, Parbat Ali, Fatehpur, Punjab 1971, Sindh 1971, East Pakistan 1971, and Kalidhar.

Sikh Light Infantry officer with Japanese war trophy 1945

Battle Honours (cont.)

Infantry Regiments (cont.)

THE BRIGADE OF THE GUARDS

This first mixed-class regiment was raised in 1949, by grouping the senior-most battalions from four senior infantry regiments. All of them had fine service records, thereby conferring on the new regiment an impressive collection of instant Battle Honours.

1ST Guards (formerly 2ND Battalion Punjab Regiment).

2ND Guards (formerly 1ST Battalion Grenadiers).

3RD Guards (formerly 1ST Battalion Rajputana Rifles).

4TH Guards (formerly 1ST Battalion Rajput Regiment).

12 extra battalions have been added to the Regiment since 1949.

Combined Battle Honours of the Battalions:
Jammu and Kashmir 1947-48, Rajasthan 1965, Punjab 1965, East Pakistan 1971, Jammu and Kashmir 1971, Akhaura, Burki, Gadra Road, Hilli, Naushera, Gurais, Shingo River Valley, Sylhet, and Ganga Sagar.

In March 1973, the then President of India, Mr. V. V. Giri, paid tributes to the stellar evolution of The Brigade of The Guards. He said, "Since Independence, no war or action has been fought without Guards having taken part in it. . . The Guards have made their indelible mark everywhere, justifying their motto, *Pahla Hamesha Pahla (Ahead Always Ahead).*"

Presidential Body Guard

THE INDIAN PARACHUTE REGIMENT

Changes of Title:

1941 Independent Parachute Brigade.
1944 44TH Indian Airborne Division.
1945 2ND Indian Airborne Division.
1952 The Indian Parachute Regiment.

Eleven infantry battalions were converted to the Parachute role and formed the Indian Airborne Division. On Partition in 1947, five of these battalions were transferred to Pakistan. Of the remaining six, only the following three continued as Parachute units:

1ST (Para) Punjab: Sikhs and Dogras.
2ND (Para) Maharatta: Maharattas, Mahars, South Indians and Bengalis.
3RD (Para) Kumaon: Kumaon and Hill Classes.

The following six newly raised battalions were added to the regiment and their class composition was:

1961 4TH Battalion: Gurkhas, Dogras, Garhwalis and South Indians.
1963 5TH Battalion: Rajput, Marathas, Ahirs and Kumaon.
1963 6TH Battalion: Sikhs, Gujars, Rajputs and Dogras.
1964 7TH Battalion: Bengalis, Oriyas, Rajputs and Jats.
1965 8TH Battalion: Sikhs, Gujars, Garhwal and Gurkhas.
1966 9TH Battalion: Mixed North Indian Classes.

Combined Battle Honours of the Battalions:
Sirinagar, Naushera, Jhangar, Jammu and Kashmir 1947-48, Hajipur 1965, Jammu and Kashmir 1965, Defence of Punch 1947-48, Chachro, Poongli Bridge, Sindh 1971, East Pakistan 1971, and Kargil 1999.

In 1951 the 60 Para Field Ambulance, a medical unit of the Regiment, served in Korea with the United Nations Forces. In 1956 the Regiment was involved in Peacekeeping duties following the Arab-Israeli War. In 1975 they were active in the annexation of Sikkim to the Indian Republic. In 1987 they fought against the Tamil Tigers in Sri Lanka, and in 1988 they repulsed the Sri Lankan mercenary assault of the Maldives.

Lt. Gen. I. S. Gill, PVSM, MC, was colonel of the regiment from 1967 to 1977.

Battle Honours (cont.)

Infantry Regiments (cont.)

THE MECHANIZED INFANTRY REGIMENT

Class composition: all India Classes.

The Mechanized Infantry Regiment was raised in 1979, initially with fourteen battalions. The regiment went on to raise nine more battalions.

The Battalions	Contributing Regiments
1ST Battalion	1ST Madras
2ND Battalion	1ST Jat Light Infantry
3RD Battalion	8TH Gurkha Rifles
4TH Battalion	1ST Sikh
5TH Battalion	14TH Kumaon
6TH Battalion	1ST Narwhal Rifles
7TH Battalion	Dogra
8TH Battalion	7TH Punjab
9TH Battalion	7TH Grenadiers
10TH Battalion	20TH Maratha
11TH Battalion	18TH Rajputana Rifles
12TH Battalion	16TH Mahar
13TH Battalion	18TH Rajput
14TH Battalion	16TH Jak Rifles

The Sikh Regiment, which contributed one of their elite battalions to the new regiment, did not regard it as an honour, and their missing battalion has not been replaced.

As a relatively new unit the Mechanized Infantry Regiment has not yet had the opportunity to earn any Battle Honours.

A Sikh soldier, typical of those who joined the Mechanized Infantry Regiment.

Corps and Services

CORPS OF SIKH PIONEERS

Class composition: Sikhs.

The first two battalions were raised during the Sepoy Mutiny. The pioneer battalions were unique because in addition to producing skilled technical troops, capable of carrying out the most complex engineering assignments, they were at the same time trained infantry battalions, armed with machine-guns and mortars and embodying such ancillary troops as signallers and medical orderlies.

Changes of Title:

1857 15TH (Pioneer) Regiment Punjab Infantry. 1922 1ST Bn. Corps of Sikh Pioneers.	1857 The Punjab Sappers (Pioneers). 1922 2ND Bn. Corps of Sikh Pioneers.
1887 34TH (Punjab) Regiment (Pioneers). 1922 3RD Royal Bn. Corps of Sikh Pioneers.	1917 2ND Bn. 23RD Sikh Pioneers. 1922 10TH Bn. Corps of Sikh Pioneers.

Combined Battle Honours of the Battalions:
Pre First World War: Delhi 1857, Lucknow, Taku Forts, Pekin 1860, Abyssinia, Peiwar Kotal, Charsiah, Kabul 1879, Kandahar 1880, Afghanistan 1878-80, Chitral, Punjab Frontier, China 1900, and Afghanistan 1919.

First World War: La Bassée 1914, Armentieres, Festubert, Givenchy, Neuve Chapelle, Ypres, St. Julian, France and Flanders 1914-15, Egypt 1916-17, Gazam, Meggido, Sharon, Nablus, Palestine 1917-18, Kut al Amara, Baghdad, Sharqat, Mesopotamia, and Aden.

In 1891 the Sikh pioneers provided volunteers to suppress the Arab slavers in central Africa.

On 10TH February 1933 all the pioneer regiments in the Indian army were disbanded. The Sikh pioneers were absorbed into the sapper regiments.

Battle Honours (cont.)

Corps and Services (cont.)

CORPS OF BOMBAY PIONEERS

Class composition: Sikhs, Maharattas and Rajputana Muslims.

Changes of Title:

1788 4TH Bombay Sepoys.
1903 107TH Pioneers.
1922 1ST Bn. 2ND Corps of Bombay Pioneers.

1842 The Regiment of Kelat-I-Ghilzai.
1903 12TH Pioneers (Kelat-I-Ghilzai Regiment).
1922 2ND Bn. Corps of Bombay Pioneers (Kelat-I- Ghilzai Regiment).

1846 28TH Bombay Native Infantry.
1903 128TH Pioneers.
1922 3RD Bn. Corps of Bombay Pioneers.

1901 48TH Bengal Pioneers.
1916 1ST Bn. 48TH Pioneers.
1922 4TH Bn. Corps of Bombay Pioneers.

1777 The Marine Battalion.
1903 121ST Pioneers.
1922 10TH Bn. Corps of Bombay Pioneers.

Combined Battle Honours of the Battalions:
Pre First World War: Abyssinia, Kandahar 1880, Afghanistan 1878-80, Tofrek, Suakin 1885, Burma 1885-87, Tirah, Punjab Frontier, and Afghanistan 1919.

First World War: Festubert 1914-15, Givenchy 1914, Neuve Chapelle, Aubers, Loos, France and Flanders 1914-15, Suez Canal, Egypt 1915, Meggido, Sharon, Palestine 1918, Basra, Shaiba, Kut al Amara 1915-17, Ctesiphon, Defence of Kut al Amara, Tigres 1916, Baghdad, Khan Baghdadi, Mesopotamia 1914-18, Persia 1918-19, and Baluchistan 1918.

On 10TH February 1933 all the Pioneer Regiments in the Indian Army were disbanded.

The Sikhs of the Bombay Pioneers were absorbed into the sapper regiments.

ROYAL BOMBAY SAPPERS AND MINERS

Class Composition: Sikhs, Rajputs, Maharattas, Mussulmans, with the levelling of Ahirs, Telegus etc.

Changes of Title:

1781 The Pioneer Corps.

1830 Engineer Corps.

1857 Corps of Bombay Sappers and Miners.

1923 Royal Bombay Sappers and Miners.

Battle Honours:
Pre First World War: Carnatic, Sholinghur 1781, Mysore 1782, Seringapatam 1792, Malacca, Maratha War 1774, Egypt 1801, Second Maratha War 1803, Assaye 1803, Gawilgarh, Aragon, Ali Garh, Dieg, Mauritius 1810, Java 1811, Nepal 1814, Third Maratha War 1818, Kirkee, Sitabaldi, Nagpur, Maheidpoor, Ashti, Asirgarh 1819, First Burma War 1824, Kemmendine, Pagoda Point, Defence of Rangoon 1824, Kokein, Bhurtpore 1825, First Afghan War 1839, Kabul Gate, Jalalabad 1841, China 1841, Sind 1843, Meanee, Hyderabad, Gwalior Campaign, Sikh War 1845, Sobraon, Second Sikh War 1848, Multan, Chillianwala, Gujarat, Second Burma War 1852, Rangoon, Sepoy Mutiny 1857, Roorkee, Meerut, Delhi, Kashmir Gate, Cawnpore, Lucknow, Central India, Second China War 1860, Bhutan 1864-65, Abyssinia 1867, Perak Expedition 1875, Second Afghan War 1878, Egypt 1882, Sudan 1884, Third Burma War 1885, Somaliland 1890, Suakin 1896, Third China War 1899, Aden 1901, Somaliland 1903, North West Frontier of India, Ambela, Black Mountains, Zakha Khel, Mahsuds, Zhob Valley, Miranzai Expedition, Hunza Nagar Expedition, Chitral, Malakand, North East Frontier, Lushai, Naga, Sikkim, Chin, Tibet, Manipur, Abor, and Mishami.

First World War: France 1914, Egypt, Palestine, East Africa, Aden, and Afghanistan 1919.

In 1943 The Corps of Sappers and Miners were merged and became part of the Royal Indian Engineers. Their Second World War Battle Honours are listed separately with the Royal Indian Engineers.

KING GEORGE V'S BENGAL SAPPERS AND MINERS

Class Composition:
1ST Company: Sikhs and Punjabi Mussulmans.

2ND Company: Sikhs and Punjabi Mussulmans.

3RD Company: Hindustanis.

4TH Company: Sikhs and Pathans.

5TH Company: Sikhs and Punjabi Mussulmans.

6TH Company: Hindustanis.

Balloon Section: Punjabi Mussulmans.

Mounted Detachment: Sikhs.

Changes of Title:

1819 Corps of Bengal Sappers and Miners.

1847 Bengal Sappers and Pioneers.

1851 Bengal Sappers and Miners.

1906 1ST Prince of Wales' Own Sappers and Miners.

1923 King George's Own Sappers and Miners.

1937 King George V's Bengal Sappers and Miners.

Battle Honours:
Pre First War: Bhurtpore, Cabool 1842, Ferozeshah, Sobraon, Mooltan, Goojerat, Punjaub, Delhi 1857, Lucknow, Ali Masjid, Charasiah, Kabul 1879, Ahmed Khel, Afghanistan 1878-80, Burma 1885-87, Chitral, Punjab Frontier, Tirah, and China 1900.

First World War: La Bassée 1914, Festubert 1914-15, Givenchy 1914, Neuve Chapelle, Aubers, Loos, France and Flanders 1914-15, Megiddo, Sharon, Damascus, Palestine 1918, Aden, Kut al Amara 1915-17, Ctesiphon, Defence of Kut al Amara, Tigris 1916, Baghdad, Khan Baghdadi, Sharqat, Mesopotamia 1915-18, Persia 1918, North West Frontier of India 1915-16-17, and Afghanistan.

In 1943 The Bengal Sappers and Miners were merged and became part of the Royal Indian Engineers. Their Second World War Battle Honours are listed separately with the Royal Indian Engineers.

ROYAL INDIAN ENGINEERS

Class Composition: all India classes.

Changes of Title:

1818 Bengal Sappers and Miners.
1847 Bengal Sappers and Pioneers.
1910 King George's Own Sappers and Miners.
1946 Royal Indian Engineers.

1780 Madras Pioneers.
1831 Madras Sappers and Miners.
1923 Queen Victoria's Own Sappers and Miners.
1946 Royal Indian Engineers.

1837 Corps Of Bombay Sappers and Miners.
1923 Royal Bombay Sappers and Miners.
1946 Royal Indian Engineers.

Battle Honours: Pre 1947
The Second World War: Kampar, Malaya 1941-42, North Africa 1940-43, Cassino II, Italy 1943-45, Yenangyaung 1942, Ngakedaung Pass, Jail Hill, Meiktila, and Burma 1942-45.

The Battle Honours for the Bengal Sappers and Miners and the Bombay Sappers and Miners up to the Second World War are listed separately.

Partition 1947: Pakistan received 34 Engineer units while India received 61 Engineer units. The Indian units became the Corps of Engineers, whose history is replete with acts of bravery and valour. General P. S. Bhagat of the Corps remains the first Indian Officer to have won the Victoria Cross in the Second World War.

CORPS OF ENGINEERS

Battle Honours: (Post 1947):
Jammu and Kashmir 1947-48, Jammu and Kashmir 1965, Punjab 1965, Rajasthan 1965, East Pakistan 1971, Jammu and Kashmir 1971, and Sindh 1971.

THE SIKH SOLDIER IN THE FAR EAST

Soon after the fall of the Sikh Kingdom and annexation of the Punjab, the fighting qualities of the Sikh soldier found expression in the far corners of the British Empire. The first Sikhs to be recruited were for the Hong Kong Police in 1867. By the 1890s Sikhs were employed in the police forces of all the Malay States including North Borneo and Sarawak. They became the backbone of the Burma Military Police battalions and served in the various Burma regiments. They became the cutting edge of the Para-Military forces from Shanghai to Singapore. Now Singaporean Sikhs are making their presence felt in the island-nation's armed forces. Ravinder Singh became the first Sikh to rise to the rank of Brigadier General and assume the command of a frontline formation - the 6TH Singapore Division. Lieutenant Colonel Deep Singh served as Singapore's first military consultant to the United Nations. In 2003, Lieutenant Colonel Sukhvinder Singh Chopra led an SAF contingent to the Middle East, as part of Singapore's contribution to the multinational reconstruction effort in Iraq. More recently, Lieutenant Colonel Jaspal Singh Sidhu was the 'Mother Goose' responsible for controlling the fighter aircraft display at the National Day Parade 2006.

Sikhs in the British North Borneo Military Police in the early 1900s.

The regiments that served in the Far East, some raised especially during the Second World War, were largely disbanded at the end of that war. These regiments had no Regimental Colours, and no Battle Honours as such were recorded. The notable military actions of these regiments are substituted.

BURMA MILITARY POLICE

Class composition: Sikhs and Punjabis of other classes.

In 1886 the Government of India sanctioned the raising of the Military Police to facilitate the withdrawal of the main part of the regular forces in Burma. The military police battalions were organized like regular army regiments, and their duties were entirely military. The Military Police at the end of 1888 included 3,937 Sikhs.

During the First World War, the Burma Military Police Battalions were milked dry for volunteers to serve in Persia and Mesopotamia. The Burma Police Battalions were bodily formed into three squadrons of Burma Mounted Rifles for service in Trans-Caspia, the region east of the Caspian Sea on the Russian/Persian border.

Burma was separated from India in 1937 but the British still effectively controlled the country. Prior to the separation there had been nine battalions of Burma Military Police. At the separation six battalions became the Burma Frontier Force and the three remaining battalions were:

1ST Rangoon Battalion, Burma Military Police.

2ND Rangoon Battalion, Burma Military Police.

The Mandalay Battalion, Burma Military Police.

At the Japanese advance, the 2ND Rangoon Battalion was transferred to the Burma Frontier Force. The remainder stayed with the retreating British forces into India, where they joined the newly raised battalions of the Burma Regiment.

Military operations:

The notable engagements were fought at:

Bhamo, Moutshobo, Kadol, Kunnah, Yinda Wango, Zemethen Salem, Tummo, Chin, Lushai, Poukhan, Tnhon, Thetta, Chinbok, Momeik, Wuntho, Tlang-Tlang, Bounghe, Irrawaddy, Chin Hills, and Kachin Hills.

The Sikh Soldier in the Far East (cont.)

BURMA MOUNTED RIFLES

Class composition: Sikhs and Punjabi Mussulmans.

The Burma police battalions were bodily formed into three squadrons of Burma Mounted Rifles for service in Trans-Caspia. The Indian troops left Trans-Caspia in 1919 for Burma, leaving behind them a reputation for discipline and gallantry which any troops might be proud of, and which they well deserved.

Military operations:
On the 5TH of July 1917 a troop under Jemadar Partab Singh encountered heavy fire but charged ahead to join a detachment engaged in a firefight against 500 robber-tribesmen. They killed 23 and the rest fled to the hills. On 21ST January 1918 they twice clashed with the robbers and encountered considerable opposition. Displaying considerable dash and spirit, they completely routed the well-armed robbers, killing about 80 of them. On 16TH June 3,200 tribesmen were repulsed with about 300 killed and wounded. Next day Sir Percy Sykes telegraphed to India expressing his high appreciation of the discipline, gallantry and soldiery spirit of the Burma Mounted Rifles.

The 'Indian Order of Merit', the highest gallantry award for Indian soldiers, was awarded to the following two Sikh officers and a Sikh Sowar of the Burma Mounted Rifles for their gallantry against the Russians and Persian Cossacks in Persia in 1917.

Sowar Uttam Singh

Risaldar Gulzar Singh I.D.S.M.

Jemadar Kishen Singh

Sikh Mounted Troopers 1914

THE BURMA FRONTIER FORCE

Class composition: Sikhs, Punjabis, Gurkhas and Burmans.

The Burma Frontier Force was formed from six battalions of The Burma Military Police in 1937.

The Burma Frontier Force was involved in settling internal disorder and frontier guard duties. They were not trained and equipped to be used as regular troops in a modern war. At the outbreak of the war in 1939, they were dispersed to take up guard duties on various airfields and supply dumps.

With the Japanese invasion, the allied retreat from Burma began. The units of the Burma Frontier Force were no match for the regular Japanese troops, and the decision was made to allow the local men to return to their homes if they so wished. The Sikhs, Punjabis and the Gurkhas continued the retreat into India where it was decided to form them into The Burma Regiment.

> When 1ST Burma Division were at Taungoo waiting to hand over to the Chinese, there occurred an incident trivial in itself, but in its way historic: the last charge of British/Indian horsed cavalry. It was led by Arthur Sandman of the Central India Horse, a Don Quixote figure, brave as a Lion, adopting the style and costume of a bygone age (in his case, Edwardian), and so short-sighted that he could not see a polo ball and had therefore taken to pig-sticking, as a boar was large enough to be visible. Never for a moment did he contemplate going to war other than on the back of a horse. So on 22ND March 1942 he was at Taungoo commanding a mounted squadron of Sikhs of the Burma frontier force. With a clink of curb-chains and a rattle of hooves on gravel, they rode out of history to reconnoiter the country to the southeast and perhaps link up with Chinese who were supposed to be there. Four or five miles out, Sandman saw what he myopically took to be Chinese, and rode towards them making allied noises. When machine-gun bullets started kicking up dust, he realized they were Japanese. He drew his sword, ordered his trumpeter to sound the charge and galloped straight at them, followed by his Sikhs yelling their war cry. None reached the enemy: most were killed.
>
> (Charles W. Trench: *Indian Army*)

The Sikh Soldier in the Far East (cont.)

THE BURMA RIFLES

This regiment was formed from the battalions of the 70TH Burma Rifles and the 85TH Burman Rifles as 20TH Burma Rifles in 1922-1923. In 1937, following the separation of Burma from India, they became the Burma Rifles, with ten Battalions. The composition was eight Battalions Burmese, and two of Indians, which are listed below.

7TH (Burma Police) Battalion.
Class Composition: Sikhs, Gurkhas, Punjabi Mussulmans.
This battalion was formed at Mandalay from a nucleus of men of the Burma Police and Burma Military Police.

8TH (Frontier Force) Battalion.
Class Composition: Sikhs and Punjabi Mussulmans
This battalion was composed of men from the Burma Frontier Force.

All the Burmese Battalions disintegrated during the Japanese invasion and were disbanded.

The wholly Indian 8TH Battalion was reduced to around 250 men by early April 1942, mainly due to battle casualties. The 8TH had fought well in the early battles and was regarded as the best of the Burma Rifles Battalions. The battalion underwent re-fitting and formed a composite battalion with The 7TH Battalion, which had reached India in May. In September the Punjabis and Sikhs were formed, with men of the 7TH Battalion, into 1ST Battalion, The Burma Regiment.

Sikh Soldiers in Burma 1945

The Sikh Soldier in the Far East (cont.)

THE BURMA REGIMENT

Class composition: Sikhs, Punjabi Mussulmans and Gurkhas.

The Burma regiment was formed in India in September 1942 from the Indian soldiers who had survived the retreat from Burma.

The six battalions raised to form the Burma regiment were:

1ST Battalion: Sikhs and Punjabi Mussulmans.

2ND Battalion: mainly Gurkhas.

4TH Battalion: mainly Gurkhas.

25TH Battalion: Sikhs and Punjabi Mussulmans.

26TH Battalion: Sikhs and Punjabi Mussulmans.

The Chin Hills Battalion: mainly Gurkhas.

In the reconquest of Burma, the 1ST Battalion fought at Kohima with the 33RD and 9TH Indian Infantry Brigades. At the end of the war the battalion went first to Singapore and then went on to serve at Palembag, Sumatra, landing in October 1945 and leaving a year later.

The Regiment was transferred to the new Burma Army in 1948.
1ST Battalion, being non-Burmese, was disbanded having had a very good war service.

Sikh Soldiers in Burma 1944

MALAY STATES GUIDES - INFANTRY AND ARTILLERY

Class composition: Sikhs and Punjabi Mussulmans, being ex-Indian Army soldiers.

The force was raised in 1875 and consisted of:

Two double companies of Infantry: Sikhs.

One double company of Infantry: Punjabi Mussulmans.

Mountain Battery of Artillery: Sikhs and Punjabi Mussulmans in equal numbers.

Military exploits:

The Guides had been more or less on continuous service within the States since 1857. During the First World War the battery and the infantry joined the Aden Defence Force from October 1915 onwards. The Battery had three Indian Officers, 54 gunners, 50 drivers and five followers, and the infantry numbered 788 all ranks. They were almost continuously in contact with the Turks, with frequent engagements, and a great deal of marching under a very hot sun.

Sikhs of the Malay States Guides Battery 1906

Sikh sharpshooters of the Malay States Guides
at a shooting competition at Bisley, England, 1910.

The Sikh Soldier in the Far East (cont.)

NORTH BORNEO DEFENCE FORCE

Class composition: Sikhs and Malays in equal numbers.

This force was essentially an armed constabulary raised in 1901. The force mounted various expeditions in what are now Sarawak, Brunei and Sabah.

The main punitive expeditions: Tambunam and Rundum.

SHANGHAI MOUNTED POLICE

In 1884 the Shanghai Police had a detachment of 558 mounted Sikh troopers. They were disbanded in 1943, when the settlement was retro ceded to Chinese control. Sikh troopers had been one of the symbols of Old Shanghai, China.

HONG KONG AND SINGAPORE ROYAL ARTILLERY

Class composition: Sikhs and Punjabi Mussulmans in equal numbers.

The battery was responsible for manning the colony's coastal defences. During the Boxer Rebellion in China, Singapore artillery served in the International Field Force.

During the First World War the battery proceeded to Egypt and saw extensive service with the Imperial Camel Corps in the Western Desert and Palestine.

During the Second World War the gunners made a gallant stand against the Japanese in Singapore. However 20 gunners were massacred at the San Wai Battery after they had surrendered.

Sikh Trooper: Shanghai Mounted Police

The Sikh Soldier in the Far East (cont.)

AZAD HIND FAUJ
(THE INDIAN NATIONAL ARMY)

Class composition: All Indian classes.

The Azad Hind Fauj or 'The Indian National Army' (INA) consisted mostly of Indian prisoners of war who had been captured by the Japanese in the course of service in the British Indian Army. Significant portions were also recruited from Indian civilians in Japanese controlled Malaya and Burma. On 17TH February 1942 one of the prisoners, Captain Mohan Singh of the 14TH Punjab Regiment, was appointed as leader, and he called upon the Indian prisoners to form an army to free India. Almost 20,000 soldiers immediately came forward to join what became the Indian National Army. They fought alongside the Japanese 15TH Army during the Japanese campaign in Burma, and in the battle of Imphal during the Second World War.

In December 1942, Mohan Singh and other INA leaders ordered the INA to disband after severe disagreement with the Japanese. Mohan Singh was subsequently arrested by the Japanese and exiled to Palau Ubin, an island off of Singapore. Thousands of INA soldiers returned to the status of POWs again. In a series of meetings between the INA leaders and the Japanese's in 1943, it was decided to cede the leadership of the INA to Subhash Chandra Bose.

The INA faced British and Allied troops in the Battle of Imphal, as well as the battles at Arakan in Burma. On 18TH April 1944 'suicide squads' of the INA broke through the British defence and captured Moirang in Manipur. The Azad Hind administration took control of this 'Independent' Indian Territory. Following the capture of Moirang, the advancing INA breached the Kohima road, posing a threat to the British positions in both Silchar and Kohima. An INA column, led by Col. Gulzara Singh, had penetrated 250 miles into India by outflanking the Anglo-American positions. However, the most serious, and ultimately fatal, limitations were the reliance on Japanese logistics and supplies. The total air dominance of the Allies, which, along with supply lines deluged by torrential rain, frustrated the joint INA and Japanese bid to take Imphal, and eventually led to their surrender to the British Indian Army.

Azad Hind Propaganda Postage Stamp.

THE FREE INDIAN LEGION

(Indische Freiwillegen - Legion Regiment 950)

Class composition: all Indian classes.

The troops of the Free India Legion were derived from German General Rommel's Indian prisoners of war captured during the battles for Tobruk. They were flown to Berlin in May 1941. Initially they were set up in Annaburg, and then transferred to Frankenburt Camp, from where they were sent to Konigsburg for training and induction. It was at Konigsburg that uniforms were issued, in German Fieldgrau with the badge of the leaping tiger of Azad Hind.

Changes of Title:

1941 Free Indian Legion.
1942 Legion Freies Indien of the Wehrmacht.
1944 Indische Freiwillegen Legion Der Waffen SS.

The Free India Legion was organized as a standard German army infantry regiment of three battalions of four companies each. The legion came to consist of:

1ST Bataillon - Infanterie Kompanien 1 to 4.
2ND Bataillon - Infanterie Kompanien 5 to 8.
3RD Bataillon - Infanterie Kompanien 9 to 12.
13TH Infanteriegeschutz Kompanie (Infantry Gun Company).
14TH Panzerjager Kompanie (Anti-Tank Company).
15TH Pionier Kompanie (Engineer Company).
Ehrenwachkompanie (Honour Guard Company).

<u>Operation Bajadere</u>

In January 1942, a detachment of about one hundred of the Freies Indian, trained by the German Special Forces, were Para dropped into eastern Persia. They were tasked to infiltrate into India through Baluchistan and to commence sabotage operations. Information passed on to Abwehr headquarters in Berlin from their office in Kabul indicates that they were successful.

<u>Holland and France</u>

The legion was transferred to Zeeland in Netherlands in April 1943 as part of the Atlantic Wall duties, and to France in September 1943, attached to 344 Infanterie Division, and later the 159 Infanterie Division of the Wehrmacht.

The ensign of Legion Freies Indien. The leaping tiger symbol was later adopted as the Flag of Azad Hind.

The Free Indian Legion (cont.)

The 1ST Battalion was reassigned to Zandvoort in May 1943 where they stayed until relieved by Georgian troops in August. In September the battalion was deployed on the Atlantic coast of Bordeaux on the Bay of Biscay. The 2ND Battalion moved to the island of Texel in May 1943 and stayed there until relieved in September of that year. From here it was deployed to Les Salles D'Ollonne in France. The 3RD battalion remained at Oldebrook as corps reserve till the end of September 1943.

Indische Freiwillegen Legion Der Waffen SS
The legion was stationed in the Lacanau region of Bordeaux at the time of the Normandy landings and remained there for four months after D-Day. On the 8TH August its control was transferred to the Waffen SS. On 15TH August 1944, the unit pulled out of Lacanau to make its way back to Germany. On the journey from Poiter to Chatrou it suffered casualties while engaging French regular troops in the town of Dun. The unit also engaged against Allied Armour at Nuis St.Georges while retreating across the Loir to Dijon, and was regularly harassed by the French Resistance. The unit moved from Remisemont, through Alsace, to Oberhohofen near the town of Heuberg in Germany in the winter of 1944, where it stayed till March 1945.

Italy
The 2ND Battalion, 9TH Company, of the Legion also saw action in Italy. Having been deployed in the spring of 1944, it faced the British 5TH Corps and the Polish 2ND Corps before it was withdrawn from the front to be used in anti partisan operations. It surrendered to the allied forces in April 1945, still in Italy.

End of the Legion Freis Legion
With the defeat of the Third Reich imminent in May 1945, the Indian Legion sought sanctuary in neutral Switzerland. The remainder of the unit undertook a desperate march along the shores of Lake Constance, attempting to enter Switzerland via the Alpine Passes. This was, however, unsuccessful and the Legion was captured by the US and French forces and delivered to British and Indian forces in Europe. They would be later shipped back to India where a number of the troops would stand trial for treason.

Sikh Free Indian Legionnaire.

SIKH PRINCELY STATES FORCES

The Cis Satluj Sikhs rose to power at the same time as the Majha Sikhs were establishing their confederacies, and did not serve under the banner of the Dal Khalsa (The Sikh Army). The Majha Sikhs had defied any authority on their rise to power, but the Cis Satluj Sikhs prudently accepted the Imperial Sovereignty. As Cis Satluj Sikhs came to maturity at the decline of the Mughal power, they faced the ambitions of the Lion of the Punjab, Maharajah Ranjit Singh. Ranjit Singh was subverting all the independent states and absorbing them to the expanding Sikh Kingdom. The Cis Satluj States were saved from annihilation by the arrival of the British.

Delhi had fallen to the British on 11TH September 1803, and they had pushed their borders to the River Jumna and then to the River Satluj, where they had a standoff with Maharajah Ranjit Singh. Ranjit Singh realised the power of the British and, with the Anglo-Sikh treaty of 1809, signed away the Cis Satluj territories. The Cis Satluj Sikhs were familiar with the concept of Imperial Authority and willingly accepted the British protection. The Cis Satluj Princely States maintained their own armed forces within their States and were obliged to make their forces available to the paramount power in the time of war or emergency. All the Cis Satluj States acceded to the union of India in 1948. At that time the bulk of the State Forces were absorbed into the Indian Army, thus losing their distinct Sikh identity.

The 1ST Patiala Infantry was probably one of the most famous of the State Forces regiments. It won an impressive number of awards, including two DSOs, and eight MCs. The Battalion Commander, Brigadier Balwant Singh Sidhu, was identified as being an excellent commander; he was one of the few Indian States Forces officers to command a battalion in action. He also became an Acting Brigade Commander during the Burma campaign.

Brigadier Balwant Singh Sidhu receives the DSO from
Field Marshall Sir Claude Auchinleck in Burma in 1945.

Sikh Princely States Forces (cont.)

PATIALA INFANTRY

Class composition: Sikhs.

Maharajah Ala Singh founded the Patiala State in 1714 and it became the most powerful state in the Cis Satluj territories. The State's armed contingent (Patiala Jatha) was the forerunner of the Patiala infantry regiments, and when the State sought British alliance in 1809, it was obliged to make the State Forces available to the British in time of war.

Changes of Title:

1714 Patiala Jatha.
1922 1ST Patiala Infantry (Rajindra Sikhs).
1950 15TH (Patiala) Punjab Regiment.

1714 Patiala Jatha.
1922 2ND Patiala Yadavindra Infantry.
1950 16TH (Patiala) Punjab Regiment.

1714 Patiala Jatha.
1819 3RD Patiala Infantry.
1948 Disbanded.

1714 Patiala Jatha.
1819 4TH Patiala Infantry.
1948 Disbanded.

Combined Battle Honours of the Battalions:
Pre First World War: Barnala 1723, Bhatti 1738, Sirhind 1761, Maler Kotla 1767, Pinjore 1768, Maratha War 1784, Gurkha War 1814, Nalagara, Sepoy Mutiny 1857, Second Afghan War 1878, and Tirah 1897-98.

First World War: Suez Canal, Egypt, Gaza, and Palestine.

Second World War: Burma, Malaya, Java, and Sumatra.

During the Second World War, the Patialas were on active service for six years and performed prodigal feats against the Japanese in Burma.

The Patiala Infantry Battalions were merged into the Indian Army in 1954, thus losing their distinct Sikh identity, and re-designated 15TH and 16TH (Patiala) Battalions, The Punjab Regiment.

Coat of Arms of the State of Patiala.

Sikh Princely States Forces (cont.)

JIND INFANTRY

Class composition: Sikhs.

Raja Gaja Singh joined the Sikh Confederate Army in 1763. During the struggle and the expulsion of the Afghans, he seized large tracts of the country, and founded the Independent State of Jind in 1772. His successor, Raja Bhag Singh, was one of the first Cis Satluj chiefs to seek British alliance, and the State's forces were made available to the British in time of war. The State's armed contingents went through several changes and re-merged as the Jind Infantry in 1940.

Changes of Title:

1763 Jind Jatha
1889 Jind Lancers.
1923 Jind Bodyguard Cavalry.
1940 Jind Infantry.

1772 Jind Jatha.
1837 Suraj Mukhi.
1923 Jind Infantry Battalion.
1940 Jind Infantry.

1772 Jind Jatha.
1889 Jind Infantry.
1940 Jind Infantry.

Combined Battle Honours of the Battalions:
Pre First World War: Maler Kotla 1767, Bhatinda 1771, Sangur 1774, Defeat of Mughal Governor Rahim Dad Khan 1775, Hansi 1801, Balawali 1815, First Sikh War 1845, Second Sikh War 1848, Sepoy Mutiny 1857, Karnal, Bhagpat, Panipat, Badliserai, Delhi 1857, Dadri 1864, Mankinas, Jhanjus, Afghanistan 1878-80, Tirah 1897, and Frontier War 1897.

First World War: During The First World War the Regiment was on active service in British East Africa for three years.

Second World War: Singapore.

Jind infantry battalions were merged into the Indian Army in 1951, thus losing their distinct Sikh identity, and re-designated 13TH (Jind) Punjab Regiment.

Coat of Arms of the State of Jind

NABHA AKAL INFANTRY

Class composition: Sikhs.

Gurdit Singh laid the foundations of the House of Nabha. His grandson Raja Hamir Singh consolidated and extended the possessions and by the year 1760 had put the independent principality on a firm footing. His successor Raja Jaswant Singh sought British alliance in 1809. At the time he was in possession of one Cavalry Regiment, two Infantry Battalions and two Batteries of Horse Artillery. They all saw service in the Second Afghan War of 1878, however at the re-organisation of 1889, only one infantry battalion survived.

Changes of Title:

1760 1ST Nabha Akal Infantry.

1760 2ND Nabha Akal Infantry.

In 1889. The two battalions were merged to form:

Nabha Akal Infantry.

Combined Battle Honours of the Battalions:

Pre First World War: Sirhind, Rori 1776, Gurkha War 1814, Bikanir 1818, Sepoy Mutiny 1857, Philaur, Delhi 1857, Afghanistan 1878-79, and Tirah 1897-98.

First World War: Afghanistan 1919.

Second World War: Eritrea, Cyprus, and Italy.

In Italy, soldiers of the Regiment were awarded a cluster of Military Medals.

In 1954 the Nabha Akal Regiment infantry battalion was merged into the Indian Army, thus losing its distinct Sikh identity, and re-designated 14TH (Nabha) Battalion, The Punjab Regiment.

Coat of Arms of the State of Nabha.

Sikh Princely States Forces (cont.)

KAPURTHALA INFANTRY

Class composition Sikhs.

The founder of the Kapurthala state, Jassa Singh Ahluwalia, was one of the Chief architects of Sikh power in the Punjab. He laid the foundations of an Independent State in 1779, when he wrested Kapurthala from Rai Ibrahim Bhatti. At the conclusion of the First Sikh War Kapurthala came under British protection. The State's forces were put at British disposal.

Changes of Title:

1890 Kapurthala I.S. Infantry.	1890 Kapurthala 2ND Line Infantry.
1911 Kapurthala Jagjit Infantry.	1928 Kapurthala Parmjit Infantry.
1939 Kapurthala Infantry.	1939 Kapurthala Infantry.

Kapurthala had two infantry battalions in 1939 and formed a composite battalion for service in Malaya.

Combined Battle Honours of the Battalions:
Pre First World War: Maler Kotla, Lahore 1761, Sarhind 1762, Katagarhi 1763, Sarhind 1764, Occupation of Kapurthala 1779, Red Fort Delhi 1783, Haidru 1813, Multan 1818, Mankera 1821, Jalalabad 1842, Aliwal 1846, Buddowel 1846, Sepoy Mutiny 1857, Lucknow 1857, Oude 1858, Afghanistan 1878-79, and Punjab Frontier 1897-98.

First World War: East Africa 1914, and Afghanistan 1919.

Second World War: Malaya.

Coat of Arms of the State of Kapurthala

Sikh Princely States Forces (cont.)

FARIDKOT SAPPERS AND MINERS

Class composition: Sikhs.

Sukha was the first independent chief of Faridkot. In 1809, to check Maharajah Ranjit Singh's expanding Sikh Kingdom, the British induced Faridkot to accept British alliance and thereby the state was obliged to make its forces available to the British in time of war or emergency.

Changes of Title:

1900 Faridkot Sappers (From Ex-Cavalry and Infantry).
1926 Faridkot Sappers and Miners.
1944 1ST Field Company, Faridkot Sappers and Miners.

1900 Faridkot Sappers (From Ex-Cavalry and Infantry).
1926 Faridkot Sappers and Miners.
1944 2ND Field Company, Faridkot Sappers and Miners.

Combined Battle Honours of the Battalions:
Pre First World War: Kot Kapura, Faridkot, Mari, Mudki, Muktsar, Ranadatta, Buhkboda, Dharamkot, Karman, Mamdot, First Sikh War 1846, Second Sikh War 1848, and Sepoy Mutiny 1857.

First World War: Francc and Flanders 1914, Kilimanjaro, Beho Beho, and East Africa 1914-18. The Faridkot Sapper Company provided reinforcements to the 39TH Garhwal Rifles in France and fought as Infantry. The Sappers were particularly commended for their service in East Africa.

Second World War: Burma 1941.

Both Field companies of Faridkot Sappers and Miners were absorbed into the Indian Army in 1948:

2ND Faridkot Field Co. became the 94TH Fd. Co. (Faridkot) Bengal Group.

1ST Field Co. became the 368TH Fd. Co. (Faridkot) Bengal Group.

Coat of Arms of the State of Faridkot.

SIKH SOLDIER IN AFRICA

The African tribal chiefs and the Arabs dominated the slave trade in Central Africa. To contain them the British administration sought to borrow Sikh soldiers from the Indian Army to form the Central African Rifles. These soldiers were the first regular army troops ever to operate in East and Central Africa. They carried the fight to the slavers and the operations were very violent and required several years to complete. Their outstanding conduct and bravery made them the backbone of several African regiments. They were always used in the forefront of all the military actions. The fighting took them from Nyasaland to Kenya, Uganda, Northern Rhodesia, Somaliland and circumnavigated the Cape to co-operate in the Ashanti campaign.
In the early days of colonial warfare, units took part in many minor and major expeditions, sometimes involving heavy fighting and always involving considerable hardship, for which medals but no battle honours were given.

Winston Churchill stated, in 1906, "The guardian over all stands the Sikh, who being immune to local influence of all kinds, constitutes the 'motor muscle' of imperial authority as he stands erect besides his rifle on guard over British interests 6,000 miles from the Punjab. He is a picked volunteer from all the Sikh regiments. If at any time considerations of expense or desire to obtain complete homogeneity in the military forces of the protectorate should lead to the disbandment of these companies, those who take the decision will have incurred a responsibility which few would care to share with them."

Sikh soldier in Central Africa 1891.

EAST AFRICAN RIFLES

Class composition: Sikhs, Punjabi Mussulmans, Swahilis, and Sudanese.

In 1888 the Imperial British East Africa Company (IBEAC) received a Royal Charter to take over the British concessions negotiated with the Sultan of Zanzibar. In 1895 Protectorate was proclaimed over East Africa (Kenya). In 1902 Kenya became a Crown Colony, and in 1963 finally became an Independent Republic.

1870 - The Sultan of Zanzibar's mercenary force was stationed at Zanzibar and the coastal ports of Lamu and Mombasa.
1877 - Lt. Mathews, R.N. raised a force of Askaris and was seconded to the Sultan's forces as Brigadier General.
1882 - The IBEAC sought the Sultan's assistance for maintaining order on the coast. The arrangement was not satisfactory, and troops from India were recruited.
1895 - The IBEAC's troops totalled 300 Punjabis (Sikhs and Punjabi Mussulmans), 300 Swahilis and 100 Sudanese.
1895 - The force was named East African Rifles.
1900 - An appeal was made for more Indian troops (especially Sikhs). The India Office complained that the continued demand from Africa for Sikh troops was prejudicial to the efficiency of the Indian Army. Military authorities wrote in the highest terms of the exemplary conduct of these troops throughout their service in East Africa. All of the Indian soldiers of the East African Battalion returned to India in 1900.

Changes of Title:

1895 East African Rifles.
1902 3RD Battalion King's African Rifles.
1963 The Kenya Rifles.

Military Operations:
During its brief history the East African Rifles took part in four major campaigns: the Uganda Mutiny; campaigns against the rebel Mbaruk of Takaungu and Ogadan Somalis in Jubaland; the Mazuri Expedition 1895-1896; punitive operations against Takaungu, Mwele, Ngobani, and Mtwapas, where the rebels were killed and dispersed. The East African Rifles also manned the Police forts dotted around the protectorate from where they made systematic operations against the rebel villages.

In 1902 the East African Rifles became the part of the King's African Rifles.

The regimental history of the King's African Rifles is listed separately.

Sikh Soldier in Africa (cont.)

CENTRAL AFRICAN RIFLES

Class composition: Sikhs and Africans.

In 1884 the African Lakes Company was founded in Nyasaland, over which British Protectorate was proclaimed in 1891. In 1895 Nyasaland became a Crown Colony called British Central Africa. The name was changed back to Nyasaland in 1907, and in 1964 Nyasaland became the Independent Republic of Malawi.

The Arab and African slave traders dominated Central Africa. To contain them the British administration sought to borrow Sikh soldiers from the Indian Army to form the Central African Rifles. These soldiers were the first regular army troops ever to operate in East and Central Africa.

Changes of Title:

1891 Central African Rifles.
1900 1ST Bn. Central African Rifles.
1899 Central African Rifles (2ND Bn.).
1899 2ND Bn. Central African Rifles.

Military Operations:
1891 Central African Slavers War (Mlanje, Chimkumbu), August 1891 Makanjira, November 1891 Kawinga, November 1891 Zarafi, February 1892 The Upper Shire, February 1893 Mlanje, Nyassera and Mkanda, October 1893 Makanjira, December 1893 Chirandzulu and Liwonde, 1893 Fort Johnson, 1894 Kawinga, 1895 Mlozi, Mwazi and Tambala, 1896 Odeti, Mkoma, Chikusi and Chilwa, 1897 Mpezeni (Present Zambia), 1898 Angoniland, 1898 Central Africa, 1894-98 Nkwamba, 1899 North East Rhodesia against Kazembe and Kalulu, 1900 Ashanti, 1901 Somaliland, 1904 Kisu Expedition, 1905 Nandi, and 1908 Somaliland.

The regimental history of the King's African Rifles is listed separately.

Sikh Contingent, Central African Rifles 1890

Sikh Soldier in Africa (cont.)

UGANDA RIFLES

Class composition: Sikhs, Sudanese and Somalis.

Capt. Lugard of the British Army arrived in 1890 from Kenya with soldiers to impose the Imperial British East Africa Company's rule on the Kabaka (king) of Buganda. Lugard made a treaty with the Kabaka and went on to annex Ankole and Toro. In 1895 British Protectorate was declared over Uganda. Subsequently Unyoro, Busoga, and Ankole were annexed to the protectorate. Uganda became an independent republic in 1962.

Changes of Title:

The force was originally Sudanese and Somalis with armed porters. In 1892 they were supplemented by Sikh volunteers.
1895 Uganda Rifles (with a contingent of 402 Sikh volunteers).

Military operations:
1895 Operations against the Nandi tribe, 1897 Sudanese Mutiny where Sikhs and Swahilis attacked and dispersed the mutineers at Lubwa, 1897 Final thrust against the mutineers taking 1,485 prisoners, and operations continued against those chiefs who supported the rebellion. The Uganda Rifles had fought five major and seven minor engagements and 35 skirmishes.

The arduous nature of the campaigning in Uganda can be visualized from the following description written by one of the officers who took part. "Passing through one of these swamps is a most tiring experience. Now clutching hold of the papyrus at the side, now stepping from one bit of floating vegetation to another, one tries in vain to save oneself from sinking deeper than necessary, until at last a treacherous root gives way, and down one goes into a quagmire of evil-smelling mud and water, only to recommence the whole process again. Except where the papyrus and weeds have been beaten down in forming a passage across them, there is no water to be seen, and from a distance one of these sluggish river swamps appears like a beautiful green lawn of varying shades. This appearance is in reality caused by the great heads of the papyrus with their innumerable little delicate spikes, supported four or five feet above the level of the marsh by the long thin stems growing out of the tangled mass of vegetation, the troops made many arduous marches throughout an area exceeding 40,000 square miles."

In 1902 the Uganda Rifles became the part of the King's African Rifles.

The regimental history of the King's African Rifles is listed separately.

Sikh Soldier in Africa (cont.)

SOMALILAND CAMEL CORPS

Class composition: Sikhs and Somalis.

Mohammed Abdille Hasan, the Mullah (religious leader), fought for a quarter of a century to keep Somaliland free of European control. He inspired his followers 'the Dervishes' so that whatever the odds, however terrible the losses, however complete the defeats in battle, they were always willing to die for him and his cause. The English called him the 'Mad Mullah'.
Opposing them the Sikhs were also mad, with their courage and self-sacrifice thousands of miles away from their homeland. The Mullah died on 23RD November 1920, sounding the death knell of the dervish movement. Disintegration soon followed and the Mullah's followers returned to their tribal areas and the Sikhs back to the Punjab.

Changes of Title:
1910 Somaliland Camel Constabulary (formed from the Sikh element of the disbanded 6TH Battalion, King's African Rifles).
1912 The Camel Corps (included 150 Somalis with Sikh Instructors).
1914 Somaliland Camel Corps (with 450 Somalis and 150 Sikhs).

The Sikh contingent of 150 Cameleers were eventually increased to 350 and operated as an integral part of the corps. The King's African Rifles Camel Battery, raised in 1903, also operated as an integral part of the corps, and was entirely manned by Sikhs.

Military Operations:
During 1912-13, the Corps constantly operated over a large area and forced a settlement on the feuding tribes and the return of looted stock. At the desperate battle of Dul Maduba on 9TH August 1913, a contingent of 110 Cameleers repelled an attack by 2,000 dervish riflemen, 150 horsemen, and 150 spearmen. The dervishes lost 600 dead and wounded, and only 30 of the Cameleers survived.
The Camel Corps was constantly engaged in the pursuit and destruction of the dervish bands right up to the death of the Mullah in 1920. The last of the time-expired Sikhs left the corps in 1922.

Sikh Soldiers of Somaliland Camel Corps 1892

Sikh Soldier in Africa (cont.)

KING'S AFRICAN RIFLES

The Central African Rifles, Uganda Rifles and East African Rifles were amalgamated into the King's African Rifles on 1ST January 1902.

Composition:
1ST (Central Africa) Bn. King's African Rifles.

2ND (Central Africa) Bn. King's African Rifles.

3RD (East Africa) Bn. King's African Rifles.

4TH (Uganda) Bn. King's African Rifles.

5TH (Uganda) Bn. King's African Rifles.

6TH (Somaliland) Bn. King's African Rifles.

Battle Honours:
First World War: Kilimanjaro, Narungombe, Nyangao, and East Africa 1914-18.

Military Operations:
The main exploit of the King's African Rifles, from the raising in 1902 to 1922, when the last Sikh soldier left the regiment, was the 'Mad Mullah' campaign in Somaliland.
Lt. Col. Swayne led the first expedition. He advanced to Zamara where he built a Zariba, a temporary stronghold. The Mullah attacked the Zariba, but was driven off with the loss of 600 men. Swayne pursued the Mullah's forces to Ferdidden and completely routed them, forcing them to make a dash over the border to the Italian territory. In 1901, the Mullah was back in British territory, proclaiming Holy War against the British. In October 1902 the Mullah's forces attacked the British at Erigo, who were hard fought to repulse the attack. During this campaign the King's African Rifles inflicted up to 1,400 casualties on the Mullah's forces. In all the expeditions the Sikh soldier was well in the forefront.

The Sikh soldier was also present in the especially formed Indian regiments operating in Somaliland. These were the 2ND Sikh Regiment, Punjab Frontier Force and Punjab Mounted Infantry.

Sikh Infantry charge at the battle of Daratola 1903

ARTILLERY

MOUNTAIN ARTILLERY

Class composition: Sikhs and Punjabi Mussulmans in equal numbers.

At the conclusion of the First Sikh War, the Punjab ceded land, reduced its army and became a British Protectorate. The British inherited the Kingdom's borders to the mountain ranges, the North West Frontier. In 1846 a Frontier Brigade consisting of a Corps of Guides, four regiments of Sikh Local Infantry and a Light Battery of Artillery was formed to guard the frontier and to police the truculent mountain tribes. All of the volunteers were soldiers and gunners of the disbanded Sikh Army .The expansion of the force was delayed because of the commencement of the Second Sikh War. After the terrifically hard fought battles and the annexation of the Punjab, the Frontier Brigade was strengthened in 1849. The new establishment included three Light Batteries of Artillery, which were bodily transferred from the disbanded Sikh Horse Artillery. For the next 100 years this artillery force, now the Mountain Artillery, were constantly taking part in some sort of war, punitive expedition or frontier engagement. The Mountain Gunners, as they were known, continuously distinguished themselves on the North West Frontier of India and went on to serve in Afghanistan, Kurdistan, Tibet, Assam, Burma, Malaya, Java, Persia, Mesopotamia, Egypt, Palestine, Gallipoli, West Africa, Abyssinia, and East Africa.

Combined Battle Honours of the Battalions:
Pre First World War: Punjaub, Multan, Peiwar Kota, Kabul 1879, Afghanistan 1878, Charasiah, Kandahar, Afghanistan 1880, Ali Masjid, Burma 1885, Lushai 1889, Chin-Lushai 1890, North East Frontier 1891, Chin Hills 1892, Kachin Hills 1893, Chitral, Punjab Frontier, Tirah, Malakand 1897, Relief of Chitral 1895, Samana 1897, North West Frontier of India 1908, Tibet 1903, Mekran 1898, Persian Gulf, Somaliland 1902, Jidbali, and Jubaland.

First World War: Anzac, Landing at Anzac, Defence of Anzac, Suvla, Saribar, Gallipoli 1915, Suez Canal, Egypt 1915, East Africa 1914-18, Narugombe, Kilimanjaro, Nyangao, Mesopotamia 1914-18, Persia 1918, Basra, Shaiba, Tigres 1916, Palestine 1918, Megiddo, Nablus, North West Frontier of India 1917, Baluchistan 1918, Afghanistan 1919, and North West Frontier of India 1936-37.

The Mountain Artillery was transferred to The Regiment of Artillery, Indian Army on 1ST August 1939.

THE REGIMENT OF ARTILLERY, INDIAN ARMY

Class composition: all India classes.

The Regiment was raised in 1935 by the formation of 'A' Field Brigade, made up of four field batteries. Prior to 1935 the only Indian artillery had consisted of six regiments of the Mountain Artillery. They were all finally absorbed into the newly raised Regiment of Artillery, Indian Army, in 1939.
At the conclusion of the Second World War the Indian artillery had expanded to sixty-four regiments. The post-war run down in strength left them with twenty-eight regiments.
Following the 2:1 split of the regiments on Partition in 1947, India received eighteen and a half whilst Pakistan received nine and a half regiments.

Military Operations:
During the Second World War, Indian gunners served in East Africa, Malaya, the Middle East, Italy and Burma.

For post-war operations in Indo-China, Java and Sumatra, they were awarded the British General Service Medal, with clasp 'South-East Asia 1945-46'. Havildar Umrao Singh was awarded the Regiment's only Victoria Cross for his supreme and sustained gallantry in the Kaladan Valley during a Japanese attack on the 16TH December 1944.

Battle Honours (Post 1947):
Srinagar, Tithwal, Jammuand and Kashmir 1947-48, Congo 1961, Goa 1961, Operations against the Chinese 1962, Burki, Punjab 1965, Jammu and Kashmir 1965, Defence of Punch, Siramani, Parbat Ali, Punjab 1971, Sindh 1971, and East Pakistan 1971.

Lieut-General Prem Singh Gyani was the first Director General of the Indian Artillery.

Sikh Gunner,
Mountain Battery, 1890.

INDIAN NAVY

Class composition: all India classes.

The Bombay Marine was the fighting Navy of the East India Company in Asian waters, which became the Royal Indian Marine in 1892, and the Royal Indian Navy in 1935. During the Second World War it expanded rapidly and by the end of the war had 117 vessels.
In 1947, after Indian Independence, the Royal Indian Navy was divided between Indian and Pakistan.
On 26 January 1950 the prefix "Royal" was dropped, as India became a Republic. Today it is the world's fifth largest navy and currently operates more than 155 vessels, including the aircraft carrier INS *Viraat*. In conjunction with the other armed forces of the union, it acts to deter or defeat any threats or aggression against the territory, people or maritime interests of India, both in war and peace.

Combined Battle Honours of the Naval Ships (Pre 1947):
Hokoku Maru 1942, North Africa 1942, Atlantic 1943, Sicily 1943, Salerno 1943, Anzio 1944, South of France 1944, Adriatic 1944, and Burma 1944.

Battle Honours (Post 1947):
Kathiawar Coast, Junagadh, Goa, Daman, and Diu.

Naval Operations:
<u>Operation Cactus 1988.</u>
This operation was instrumental in overthrowing the coup attempt by mercenaries in the Maldives by pouring troops into there in 1988.
<u>The Kargil War 1999.</u>
The Indian Navy readied itself for a blockade of Pakistani ports. Thirty Indian ships parked themselves outside Karachi, just 13 nautical miles from the harbour. It did the trick. It conveyed to Pakistan what the warfare in the Himalayas and diplomatic channels could not spell out. The Pakistanis started pulling out of Kargil.

Sikhs, not being a seafaring nation, nevertheless made a considerable contribution to the ranks of the Indian Navy, including:

Admiral Harinder Singh.
Rear Admiral Satyindra Singh.
Rear Admiral Kirpal Singh.
Rear Admiral S. Singh Sodhi.

SIKHS IN THE AIR

Hardit Singh Malik.

Hardit Singh Malik was the first Sikh to fly in action. Born on 23RD November 1894, Hardit was educated at a public school, Eastborne College, and went on to Balliol College, Oxford. When the First World War broke out in 1914 he volunteered to join the Royal Flying Corps, the first Sikh or Indian ever to do so. Hardit wore a specially designed helmet over his turban. He went 'solo' in a Cauldron after just two and half hours of instruction, and obtained his wings in under a month. Hardit fought against the legendary 'Red Baron', Manfred von Richthofen's Staffel, and became a fighter ace with 9 victories. He was recalled to India in 1944 to become Prime Minister of the predominantly Sikh state of Patiala. He later became India's first High Commissioner to Canada, and then Ambassador to Paris. In 1952 he was awarded the Legion D'Honneur, personally presented by president Coty of France.

Lieutenant Hardit Singh Malik who flew combat missions for the Royal Flying Corps during the First World War.

Mehar Singh.

Air Commodore 'Baba' Mehar Singh MVC, DSO was commissioned as a Pilot Officer on 1ST August 1936, passing out from Cranwell, and remains one of the greatest legends. His extraordinary and inspired flying skills and his leadership were at their most brilliant during the traumatic months before the 1947 Partition, and then immediately thereafter during the Kashmir operations of 1947-1948.

Harjinder Singh.

Air Vice Marshall Harjinder Singh OBI, PSVM was amongst the first nine airmen to be selected to join the Indian Air Force in November 1930. Harjinder Singh eventually became Air Vice Marshall of the Indian Air Force, and in the early 1960s laid the foundations for a civil aircraft industry, based at Kanpur.

Shidev Singh.

Air Marshal Shidev Singh served with the famous XV Squadron flying Stirling bomber raids over Germany, including night attacks on the German submarine pens at Kiel. Shivdev Singh had a most distinguished career rising to Air Marshal and becoming Vice Chief of Air Staff.

Sikhs in the Air (cont.)

Bhupinder Singh and Amarjit Singh.
Bhupinder Singh passed the rigorous selection examination for admission to the Royal Air Force College at Cranwell, followed immediately by his cousin, Amarjit Singh. After getting their "wings" in July 1932, they were the pioneers who formed "A" Flight of No. 1 Squadron of the Indian Air Force on 1ST April 1933. Tragically, both were killed in an air accident six months later during an air exercise near Hyderabad-Sind.

Arjan Singh.
In 1964 Arjan Singh DFC became the first Sikh Chief of the Air Staff and, in 1965, in recognition of his services to the Nation, he was awarded India's second highest civilian honour, the Padma Vibhushan. The Government of India conferred the rank of Marshal of the Air Force on Arjan Singh in January 2002, making him the first and only 'five star' rank officer with the Indian Air Force.

Dilbagh Singh.
Air Chief Marshal Dilbagh Singh PVSM, AVSM, VM was the second Sikh Chief of Air Staff of the Indian Air Force, and was an outstanding fighter pilot. He flew over 5,000 hours, mostly on fighters, ranging from Second World War vintage aircraft to supersonic MiGs. During his 37-year tenure in the Indian Air Force he had the distinction of being the first to command both the transonic and supersonic squadrons. Between 1985 and 1987, Dilbagh Singh served as India's Ambassador to Brazil.

Man Mohan Singh.
Man Mohan Singh was the first Sikh aviator and the first Indian to fly solo in a light aircraft from England to India, and in 1934-35, from England to South Africa. At the outbreak of the Second World War, Man Mohan Singh joined the Indian Air Force Volunteer Reserve as a Pilot Officer. He was selected as leader of an Indian Air Force batch of fliers sent to England for training and active duty. He was later promoted to Flying Officer and assigned operations in the Philippines and Indonesia, and given the command of a Catalina aircraft. Man Mohan Singh was killed in a flying accident in West Australia on 3RD March 1942.

Mohinder Singh Pujji.
Mohinder Singh Pujji was posted to No. 253 Squadron RAF, flying Hurricane fighters from RAF Kenley in England. The Hurricanes were flown day and night to intercept German aircraft. He was later attached to No.43 Squadron, flying Hurricanes from Martlesham. The squadron converted to Spitfires and he was promoted to Flight Commander. Their operational tasks included fighter sweeps over occupied Europe, low-level attacks on enemy targets, and fighter escort to RAF bombers. During these operations Mohinder Singh Pujji was involved in many dogfights with Luftwaffe fighters, and his total tally was two Messerschmitt Me 109s confirmed as shot down, and three damaged.

Sikhs in the Air (cont.)

FLYING OFFICER NIRMAL JIT SINGH SEKHON PVC

"Flying Officer Nirmal Jit Singh Sekhon was born on 17TH July 1943, in Ludhiana, Punjab. He was commissioned into the Indian Air Force on 4TH June 1967. During the 1971 Operations, Flying Officer Sekhon was with No.18 "Flying Bullets" Squadron flying the Folland Gnat Fighter based at Srinagar. In accordance with the international agreement dating back to 1948, no Air Defence aircraft was based at Sirinagar, until the outbreak of hostilities with Pakistan. Flying Officer Sekhon was, therefore, unfamiliar with the terrain and was not acclimatized to the altitude of Srinagar, especially with the bitter cold and biting winds of the Kashmir winter. Nevertheless, from the onset of the war, he and his colleagues fought successive waves of intruding Pakistani aircraft with valour and determination, maintaining the high reputation of the Gnat aircraft.

Early in the morning of 14TH December 1971, Srinagar Airfield was attacked by a wave of six enemy Sabre aircraft. Flying Officer Sekhon was on readiness duty at the time. However, he could not take off at once because of the clouds of dust raised by another aircraft, which had just taken off. By the time the runway was fit for take-off, no fewer than six enemy aircraft were overhead, and strafing of the airfield was in progress. Nevertheless, in spite of the mortal danger of attempting to take off during an attack, and in spite of the odds against him, Flying Officer Sekhon took off and immediately engaged a pair of the attacking Sabres. He succeeded in damaging two of the enemy aircraft. In the fight that followed, at treetop height, he all but held his own, but was eventually overcome by sheer weight of numbers. His aircraft crashed and he was killed.

In thus, sacrificing himself for the Defence of Srinagar, Flying Officer Sekhon achieved his object, for the enemy aircraft fled from the scene of the battle without pressing home their attack against the town and the airfield. The sublime heroism, supreme gallantry, flying skill and determination, above and beyond the call of duty, displayed by Flying Officer Sekhon in the face of certain death, set new heights to Air Force traditions."

Nirmal Jit Singh Sekhon is the only officer of the Indian Air Force to be awarded the Param Vir Chakra.

Flying Officer Nirmal Jit Singh Sekhon.

PREM PAL SINGH, AIR VICE MARSHAL PVSM, MVC

In the Indo-Pak conflict of 1965, Wg. Cdr. P. P. Singh was the Commanding Officer of an operational bomber squadron. During the period 6TH to 9TH September, he undertook six major offensive and tactical close support operations, which included reconnaissance over the Sargodha airfield complex, Dab, Akwal and Murid airfields, marking of Peshawar airfield and bombing of Pakistani troop and Armour concentrations in various sectors. Disregarding personal safety, in these very dangerous operations in the face of heavy enemy anti-aircraft fire, he led a number of bombing and reconnaissance missions with courage, determination and tenacity. Throughout the operations, Wg. Cdr. P. P. Singh displayed a high sense of duty, professional skill and gallantry in the best traditions of the Indian Air Force.

Operational History of the Indian Air Force

First Kashmir War 1947. Congo Operation 1961, Indo-China Conflict 1962, Second Kashmir War 1965, Bangladesh Liberation War 1971, Operation Cactus 1988, and Kargil 1999.

The Maha Vir Chakra (MVC) is the second highest military decoration in India and is awarded for acts of conspicuous gallantry in the presence of the enemy. The following Sikh Indian Air Force officers were awarded the Mahavir Chakra:

Wing Commander Harcharan Singh Mangat MVC.
Air Commodore Mehar Singh MVC.
Group Captain Man Mohan Bir Singh Talwar MVC.

"These are myriad examples of legendary flying Sikhs in the Indian Air Force and, indeed, in the air arms of other fighting Services in India. Flying Officer Lal Singh Grewal joined the last IAF formation raised during World War II, No.10 Squadron, with whom he flew Hurricane II Cs in the Arakan in 1944-45. After the war, and conversion to multi-engine aircraft, he was amongst the first to fly troops into the Vale of Kashmir in October 1947 and, in November 1948, formed No.5 Squadron, the IAF's first heavy bomber unit with B-24 Liberators. In 1963, and the aftermath of the frontier war with China, Lal Singh Grewal was handpicked to establish the Aviation Research Centre (ARC) for special operations, about which very little has still been revealed. Air Marshal Lal Singh Grewal later rose to be the Vice Chief of Air Staff. There have been other Sikh Vice Chiefs of the Air Force, including Air Marshals Shivdev Singh and Air Marshal Prem Pal Singh. The present (April 1999) Vice Chief is Air Marshal Pritam Singh "Ben" who, in 1982, had formed the IAF's first dedicated formation aerobatic team the Thunderbolts, flying Hunters."
(from the forthcoming *History of the Indian Air Force* by Pushpindar Singh)

CHRONOLOGY OF SIKH BATTLE HONOURS

The Sikh kingdom of the Punjab was expanded and consolidated by Maharaja Ranjit Singh during the early years of the nineteenth century. Ranjit Singh died in 1839 and almost immediately his kingdom fell into disorder. The army was expanding rapidly in the aftermath of Ranjit Singh's death and proclaimed itself to be the Khalsa, or embodiment of the Sikh nation. The sovereign and ruling clique felt their power threatened as the Khalsa leaders assumed all executive, military and civil authority in the State.

The British-controlled territories were expanding by conquest or annexation to the borders of the Punjab. "It seemed to the precarious rulers that their only chance of retaining power was to break the army in a contest with the British. . . . . . A powerful, well-trained, and confident Sikh army prepared for war under the leadership of a Commander-in-Chief under orders from a Vizier, and watched from the sidelines by a powerful and clever chieftain. All three men dedicated to the defeat of the army they lead, and secretly informing their British opponents of that fact!" (Donald Featherstone: *At Them With a Bayonet*).

With the turmoil in the Punjab, and their under-estimation of the fighting qualities of the Sikh soldier, the British started massing their armies; the largest force ever assembled in India, on the Kingdom's borders. The British Generals, although they had had the co-operation of the Sikh commanders, had won the Anglo–Sikh wars at enormous cost. Commander in Chief General Gough paid tribute to the gallantry of the Khalsa soldiery: "Policy precluded me publicly recording my sentiments on the splendid gallantry of our fallen foe, or record the acts of heroism displayed, not only individually, but almost collectively, by Sikh Sardars and the army." The Sikhs were considered the finest soldiers in the East. "If I had anything to say to annexation," Harding had commented "I should enlist whole regiments of Sikhs into our service."

The British decided to enlist many battalions of Sikh forces. Sikhs readily volunteered for military service, displaying an enthusiasm for martial adventure, much of it involving lengthy tours of duty overseas. They became a conspicuous element within numerous regiments of infantry, cavalry and artillery battalions.

This staunch and loyal Sikh support was to show itself during the great wars.

During World War One, they fought in China, France and Flanders, Mesopotamia, Persia, Egypt, Palestine, Gallipoli, East Africa, and numerous other battlefields in nearly all theatres of the war.

During the Second World War they fought in the Western Desert, the Middle East, Eritrea, Ethiopia, Italy, and took part in the liberation of Greece. But against Japan in the east, they played their greatest role from the reverses of 1942 to the final overwhelming victory of 1945.

Chronology of Sikh Battle Honours (cont.)

There follows detailed descriptions of the battles of the Anglo–Sikh wars demonstrating the gallantry of the Sikh soldier before battle honours were awarded. Then there are the Regimental battle honours earned by the Sikh soldier as part of the British Indian Army, and the battle honours earned in the defence of his homeland since 1947.

Below the description is listed the units that were awarded the honour and in brackets is the title of the unit after partition in 1947, together with the country it was assigned to.

Moodkee (Mudki), 1845 (Punjab).

This was the opening battle of the First Anglo-Sikh War. The Sikh commander, Lal Singh, took a detachment of 3,500 cavalry, 2,000 infantry and 20 guns from the main force. He advanced to confront the British force of 12,000 men with 48 guns and four troops of horse artillery. They sighted the British forces on 18TH December 1845, near the villages of Moodkee and attacked immediately. As soon as the attack started, Lal Singh (who was in league with the British) deserted his men and retreated to the camp at Ferozeshah. Though outnumbered, the Sikhs fought the enemy to a standstill. Wheeler's Brigade, so terrified at the sight of the Sikh cavalry, formed squares and would not obey orders to reform and advance. In the fierce encounter, the Sikh gunners nobly served their beloved guns and the Khalsa took on the numerous enemies in grim hand-to-hand fighting. Having lost almost half of their force and fifteen guns, the leaderless Khalsa withdrew back to the main force at Ferozeshah.

Ferozeshah, 1845 (Punjab).

The most terrible defeat in the annals of British Indian history occurred at Ferozeshah in December 1845. The British commander, General Gough, decided on a frontal attack. The attacking force amounted to 17,674 men and 69 guns. The British Divisional attack, under General Littler, was repulsed with terrible slaughter. The British native regiments scattered to the wind and the British 62ND Foot came to a standstill and hastily retreated. The whole division retreated and stayed out of action for the rest of the day. Gough, in desperation, poured all of his cavalry, infantry and artillery into the jaws of death. The Khalsa repulsed every British charge and decimated the parties that had penetrated their lines. The British had suffered 2,415 casualties, the bulk of their artillery was out of action without any ammunition and the men were cold, tired and hungry with no reserves and reinforcements. The next morning, as the battered British force gathered itself, battalions and battalions of Khalsa army with heavy guns appeared on the battlefield. The Sikh guns opened fire; there was no reply from the British artillery. As the British steeled themselves to be slaughtered, the Sikh commander, Tej Singh (who was also in league with the British), wheeled away the Sikh Army and abandoned the battlefield.

Chronology of Sikh Battle Honours (cont.)

Baddowal, 1846 (Punjab).

After the battle of Ferozeshah the British force had already been considerably weakened and did not intend to engage the Sikhs. The British were seeking reinforcements from all quarters and troops with heavy guns were on their way from Meerut, Ambala and Delhi, and much-needed supplies were moving towards Ludhiana and then Ferozepore. The Sikh commander Ranjodh Singh Majithia, with a force of 8,000 men and 70 guns, crossed the River Satluj, sacked the forts of Fatehgarh, Dharamkot, Gangarana and Buddowal and raided Ludhiana. Gough immediately ordered General Harry Smith's division to Ludhiana. Harry Smith's force collided with the moving column of the Khalsa. The British force would not give battle and hastily retreated. The Sikhs closed in on the retreating force, captured their baggage train and stores, inflicting 137 casualties and taking 77 prisoners. Ranjodh Singh re-crossed the Satluj, as there was a danger of being trapped between Gough and the advancing reinforcements.

Aliwal, 1846 (Punjab).

This battle was fought in January 1846 between a British force detached from the main army, under Sir Harry Smith, and a portion of the Sikh army, under Ranjodh Singh, which had been threatening Ludhiana. As Smith attacked the Sikhs and carried their entrenchments, the Sikh commander and his officers deserted the troops. At the repeated cavalry charges, the leaderless men refused to retreat. 3,500 were killed and 54 guns were lost. Eventually they abandoned all their posts south of the River Satluj, except for the bridgehead at Sobraon.

Sobraon, 1846 (Punjab).

This was the decisive battle of the First Anglo-Sikh War. To check the British advance, a force commanded by Tej Singh was entrenched near the village of Sobraon on the River Satluj. Another force of artillery and infantry commanded by Lal Singh was kept away from the battlefield about four miles upstream. The Khalsa had constructed formidable entrenchments with 70 heavy guns and battalions of infantry in treble trenches. All the formations were defensive. On 18TH February Gough received his reinforcements of men, ammunition, stores and heavy guns, including Harry Smith's Division. Gough took two days to prepare for battle and then launched a frontal attack on the Sikh entrenchments. As the Sikh guns were silenced for the lack of powder and shell, Gough threw the full weight of the three divisions and field guns onto the entrenchments. Tej Singh fled from the battlefield and treacherously destroyed the pontoon bridge to cut off the Sikh retreat. Lal Singh had decamped soon after the first assault. Sardar Sham Singh Attariwala organized a last stand but gallantly as they fought, they were overwhelmed. The British casualties were 2,403. The Sikhs had 3,125 killed. The British Generals, although they had the co-operation of the Sikh commanders, had won the war at enormous cost.

Chronology of Sikh Battle Honours (cont.)

Ramnagar, 1848 (Punjab).

In the Second Anglo-Sikh War the Sikh commander Sher Singh had withdrawn across the River Chenab to the village of Ramnagar. The British commander, Brigadier General Campbell, with an infantry division, a cavalry division and Horse artillery under Brigadier General Cureton, was ordered to attack the Sikhs. Their attack met with disaster. The withering cannonade from the Sikh guns compelled the attackers to make a hasty retreat, abandoning a heavy gun and wagons of ammunition. The Sikh cavalry crossed the Chenab and checked and routed the attack of the 14TH Light Dragoons and the 5TH Light Cavalry. The whole British attacking force retreated from the field. Ninety British officers and men were killed in the attack, including Lieutenant Colonel Havelock and Brigadier General Cureton. The commander of the 14TH Dragoons was reported missing, presumed dead.

Sadullapur, 1848 (Punjab).

After the British reverse at Ramnagar, Gough waited for a week for his heavy guns to come up. On their arrival, he pushed forward to the riverbank and opened up a cannonade on the Sikh front. At the same time, he detached two brigades, commanded by General Thackwell and Brigadier Godby respectively, to cross the river and take the Sikhs on the flank. The Sikh guns opened up on Thackwell's Brigade and checked his advance, while the Sikh Cavalry blocked Godby's advance. The British attacking forces had been brought to a standstill. The cannonade from either side lasted for two hours until the dusk, when all the guns fell silent.

Chillianwala, 1849 (Punjab).

The main Sikh force moved to Lollianwala on the River Jhelum and entrenched in a strong position commanded by the artillery. They established strong picket lines in the surrounding villages. The total Sikh strength was about 10,000 men and 54 guns. The total strength of the invading force was about 12,000. On 13TH January the British approached the village of Chillianwala and came under heavy artillery fire. The British heavy guns and field batteries opened up and belched their cannonade for about an hour. Then they launched both divisions simultaneously on the Sikh positions with disastrous results. The British divisions completely lost their formations in the dense jungle. The Sikh infantry and cavalry fell on Campbell's Brigade, decimated their ranks and drove them back at bayonet point. The dreaded Sikh Irregular Light Cavalry charged Pope's Cavalry Brigade. The entire British Cavalry Brigade fled from the Khalsa attack and disappeared from the field, abandoning four of their guns and leaving their comrades at the mercy of the Sikhs. In another direction Pennyquik's Brigade, advancing through the thick forest, was trapped and shattered by the Sikh artillery. The shattered ranks of the British Brigade fled the deadly destruction of the Sikh artillery, leaving behind their commander and field officers dead on the field. The Khalsa drove the brigade back with heavy losses.

Chronology of Sikh Battle Honours (cont.)

Gujarat, 1849 (Punjab).

The last battle of the Second Anglo-Sikh War was fought at Gujarat on 21ST February 1849 and resulted in the decisive defeat of the Sikh Army. Gough at last had superiority in artillery and the advance was preceded by a sustained bombardment, the subsequent assault carrying all before it.

Punjaub, 1849 (Punjab).

This was the Campaign Honour for the Second Anglo-Sikh War, which resulted in the annexation of the Punjaub (Punjab). On 29TH March 1849, Maharajah Dalip Singh took his seat on the throne for the last time. The Punjaub was annexed to British India, the Sikh Kingdom ended, and Maharajah Dalip Singh was pensioned off to England.

BRITISH INDIAN ARMY

In 1849, after the fall of the Sikh Kingdom, the disbanded Sikh soldiery was welcomed into all arms of the East India Company's armies, thus joining the British Imperial forces. They were keenly recruited for their unsurpassed fighting qualities, and came to be known as 'The Sword Arm of the Empire'.

Pegu, 1852 (Burma).

The Second Anglo-Burmese War took place in 1852 and ended in 1853. It was one of the three wars fought between Burma and the British during the 19TH century with the outcome of the gradual extinction of Burmese sovereignty and independence. In 1852, Commodore Lambert was dispatched to Burma over a number of minor issues related to the 1826 Treaty of Yandabo between the countries. Lambert eventually provoked a naval confrontation in extremely questionable circumstances by blockading the port of Rangoon and thus started the Second Anglo-Burmese War. The British took Martban and Rangoon in April, Bassein in May, Prome in October and Pegu in November. This action ended in the annexation of the province of Pegu, which included Rangoon.

4TH Sikh Local Infantry	(12TH Frontier Force Regiment, Pakistan)
3RD Light Field Battery	(2ND Mountain Battery, India)

Battle of Gujrat

Chronology of Sikh Battle Honours (cont.)

Delhi, 1857 (India).

In 1857 Bahadur Shah Zafar proclaimed himself the Emperor of the whole of India. Most contemporary and modern accounts suggest that he was coerced by the Sepoys and his courtiers to sign the proclamation against his will. The civilians, nobility and other dignitaries took the oath of allegiance to the Emperor. The Emperor issued coins in his name, one of the oldest ways of asserting Imperial status, and he was accepted by the Muslims as their King.

The Sikhs of the Punjab did not support this rebellion as they did not want to return to Islamic rule, having fought many wars against the Mughal rulers. The Sikh princes backed the East India Company by providing both soldiers and support.

At the outbreak of the Sepoy Mutiny in 1857, the Mutineers seized Delhi, the old Mughal capital, and it was essential for the British to recapture it. A force, mainly drawn from the Punjab, established itself on the Ridge outside the walls. The greatly outnumbered troops on the Ridge fought off numerous assaults from the Mutineers, and then on 6TH September stormed the city. Dheli was recaptured after six days of tough fighting.

9TH, 10TH Bengal Cavalry	(4TH Horse, India)
32ND Sikh Pioneers	(The Sikh Light Infantry, India)
2ND and 5TH Punjab Cavalry	(Armoured Corps, India)
4TH Sikhs Infantry	(12TH Frontier Force, Pakistan)
1ST, 2ND, 4TH Punjab Infantry	(13TH Frontier Force, Pakistan)
Guides Cavalry	(10TH Guides Cavalry, Pakistan)
1ST Punjab Cavalry	(11TH Cavalry, Pakistan)

Lucknow, 1857 (India).

News of capture of Delhi by mutineers reached Lucknow on 12TH May 1857. On receiving the news the local native garrison also mutinied and besieged the British Residency at Lucknow.

This Battle Honour covers the defence of the Residency, which was besieged by 130,000 mutineers, many of who had been regular Sepoys. The first attempted relief was in September by Generals Havelock and Outram, whose troops reinforced the original Residency garrison. The second attempt by Sir Colin Campbell in March 1858 was successful and relieved the garrison. The 14TH Ferozepore Sikhs were at Mirzapore and became part of the British column for the relief of Lucknow. During this course the battalion fought a series of actions, the most noteworthy being the attack on Little Imambara. It was after this action that the battalion was permitted to wear the red turban as a mark of valour and distinction. The red turban is now part of the regimental uniform of the entire Sikh Regiment. Another gallantry award was the grant of one rank higher for all ranks.

Chronology of Sikh Battle Honours (cont.)

Lucknow, 1857 (India). (cont.)

14TH Ferozepore Sikhs (1ST Battalion, 4TH Mechanised Infantry, India)
32ND Sikh Pioneers (The Sikh Light Infantry, India)
2ND, 5TH Punjab Cavalry (Armoured Corps, India)
9TH, 10TH Bengal Cavalry (4TH Horse, India)
11TH Bengal Cavalry (5TH Horse, Pakistan)
1ST Punjab Cavalry (11TH Cavalry, Pakistan)
2TH, 4TH Punjab Infantry (13TH Frontier Force, Pakistan)
Bengal Sappers and Miners (Bengal Engineers, India)

Behar and **Defence of Arrah, 1857 (India).**

During the Sepoy Mutiny a Sikh Military Police Battalion did much good work in the province of Behar. A particular highlight of its performance being the defence of a house at Arrah by a detachment of sixty men for ten days against three battalions of mutinous Sepoys. For this action and for hunting down the mutineers in the province of Behar, the Battalion was awarded these two Battle Honours. In 1864, the Battalion became a regular unit of the Bengal Army and in 1874, became the famous 45TH (Rattray's Sikhs) Bengal Native Infantry.

Mooltan (Multan), 1857-1858 (India).

This Battle Honour was earned by Gardner's Horse in recognition of success in maintaining order in the Multan district of Punjab, where disarmed regiments broke out and attempted insurrection.

Taku Forts, 1860 (China).

The aim of the Anglo-French Expeditionary Force of 1860 was to compel the Chinese court at Peking to observe the trading treaties signed between their governments at Tientsin in 1858. At the Chinese refusal to ratify the treaty, Taku Forts, at the mouth of the Peiho River in North China, were stormed by an Anglo-French force under Sir Hope Grant, and Tientsin was opened to trade. The bravery of the Indian troops impressed everyone involved and 1ST Sikh Cavalry were said to have "performed their work most admirably. On more than one occasion they successfully charged a vastly superior force of the enemy's cavalry."

23RD Sikh Pioneers (The Sikh Light Infantry, India)
1ST Sikh Cavalry (5TH Horse, Pakistan)
19TH Bengal Cavalry (19TH Lancers, Pakistan)
20TH Bengal Infantry (2ND Btn. 14TH Punjab Regiment, Pakistan)

Chronology of Sikh Battle Honours (cont.)

Pekin, 1860 (China).

After the fall of the Taku Forts, the Chinese again refused to ratify the treaties, and the allies resumed hostilities. They captured Peking, and burned the emperor's summer palace, thus bringing the war to a successful conclusion. In 1860 the Chinese signed the Peking Convention, in which they agreed to observe the treaties of Tientsin and agreed to have Legations at Pekin and to open another ten ports for trade.

23RD Sikh Pioneers (The Sikh Light Infantry, India)
1ST Sikh Cavalry (5TH Horse, Pakistan)
19TH Bengal Cavalry (19TH Lancers, Pakistan)
20TH Bengal Infantry (2ND Btn. 14TH Punjab Regiment, Pakistan)

China, 1860-1862. (Campaign Honour)

This Campaign Honour was awarded for operations in China that included those against the Taiping rebels and the capture of Tsingpo. The large-scale Taiping Rebellion against the Qing Dynasty lasted from 1850 to 1864. The rebel army was led by heterodox Christian convert Hong Xiuquan. He established the Taiping Kingdom with its capital at Nanjing and gained control of significant parts of southern China, at its height ruling over about 30 million people.

The Taiping Kingdom was constantly besieged and harassed by Qing forces aided by the French and British, and they eventually put down the rebellion. The Guinness Book of World Records calls this the bloodiest civil war in history, with an estimated death toll of between 20 and 30 million people.

15TH Ludhiana Sikhs (2ND Btn. 11TH Sikh Regimen, India)
22ND Bengal Infantry (3RD Btn. 14TH Punjab Regiment, Pakistan)
27TH Bengal Infantry (3RD Btn. 15TH Punjab Regiment, Pakistan)

Abyssinia, 1868. (Campaign Honour)

In 1868 a combined British and Indian force invaded Abyssinia to secure the release of captives held hostage by King Theodore. The force advanced over 380 miles of difficult country to the capital, Magdala, near Apogee, where the decisive action was fought. A detachment of 23RD Sikh Pioneers charged forward and met the enemy in close combat. The Abyssinian courage could not stand up to the Sikh bayonets and they were beaten off with very heavy losses.

"The battle had been all along the Apogee Valley. The Abyssinians were in rapid retreat, and the blood of the Sikhs was fairly up. They fixed Bayonets and charged with cold steel, with which they were doing fearful execution, having penned their antagonists into one of the ravines running down from the heights of Selassie and Fahla."

Chronology of Sikh Battle Honours (cont.)

Abyssinia, 1868. (cont.)

Native Artillery	(5TH Mountain Battery, India)
Bombay Sappers and Miners	(Bombay Engineers, India)
23RD Sikh Pioneers	(The Sikh Light Infantry, India)
12TH Bengal Cavalry	(5TH Horse, Pakistan)
21ST Bengal Infantry	(10TH Btn. 14TH Punjab Regiment, Pakistan)

Afghanistan, 1878-1880. (Campaign Honour)

The Second Afghan War was fought, as had been the First, to eliminate Russian influence in Afghanistan. In 1878 two British forces advanced towards Kabul through the Khyber Pass and the Kurram Valley respectively, and the Afghans, having been defeated, agreed to receive a British Envoy. The following year the Afghans attacked the British Residency in Kabul and the Envoy and his escort of seventy Guides were killed, after resisting literally to the last round. The British advanced again and this time occupied Kabul. There they were virtually besieged, but eventually drove off their opponents. In 1880 trouble arose at Kandahar, previously occupied with little opposition, following the British defeat at Maiwand. Roberts, who was commanding at Kabul, was due to evacuate the country and he did so by marching part of his army to Kandahar and defeating the Afghans in that area before returning to India. All Second Afghan War Honours were granted in 1881.

14TH Ferozepore Sikhs	(1ST Battalion, 4TH Mech. Infantry, India)
45TH Rattray's Sikhs	(3RD Battalion, 11TH Sikh Regiment, India)
23RD Sikh Pioneers	(The Sikh Light Infantry, India)
32ND Sikh Pioneers	(The Sikh Light Infantry, India
1ST Bengal Cavalry	(1ST Horse, India)
4TH Bengal Cavalry	(2ND Lancers, India)
8TH Bengal Cavalry	(3RD Cavalry, India)
14TH, 15TH Bengal Lancers	(4TH Horse, India)
15TH Lancers	(Armoured Corps, India)
12TH Cavalry	(Armoured Corps, India)
2ND Punjab Mountain Battery	(2ND Mountain Battery, India)
3RD Punjab Mountain Battery	(3RD Mountain Battery, Pakistan)
4TH Punjab Mountain Battery	(4TH Mountain Battery, India)
Bengal Sappers and Miners	(Bengal Engineers, India)
Bombay Sappers and Miners	(Bombay Engineers, India)
12TH Bengal Cavalry	(5TH Horse, Pakistan)
13TH Bengal Cavalry	(6TH Lancers, Pakistan)
Corps of Guides	(10TH Guides Cavalry, Pakistan)
1ST Punjab Cavalry	(11TH Cavalry, Pakistan)
19TH Bengal Cavalry	(19TH Lancers, Pakistan)

Chronology of Sikh Battle Honours (cont.)

Afghanistan, 1878 - 1880. (cont.)

1ST Punjab Mountain Battery	(1ST Mountain Battery, Pakistan)
2ND Bombay Mountain Battery	(6TH Mountain Battery, Pakistan)
2ND Sikh Infantry	(12TH Frontier Force Regiment, Pakistan)
5TH Punjab Infantry	(13TH Frontier Force Rifles, Pakistan)
21ST, 24TH, Bengal Infantry	(14TH Punjab Regiment, Pakistan)
28TH,29TH,Bengal Infantry	(15TH Punjab Regiment, Pakistan)
3RD Punjab Cavalry	(11TH Cavalry, Pakistan)
2ND Bombay Cavalry	(13TH Lancers, Pakistan)
18TH Bengal Cavalry	(19TH Lancers, Pakistan)

Ali Masjid, 1878 (Afghanistan).

Ali Masjid fort in the Khyber Pass was attacked and captured by a force under Sir Sam Browne during their initial advance in Afghanistan, thus opening the main road to Kabul. British casualties were 58. Afghan casualties are unknown but will have been around 1,000 including 500 captured during the retreat.

4TH Punjab Mountain Battery	(4TH Mountain Battery, India)
Bengal Sappers and Miners	(Bengal Engineers, India)
14TH Ferozepore Sikhs	(1ST Battalion, 4TH Mech. Infantry, India)
45TH Rattray's Sikhs	(3RD Battalion, 11TH Sikh Regiment, India)
11TH Bengal Lancers	(5TH Horse, Pakistan)
Corps of Guides	(10TH Guides Cavalry, Pakistan)
1ST Sikh Infantry	(12TH Frontier Force Regiment, Pakistan)
20TH Bengal Infantry	(14TH Punjab Regiment, Pakistan)
27TH Bengal Infantry	(15TH Punjab Regiment, Pakistan)

Peiwar Kotal, 1878 (Afghanistan).

As Kurram Field Force, under Sir Fredrick Roberts, moved up the Kurram valley, the Afghans, 1,800 in number with 12 guns, retreated before them until they reached Peiwar Kotal. They joined the strongly entrenched existing garrison so that 4,000 Afghans and 23 guns held the 4 mile long fortified position centred on the Kotal, which guarded the entrance to the Kurram Valley route to Kabul. Sir Roberts, by excellent manoeuvring, managed to defeat the Afghans and routed them from their strong positions. In doing so he also captured their 11 artillery pieces. Kurram Field Force then continued onwards towards Kabul.

23RD Sikh Pioneers	(The Sikh light Infantry, India)
12TH Bengal Cavalry	(5TH Horse, Pakistan)
1ST Punjab Mountain Battery	(1ST Mountain Battery, Pakistan)
2ND, 5TH Punjab Infantry	(13TH Frontier Force Rifles, Pakistan)
29TH Punjabis	(15TH Punjab Regiment, Pakistan)

Chronology of Sikh Battle Honours (cont.)

Charasiah, 1879 (Afghanistan).

Charasiah is situated about six miles from Kabul. The Kabul Field Force, under Sir Fredrick Roberts, advancing to exact retribution for the massacre at the British Residency, and routed the Afghan Field Army. With him he had four cavalry regiments, two infantry brigades, and two mountain batteries of 4 guns each: a total of about 6,500 men including the Punjab infantry and cavalry; and the 14TH Bengal Lancers. On 6TH October 1879, he found his path blocked at Charasia by 13 regiments of Afghan regulars led by Sirdar Nek Mohammed and supported by the usual tribesmen. The British attacked in an uphill flanking manoeuvre and soon defeated the Afghans, pushing them from the ridge they defended.

14TH Bengal Lancers (20TH Lancers, India)
5TH Punjab Cavalry (Armourded Corps, India)
2ND Punjab Mountain Battery (2ND Mountain Battery, India)
Bengal Sappers and Miners (Bengal Engineers, India)
23RD Sikh Pioneers (The Sikh Light Infantry, India)
12TH Bengal Cavalry (5TH Horse, Pakistan)
5TH Punjab Infantry (13TH Frontier Force Rifles, Pakistan)
28TH Punjabis (15TH Punjab Regiment, Pakistan)

Kabul, 1879 (Afghanistan).

During December 1879 there was a general uprising of the Afghan tribes, and they closed in on the British troops in the Sherpur Cantonment outside Kabul. An Afgan army under the command of Mohammed Jan, who had denounced Yaqub Khan as a British puppet and instead declared Musa Jan the new Amir, gathered in the area north of Kabul. On December 15TH, his forces began to besiege the British forces entrenched in the Sherpur Cantonment. After some three weeks fighting, a mass assault on the British positions was beaten off on 23RD December, and a cavalry pursuit turned the repulse into a decisive victory. No quarter was given to the Afghans found in the area with weapons.

14 Bengal Lancers (20TH Lancers, India)
5TH Punjab Cavalry (Armoured Corps, India)
2ND Punjab Mountain Battery (2ND Mountain Battery, India)
4TH Punjab Mountain Battery (4TH Mountain Battery, India)
Bengal Sappers and Miners (Bengal Engineers, India)
23RD Sikh Pioneers (The Sikh Light Infantry, India)
12TH Bengal Cavalry (5TH Horse, Pakistan)
1ST Punjab Mountain Battery (1ST Punjab Mountain Battery, Pakistan)
3RD Sikh Infantry (12TH Frontier Force Regiment, Pakistan)
5TH Punjab Infantry (13TH Frontier Force Rifles, Pakistan)
28TH Punjabis (15TH Punjab Regiment, Pakistan)

Chronology of Sikh Battle Honours (cont.)

Ahmed Khel, 1880 (Afghanistan).

In April 1880, a British force under General Stewart set out from Kandahar to secure Ghuzni and reopen the road to Kabul. At Ahmad Khel about 15,000 Ghilzais attacked it. A rush of 3,000 Ghazis was successfully repulsed, and the enemy defeated and driven off, leaving 1,000 dead on the field. The British lost 17 only. The British force then marched on to Kabul.

2ND Punjab Cavalry (Armoured Corps, India)
Bengal Sappers and Miners (Bengal Engineers, India)
45TH Rattray's Sikhs (3RD Battalion, 11TH Sikh Regiment, India)
1ST Punjab Cavalry (11TH Cavalry, Pakistan)
19TH Bengal Lancers (19TH Lancers, (Pakistan)
2ND Sikh Infantry (12TH Frontier Force Regiment, Pakistan)
19TH Punjabis (14TH Punjab Regiment, Pakistan)
25TH Punjabis (15TH Punjab Regiment, Pakistan)

Kandahar, 1880 (Afghanistan).

After the disastrous defeat at Maiwand, the remnants of battle-wearied army began the 45 mile retreat to the city of Kandahar. Of the 1,500 (approx) British and Indian troops at Maiwand, a little over 1,340 succumbed in either the battle or the ensuing retreat. Only 160 of the wounded reached the citadel of Kandahar on the 28TH, raising the garrison numbers to 4,360. With the abandonment of the cantonments, the whole garrison withdrew behind the walls of the fortified city and organized preparations for its defence. On 8TH August, Ayub Khan, the victor at Maiwand, opened fire on the citadel from Picquet Hill north west of the city; a few days later other guns volleyed forth from the villages of Deh Khoja and Deh Khati on the east and south. Part of the main Kabul Field Force was now brought in after a forced march of 500 Kilometers lasting 22 days, and decisively defeated the Afghans outside the city on 1ST November. The Battle of Kandahar brought a close to the Second Anglo-Afghan War. Ayub Khan had been decisively beaten. He had lost the whole of his artillery, his camp, enormous quantities of ammunition and about 1,000 men killed. Ayub Khan became a fugitive along with small remnants of his battered army. The British appointee Abdur Rahman was thus securely established as emir of Afghanistan, under a protectorate which gave Britain control of Afghanistan's foreign policy.

3RD Bengal Cavalry (1ST Horse, India)
2ND Punjab Mountain Battery (2ND Mountain Battery, India)
Bombay Sappers and Miners (Bombay Engineers, India)
15TH Ludhiana Sikhs (2ND Battalion, 11TH Sikh Regiment, India)
23RD Sikh Pioneers (The Sikh Light Infantry, India)
3RD Punjab Cavalry (11TH Cavalry, Pakistan)
2ND, 3RD Sikh Infantry (12TH Frontier Force Regiment, Pakistan)
24TH Punjabis (14TH Punjab Regiment, Pakistan)
25TH Punjabis (15TH Punjab Regiment, Pakistan)

Chronology of Sikh Battle Honours (cont.)

Tel el Kebir, 1882 (Egypt).

The importance of Egypt to Britain rose dramatically after the opening of the Suez Canal in 1869. At a stroke there was a new route from Europe to the Far East that halved the journey time between Britain and India. To safeguard their interests Anglo-French control was established in Egypt in 1876. In 1881 a military dictator, Arabi Pasha, had seized power in Egypt, and Britain intervened to restore order and protect foreign lives and property. Alexandria was occupied after a naval bombardment and an expedition landed in the Suez Canal area. British landing parties entered Alexandria on 13TH July, two days after the bombardment. The city had been partially destroyed by fire and following the departure of Arabi's soldiers, law and order had collapsed. Arabi's troops were encamped outside Alexandria and the British feared for the security of the Suez Canal. Britain's response was to send an expeditionary force to restore order and install a new administration. Between 13TH July and 6TH September 1882, two armies, one from Britain and the other from India, converged on Egypt. On 21ST August, troops were landed at Ismailia and advanced on Tel el Kebir, which was taken in a dawn attack on 13TH September. The actual fighting was over quickly and the cavalry exploited success by riding on to Cairo, 64 miles away, reaching there the same evening. Britain retained control of the country for the next sixty years.

2ND Bengal Cavalry	(2ND Lancers, India)
6TH Bengal Cavalry	(18TH Cavalry, India)
13TH Bengal Lancers	(6TH Lancers, Pakistan)
20TH Punjabis	(14TH Punjab Regiment, Pakistan)

Suakin, 1885 (Sudan).

An Arab of Dongola, a Moslem fanatic, who had been accepted by many of the Arabs as the Mahdi or prophet, the expected Messiah of Islam, had, as far back as 1881, resisted and defeated the Egyptian forces. During 1882, by repeated successes, he had largely increased his power and the number of his adherents.

In 1883 the Egyptian Government collected and dispatched an army of over 10,000 men against the Mahdi under the command of Colonel Hicks. After three days' fighting Mahdi's followers annihilated the Egyptian army with great slaughter and overran the whole of the Sudan. The British Government placed General Sir G. Graham in command of a strong force collected at Suakin, with instructions to destroy the power of the Mahdi. Among the components of this force were Indian troops, both the cavalry and infantry. From the very first the Arabs offered fierce resistance to the advance of the expedition but were narrowly defeated in an action on 22ND March 1885.

9TH Bengal Lancers	(4TH Horse, India)
15TH Ludhiana Sikhs	(2ND Battalion, 11TH Sikh Regiment, India)
17TH Punjabis	Disbanded 1921

Chronology of Sikh Battle Honours (cont.)

Tofrek, 1885 (Sudan).

The British force and Indian Contingent marched from Suakin towards Tamai, Sudan, to build three Zaribas (*fortified bases*). While still unfinished, they were heavily attacked by Arabs of the Hadendoa tribe. In one action an Indian regiment broke and retreated, while elements of the Berkshire regiment were pursued by the yelling Arabs. Fortunately the Sikh outposts kept their heads and retired steadily and in good order, which just gave the Berkshires time to reach safety. Even so a few of the slower ones would have been overtaken, had not a very gallant Sikh Subedar turned back single handed and killed several of their pursuers with his sword. After severe fighting the enemy were driven off, losing 3,000 killed or died of wounds.

"Two soldiers of the Berkshires were saved from certain death by the magnificent daring of Subedar Gurdidt Singh of the 15TH Sikhs, who, placing himself between the pursuers and their prey, killed three Arabs in succession by rapid sword cuts." (From: *Frontier and Overseas Expeditions from India*)

15TH Ludhiana Sikhs	(2ND Battalion, 11TH Sikh Regiment, India)
17TH Punjabis	Disbanded 1921

Burma, 1885-1887. (Campaign Honour)

The Burmese King Thebaw harassed British trading concerns, and the British fear of another European power seeking influence near their Empire, led to the Third Burma War. An ultimatum demanding his protection for British subjects was rejected by King Thebaw, so war was declared on the 8TH November 1885. The Indian Government sent an expedition that advanced up the River Irrawaddy and confronted and destroyed the Burmese Army. They went on to annex the country. There followed, however, a great deal of trouble with the dacoits (bandits) and it was a considerable time before Burma was pacified by the Burma Military Police, a militia which contained a large number of Sikh ex-servicemen.

7TH Bengal Cavalry	(18TH Cavalry, India)
4TH Mountain Battery	(4TH Mountain Battery, India)
5TH Mountain Battery	(5TH Mountain Battery, India)
7TH Mountain Battery	(7TH Mountain Battery, India)
Bengal Sappers and Miners	(Bengal Engineers, India)
Bombay Sappers and Miners	(Bombay Engineers, India)
1ST Bombay Lancers	(13TH Lancers, (Pakistan)
8TH Mountain Battery	(8TH Mountain Battery, Pakistan)
26TH, 27TH Punjabis	(15TH Punjab Regiment, Pakistan)
33RD Punjabis	(16TH Punjab Regiment, Pakistan)

Chronology of Sikh Battle Honours (cont.)

Defence of Chitral, 1895 (India).

In 1895 a rebellion broke out in the State of Chitral in the northwest corner of India, following the murder of the Ruler. The small British garrison of the fort, which included a detachment of 88 men of the 14TH Ferozepore Sikhs, was responsible for the defence of the fort at Chitral for 46 days. Captain Townsend, in his report on the siege, wrote: "The spirit of the 14TH Sikhs won our admiration; the longer the siege lasted the more eager they became to teach the enemy a lesson. There could not be finer soldiers than these men of the 14TH Sikhs and they were our sheet anchor in the siege". Six Sikh officers and men were awarded the Indian Order of Merit (The highest gallantry award for the Indian soldier at that time) for their conspicuous gallantry, and all the men in the fort were given six months pay as bonus.

14TH Ferozepore Sikhs	(1ST Battalion, 4TH Mech. Infantry, India)

Chitral, 1895 (India).

This Battle Honour covers the campaign mounted to relieve the garrison of the Chitral fort. The 32ND Sikh Pioneers set out from Gilgit to cover 220 miles of very poor road to Chitral. The importance of the Sikh Pioneer's epic march was never fully recognized, most of the publicity and fame for the relief being lavished on the well-known British regiments like the 60TH Rifles and Gordon Highlanders. During the relief operations six Sikh officers and men of the 32ND Sikh Pioneers were awarded the Indian Order of Merit (The highest gallantry award for the Indian soldier at that time) for their conspicuous gallantry.

9TH Bengal Lancers	(4TH Horse, India)
2ND Mountain Battery	(2ND Mountain Battery, India)
4TH Mountain Battery	(4TH Mountain Battery, India)
15TH Ludhiana Sikhs	(2ND Battalion, 11TH Sikh Regiment, India)
23RD Sikh Pioneers	(The Sikh Light Infantry, India)
32ND Sikh Pioneers	(The Sikh Light Infantry, India)
34TH Sikh Pioneers	(The Sikh Light Infantry, India)
11TH Bengal Lancers	(5TH Horse, Pakistan)
Corps of Guides	(10TH Guides Cavalry, Pakistan)
4TH Sikh Infantry	(12TH Frontier Force Regiment, Pakistan)
25TH, 29TH Punjabis	(15TH Punjab Regiment, Pakistan)
30TH Punjabis	(16TH Punjab Regiment, Pakistan)

Chronology of Sikh Battle Honours (cont.)

Punjab Frontier, 1899 (India). (Campaign Honour)

This Campaign Honour was awarded to the forces that had taken part in suppressing the general rising of Pathan tribes on the North West Frontier of India in 1897-1898. The force used to suppress this great uprising was the largest ever used in the Frontier operations.

3RD Bengal Cavalry	(1ST Horse, India)
6TH Bengal Cavalry	(18TH Cavalry, India)
9TH Bengal Lancers	(4TH Horse, India)
Central India Horse	(Central India Horse, India)
2ND Mountain Battery	(2ND Mountain Battery, India)
5TH Mountain Battery	(5TH Mountain Battery, India)
Bengal Sappers and Miners	(Bengal Engineers, India)
Bombay Sappers and Miners	(Bombay Engineers, India)
Kapurthala Infantry	Disbanded
Jhind Imperial Service Infantry	(13TH Battalion, Punjab Regiment, India)
Nabha Imperial Service Infantry	(14TH Battalion, Punjab Regiment, India)
1ST Patiala Imp. Service Infantry	(15TH Battalion, Punjab Regiment, India)
15TH Ludhiana Sikhs	(2ND Battalion, 11TH Sikh Regiment, India)
45TH Rattray's Sikhs	(3ND Battalion, 11TH Sikh Regiment, India)
36TH Sikhs	(4ND Battalion, 11TH Sikh Regiment, India)
35TH Sikhs	(Sikh Regimental Centre, India)
34TH Sikh Pioneers	(The Sikh Light Infantry, India)
11TH Bengal Lancers	(5TH Horse, Pakistan)
13TH Bengal Lancers	(6TH Lancers, Pakistan)
Corps of Guides	(10TH Corps of Guides, Pakistan)
18TH Bengal Lancers	(19TH Lancers, Pakistan)
1ST Mountain Battery	(1ST Mountain Battery, Pakistan)
8TH Mountain Battery	(8TH Mountain Battery, Pakistan)
3RD Sikh Infantry	(12TH Frontier Force Regiment, Pakistan)
2ND Punjab Infantry	(13TH Frontier Force Rifles, Pakistan)
20TH, 22ND, 24TH Punjabis	(14TH Punjab Regiment, Pakistan)
30TH, 31ST Punjabis	(16TH Punjab Regiment, Pakistan)

North West Frontier of India in 1897

Chronology of Sikh Battle Honours (cont.)

Malakand, 1897 (India).

In July 1897 the garrison in the Malakand was subject to a mass attack led by the 'Mad Mullah'. Although there was a fort at Malakand, many of the men were in camps outside the fort. When the alarm sounded the British officers McRae and Major Taylor ran out with some Sikhs and engaged the attackers in a narrow defile, in which Taylor was killed. This action prevented the enemy from encircling the camp and cutting it off from the fort. The Sikhs held the right of the position against repeated day and night attacks between 26TH and 30TH July. A detachment of the 45TH Rattray's Sikhs clashed with a fanatical tribal horde advancing on the garrison. Outnumbered by swarms of tribesmen, the Sikhs disputed every yard as they retreated back to the rest of their regiment. Having had very little sleep they were required to make a desperate bayonet charge during the storm-laden night of 30TH, which scattered the tribesmen. It was all over by the time reinforcements arrived the next day; the tribesmen had fled back to the hills.

45TH Rattray's Sikhs	(3ND Battalion, 11TH Sikh Regiment, India)
35TH Sikhs	(Sikh Regimental Centre, India)
11TH Bengal Lancers	(5TH Horse, Pakistan)
Corps of Guides	(10TH Guides Cavalry, Pakistan)
8TH Mountain Battery	(8TH Mountain Battery, (Pakistan)
24TH Punjabis	(14TH Punjab Regiment, Pakistan)
31ST Punjabis	(16TH Punjab Regiment, Pakistan)

Chakdara, 1897 (India).

Defence of Chakdara Fort by six British officers and 240 Indian soldiers of the 45TH Sikhs and 11TH Bengal Lancers against 14,000 Pathan tribesmen, must rank as one of the greatest feat of arms in military history. Eventually there was tremendous execution of the tribals at Chakdara Fort.

45TH Rattray's Sikhs	(3ND Battalion, 11TH Sikh Regiment, India)
11TH Bengal Lancers	(5TH Horse, Pakistan)

Samana, 1897 (India).

At the time of the Afridi incursion into the Khyber and Samana ranges, 165 men of the 36TH Sikhs occupied the Fort Cavagnari at Gulistan. After the enemy had captured the small post at Saragarhi and annihilated the gallant Sikh garrison of 21 men, they proceeded to attack Fort Cavagnari, which was closely besieged for three days. The Sikhs conducted the defence with great gallantry and on one occasion they made a sortie from the walls and captured three of the enemy's standards. The garrison had been under continuous fire for 52 hours, suffering 44 men killed or wounded. The relief column arrived at a most opportune moment.

36TH Sikhs	(4ND Battalion, 11TH Sikh Regiment, India)

Chronology of Sikh Battle Honours (cont.)

Saragarhi, 1897 (India).

On 12TH September 1897, a detachment of 21 men of the 36TH Sikhs manned a detached, fortified, signaling post of Saragarhi. The post was surrounded by some 10,000 Afridis and Orakzais who promised the detachment safe conduct if they surrendered. The Sikhs chose to fight instead and repulsed repeated attacks for three days. The tribals set fire to the post, while the brave garrison lay dead or dying with their ammunition exhausted. Next morning the relief column reached the post and the tell tale marks of the epic fight were there for all to see. The tribals later admitted to a figure of 180 dead and many more wounded. This episode, when narrated in the British Parliament, drew from the members a standing ovation in the memory of the defenders of Saragarhi. The story of the heroic deeds of these men was also placed before Queen Victoria. The account was received all over the world with awe and admiration. All the 21 valiant men of this epic battle were awarded the Indian Order of Merit (posthumously) which at the time was one of the highest gallantry awards given to Indian troops and is considered equivalent to the present-day Mahavir Chakra. The dependants of the Saragarhi heroes were awarded 50 acres of land and 500 Rupees. Never before or since has a body of troops, that is all of them, won gallantry awards in a single action. It is indeed a singularly unique action in the annals of Indian military history. A tablet was erected in the memory of these brave men. The tablet reads: "The Government of India have caused this tablet to be erected to the memory of the twenty one non-commissioned officers and men of the 36TH Sikh Regiment of the Bengal Infantry whose names are engraved below as a perpetual record of the heroism shown by these gallant soldiers who died at their posts in the Defence of the fort of Saragarhi, on the 12TH September 1897, fighting against overwhelming numbers, thus proving their loyalty and devotion to their sovereign, the Queen Empress of India and gloriously maintaining the reputation of the Sikhs for unflinching courage on the field of battle." The Sikh Regiment celebrates 12TH September annually as "Sargarhi Day". The story of this battle of epic dimensions is taught to school children in France and is one of the eight stories of collective bravery published by UNESCO.

Tirah, 1897-1898 (India).

During the summer of 1897, along the Northwest Frontier of India, various tribes had fielded a force of close to fifty thousand men to harass and destroy British forts and villages. When they captured the Khyber Pass in August, the British Government decided they must be removed. The Army immediately fielded two Divisions to engage them. The campaign in Tirah employed one of the largest force in a Frontier Expedition. There was some hard fighting at the Khybar Pass, Tseri Kando, Maidan, and Arhanga Pass, particularly at the storming of the Dargai Heights, where the Sikhs rushed at the open and murderous fire and won the heights in forty minutes.

Tirah, 1897-1898 (India). (cont.)

2ND Mountain Battery	(2ND Mountain Battery, India)
5TH Mountain Battery	(5TH Mountain Battery, India)
Bengal Sappers and Miners	(Bengal Engineers, India)
Bombay Sappers and Miners	(Bombay Engineers, India)
Kapurthala Infantry	Disbanded
Jhind Imperial Service Infantry	(13TH Battalion, Punjab Regiment, India)
Nabha Imperial Service Infantry	(14TH Battalion, Punjab Regiment, India)
15TH Ludhiana Sikhs	(2ND Battalion, 11TH Sikh Regiment, India)
45TH Rattray's Sikhs	(3ND Battalion, 11TH Sikh Regiment, India)
36TH Sikhs	(4ND Battalion, 11TH Sikh Regiment, India)
18TH Bengal Lancers	(19TH Lancers, Pakistan)
3RD Sikh Infantry	(12TH Frontier Force Regiment, Pakistan)
2ND Punjab Infantry	(13TH Frontier Force Rifles, Pakistan)
30TH, 31ST Punjabis	(16TH Punjab Regiment, Pakistan)

Pekin, 1900 (China).

In 1900 the foreign legations in Pekin were besieged. An international force under a German commander, Count Waldersee, was assembled at Tientsin and, after initial checks, reached Pekin and relieved the Legations. The British force was the first to reach the besieged legations.

1ST Sikh Infantry	(12TH Frontier Force Regiment, Pakistan)
24TH Punjab Infantry	(14TH Punjab Regiment, Pakistan)

China, 1900. (Campaign Honour)

In 1900, the Boxers, a xenophobic movement in China, carried out a series of attacks on foreign missionaries, merchants and property. The Chinese government did little to remedy the situation and in June 1900 issued an edict, which amounted to support for the Boxers. The foreign legations in the Imperial capital Pekin (Beijing) were besieged and held out for three months, despite having a small garrison. An international relief force was organised by seven nations and in June 1900 the Taku Forts were captured. The force then moved on Pekin, which was relieved in August. Peace was concluded in January 1901. This Campaign Honour was awarded in 1903 to units who served in China during the Boxer Rising, other than those granted 'Pekin 1900'.

34TH Sikh Pioneers	(The Sikh Light Infantry, India)
Bengal Sappers and Miners	(Bengal Engineers, India)
Bombay Sappers and Miners	(Bombay Engineers, India)
14TH Ferozepore Sikhs	(1ST Btn., 4TH Mech. Infantry India)
16TH Bengal Lancers	(8TH Punjab Regiment, Pakistan)
31ST Burma Infantry	(13TH Frontier Force Rifles, Pakistan)
4TH Punjab Infantry	(14TH Punjab Regiment, Pakistan)
20TH Punjab Infantry	(14TH Punjab Regiment, Pakistan)

Chronology of Sikh Battle Honours (cont.)

Ashanti, 1873-1874 (Ghana). (Campaign Honour)

After the deposition of King Prempeh I of the Ashanti in the campaign of 1896, considerable ill-feeling in the country towards the British led to their decision to capture the Golden Stool which symbolised Ashanti royal power. The Ashanti chiefs thwarted this attempt and their people promptly rose against the British, besieging the Governor in the capital of Kumasi, now in Ghana. The rising was finally suppressed in December. The Sikhs of the Central African Rifles were most forward in their attacks. "All ranks, especially those fine soldiers the Sikhs, behaved admirably,' wrote Wilcocks in his official dispatch,' and if it were not for this impossible forest we should soon wipe out most of the Ashantis".

Central African Rifles (Malawi Rifles, Malawi)

British East Africa, 1897-1899. (Campaign Honour)

A mutiny in 1897 of the Sudanese troops used by the colonial government led Britain to take a more active interest in the Uganda Protectorate. In June 1897, a party consisting of Lieutenant Macdonald, Jemadar Bhagwan Singh and thirty N.C.O.'s and the men of the 14TH and 15TH Sikh Regiments proceeded to British East Africa. They joined an expedition formed to fight mutineers and other hostile elements in Uganda. A small force under Major J R. L. Macdonald, Royal Engineers, arrived at Lubwa Fort on Lake Victoria on the 18TH October 1897, and found it occupied by mutinous Sudanese troops. On the following day the mutineers attacked Major MacDonald's force for five hours, but were defeated and driven back into the fort. This was a remarkable feat by the Sikhs and the untrained Swahilis, ast the mutineers were led by experienced native officers. On the 11TH December, Lieutenant Macdonald and his small party were covering the activities of men delegated to destroy the rebels' plantations and gardens, when the enemy made a desperate flank attack on the working parties. Lieutenant Macdonald was shot and mortally wounded. Sepoy Sahib Singh, with the help of Sepoy Phuman Singh, defended Macdonald against overwhelming odds and carried him to a more secure position. Another force, crossing a swamp supposed to be impassable, attacked the rebel stockade at Kabagambi and carried it with great gallantry.

14TH Ferozepore Sikhs (1ST Battalion, 4TH Mech. Infantry, India)
15Th Ludhiana Sikhs (2ND Battalion, 11TH Sikh Regiment, India)

Engagement at Lubwa Hill 1897

Chronology of Sikh Battle Honours (cont.)

Somaliland, 1901-1904. (Campaign Honour)

Mohammed Abdille Hasan, the Mullah (religious leader), fought for a quarter of a century to keep Somaliland free of European control. He inspired his followers, 'the Dervishes', so that whatever the odds, however terrible the losses, however complete the defeats in battle, they were always willing to die for him and his cause. The English called him the 'Mad Mullah'. Opposing him were not only the organised regiments from India but also the Central African Regiments with Sikh contingents, The King's African Rifles Camel Battery, raised in 1903, also operated as an integral part of the corps and was entirely manned by Sikhs. In addition to the Sikhs of the Somaliland Camel Corps there was another force permanently stationed in Somaliland, the Somaliland Indian Contingent. This force consisted of one Camel and two Mounted Infantry companies, a total of 400 men, largely Sikh in composition. The Mullah died on 23RD November 1920, sounding the death knell of the dervish movement. Disintegration soon followed and the Mullah's followers returned to their tribal areas and the Sikhs back to the Punjab.

Bombay Sappers and Miners	(Bombay Engineers, India)
52ND Sikhs	(12TH Frontier Force Regiment, Pakistan)
19TH Punjab Infantry	(15TH Punjab Regiment, Pakistan)
Central African Rifles	(Malawi Rifles, Malawi)
Kings African Rifles	(Kenya Rifles, Kenya)
Somaliland Camel Corps	Disbanded 1943

Ashanti, 1900 (Ghana).

Close to the end of the 19TH century, the British attempted to colonize the Gold Coast, now known as Ghana. The British began by exiling the Ashanti's King Premph in 1896. When this did not succeed in breaking the people's spirit they demanded the supreme symbol of the Ashanti people: the Golden Stool. On March 28, 1900, the British Governor called a meeting of all the kings in and around the Ashanti city of Kumasi and ordered them to surrender the Golden Stool. Deeply insulted, the Ashanti Chiefs showed no outward reaction. Silently, they left the meeting and at once swore the Great Oath of Ashanti to fight the British until the Asantehene King Premph was set free from his exile. They moved quickly, cutting telegraph wires and blocking routes to and from Kumasi where the British had a fort. For several months the Ashanti kept the British pinned down. After sending 1,400 soldiers to put down the rebellion, the British captured the Ashanti leaders; all were exiled.

Central African Rifles	(Malawi Rifles, Malawi)

British East Africa, 1901. (Campaign Honour)

This Campaign Honour commemorates operations against the 'Mad Mullah' in British Somaliland.

Central African Rifles	(Malawi Rifles, Malawi)

Chronology of Sikh Battle Honours (cont.)

THE FIRST WORLD WAR 1914-1918

France and Flanders. (Campaign Honour)

This was the main theatre in which the 1914-1918 war was fought. The German invasion of Belgium and France in 1914 had virtually destroyed the British 2ND Corps in the first battle of Ypres. An Indian Corps (Lahore and Meerut Divisions), followed by 4TH and 5TH Cavalry Divisions destined for the Middle East were diverted to France in October, still in their tropical uniforms. Lt Col Merewether and Sir Frederick Smith wrote in *The Indian Corps in France:* "Of the Indian Corps it may be said that as much was asked of them as had been asked of any troops at any period or in any theatre of this war. They stemmed the first German onslaught through the late autumn of 1914, which ended in bitter fighting at Givenchy. They played a glorious part in the battle of Neuve Chapelle. The second battle of Ypres, the struggle for the Aubers ridge, and the desperate assaults of Loos - all claimed a toll of blood from the devoted Corps. They were asked to do much and they tried to do everything they were asked." and "The Sikhs may with justice be considered the most important class among our Indian soldiers. Not only are they the best known to Englishmen of all the fighting men of India, but they also bulk more largely than any other class in the Indian Army". Three class regiments of Sikhs formed part of Indian Corps in France: the 15TH Ludhiana Sikhs, 47TH Sikhs, and 34TH Sikh Pioneers. The community was, however, largely represented also in the 27TH, 33RD, 69TH, and 89TH Punjabis, and 57TH, 58TH, 59TH Rifles.

La Bassée, 1914 (France and Flanders).

The battle of La Bassée, 10TH October-2ND November 1914, was part of the Race to the Sea, the series of battles that established the line of the Western Front from the Aisne to the North Sea. This was the first battle for the Indian Corps in France. La Bassée is a proud battle honour for the 47TH Sikhs. The 47TH Sikhs were part of a planned group attack on the German trenches, but this attack was cancelled. Two companies of the 47TH Sikhs did not receive the cancellation order and so on October 28TH, 1914 they went into attack all by themselves and reached the German trenches where fierce hand to hand fighting took place. Out of 280 men who went into the attack only 68 returned. In spite of this heavy casualty rate the Sikhs had captured and destroyed the strongly held German feature. The British Parliament specially commended the battalion for valour during this attack.

Sikh Pioneers	(The Sikh Light Infantry, India)
Bengal Engineers	(Corps of Engineers, India)
Bombay Engineers	(Corps of Engineers, India)
47TH Sikhs	(5TH Battalion, 11TH Sikh Regiment, India)
13TH Frontier Force Rifles	(13TH Frontier Force Rifles, Pakistan)
16TH Punjab Regiment	(16TH Punjab Regiment, Pakistan)

Chronology of Sikh Battle Honours (cont.)

Armentieres, 1914 (France and Flanders).

The British 3RD Corps, after some severe fighting near Meteren, drove the Germans back and got within five miles of Lille, but was gradually forced back itself to a line just a mile east of Armentieres.

Sikh Pioneers	(The Sikh Light Infantry, India)
Bombay Engineers	(Corps of Engineers, India)
11TH Sikh Regiment	(11TH Sikh Regiment , India)
13TH Frontier Force Rifles	(13TH Frontier Force Rifles, Pakistan)
15TH Punjab Regiment	(15TH Punjab Regiment, Pakistan)

Messines, 1914 (France and Flanders).

British Cavalry had been endeavouring to close the gap between the troops in the Armentieres sector and those already near Ypres to the north. They were forced back to the Messines Ridge, fighting dismounted and reinforced by the Indian infantry. They held for a fortnight, although heavily outnumbered, before being driven off and establishing a line to the west.

13TH Frontier Force Rifles	(13TH Frontier Force Rifles, Pakistan)
16TH Punjab Regiment	(16TH Punjab Regiment, Pakistan)

Festubert, 1914 (France and Flanders).

This Battle Honour covers the repulse of German attacks on this village, which lies about two miles northwest of La Bassée and was held by the troops of the Indian Corps in late November. During the night of the 23RD November the enemy had sapped up to within five yards of the 34TH Sikh Pioneers and at dawn attacked with a shower of bombs and hand grenades. The bombs fell fast and furious near the 34TH Sikh's machine gun and many men fell. Subedar Natha Singh at once took charge and kept the gun in action for some time against the enemy who had broken in. At last the only survivor of the gun crew, Havildar Nikka Singh, carried it out alone under heavy fire. Both received the highest gallantry award for the Indian soldier. All through the night the units of Indian Divisions fought with bomb and bayonet; when the dawn came it was found that the original trenches had been practically recovered. Altogether the Sikh Pioneers lost 161 killed and 105 wounded in this fight and the Punjab Regiment had suffered 200 killed and wounded. Subedar Sant Singh was awarded the Military Cross for his conspicuous gallantry and leadership at Festubert.

34TH Sikh Pioneers	(The Sikh Light Infantry, India)
16TH Punjab Regiment	(16TH Punjab Regiment, Pakistan)

Chronology of Sikh Battle Honours (cont.)

Givenchy, 1914 (France and Flanders).

Sharp fighting broke out on 19TH December when Indian troops from the Lahore division launched an attack, successfully capturing two lines of German trenches. Defensive tactics were severely hampered by the conditions of the Indian trenches, heavily waterlogged as they were. Consequently the German force broke through and managed to occupy part of Givenchy but was driven out by counter-attacks, with the result that the village was back in British hands by the close of 20TH December.

Sikh Pioneers (The Sikh Light Infantry, India)
8TH Cavalry (8TH Cavalry, India)
4TH Horse (4TH Horse, India)
Deccan Horse (9TH Horse, India)
Bengal Engineers (Corps of Engineers, India)
Bombay Engineers (Corps of Engineers, India)
11TH Sikh Regiment (11TH Sikh Regiment , India)
13TH Frontier Force Rifles (13TH Frontier Force Rifles, Pakistan)
16TH Punjab Regiment (16TH Punjab Regiment, Pakistan)

Neuve Chapelle, 1915 (France and Flanders).

This village, about three miles north of Givenchy, was the scene of the first British offensive of 1915, launched on 10TH March after what was until then the heaviest bombardment of the war. The village was captured and all the first objectives achieved - an advance of two thousand yards being made on a front of two miles, but the British were unable to exploit their success and seize the high ground of Aubers Ridge, being held up mainly by machine-gun fire.

Sikh Pioneers (The Sikh Light Infantry, India)
Bengal Engineers (Corps of Engineers, India)
Bombay Engineers (Corps of Engineers, India)
11TH Sikh Regiment (11TH Sikh Regiment , India)
13TH Frontier Force Rifles (13TH Frontier Force Rifles, Pakistan)

Ypres, 1915 (France and Flanders).

Failure to take the Aubers Ridge after Neuve Chapelle exposed British weakness, which the Germans decided to exploit with an attack for the capture of Ypres. Using poison gas for the first time, which drifted across the front of the Ferozepore Brigade and checked their advance everywhere, the enemy redoubled his fire. The Indian troops, who were without any means of protection, suffered very heavily and fell back in confusion. At night the Jullunder and Ferozepore Brigades were relieved by the Sirhind Brigade, which immediately consolidated the line. The Germans, after fierce fighting, gained some ground but could not capture Ypres. The fighting continued for a month. Although the Germans gained ground they failed to achieve their objective.

Chronology of Sikh Battle Honours (cont.)

Ypres, 1915 (France and Flanders). (cont.)

Sikh Pioneers	(The Sikh Light Infantry, India)
11TH Sikh Regiment	(11TH Sikh Regiment, India)
Bombay Engineers	(Corps of Engineers, India)
13TH Frontier Force Rifles	(13TH Punjab Regiment, Pakistan)
14TH Punjab Regiment	(14TH Punjab Regiment, Pakistan)
16TH Punjab Regiment	(16TH Punjab Regiment, Pakistan)

St. Julien, 1915 (France and Flanders).

This Battle Honour covers the British counter–attacks to recover the ground lost in the opening phase of the battle and refers to the village around which there was particularly hard fighting at the cost of severe British casualties. Further German progress was halted, but the British had to withdraw after suffering heavy casualties.

Sikh Pioneers	(The Sikh Light Infantry, India)
Bombay Engineers	(Corps of Engineers, India)
11TH Sikh Regiment	(11TH Sikh Regiment, India)
13TH Frontier Force Rifles	(13TH Frontier Force Rifles, Pakistan)
14TH Punjab Regiment	(14TH Punjab Regiment, Pakistan)
16TH Punjab Regiment	(16TH Punjab Regiment, Pakistan)

Aubers, 1915 (France and Flanders).

While the Second Battle of Ypres was being fought, the British launched an attack in the Neuve Chapelle sector on 9TH May with the object of capturing Aubers Ridge. Three successive assaults were thrown back with heavy loss and the effort was abandoned the same night.

Sikh Pioneers	(The Sikh Light Infantry, India)
Bengal Engineers	(Corps of Engineers, India)
Bombay Engineers	(Corps of Engineers, India)
11TH Sikh Regiment	(11TH Sikh Regiment, India)
13TH Frontier Force Rifles	(13TH Frontier Force Rifles, Pakistan)
14TH Punjab Regiment	(14TH Punjab Regiment, Pakistan)
16TH Punjab Regiment	(16TH Punjab Regiment, Pakistan)

Sikh Soldiers in France 1914

Chronology of Sikh Battle Honours (cont.)

Festubert, 1915 (France and Flanders).

A week after the repulse at Aubers Ridge a further British attack was made in the Festubert sector. Preceded by a four-day artillery bombardment by over 400 guns firing 100,000 shells, the attack around the village of Festubert was launched at night on 15TH May by two divisions of mostly Indian infantry. They made rapid initial progress, despite the failure of the preliminary bombardment to effectively destroy the German Sixth Army front line defences. Under attack, the Germans retreated to a line directly in front of the village. The battle lasted ten days and resulted in an advance of about six hundred yards over most of the front attacked, but much of the ground gained was lost to counter-attacks. These operations were taken mainly to assist the French thrusts in the vicinity of Vimy Ridge further south and were hampered by a serious shortage of shells. Renewed attacks by the Allied forces between 20TH–24TH May resulted in the capture of Festubert village itself, a position held until the German advance of spring 1918. Despite having captured Festubert, however, the Allied forces had advanced less than a kilometre; consequently the attack was ended on 27TH May, with the British having suffered some 16,000 casualties during the action.

11TH Sikh Regiment	(11TH Sikh Regiment, India)

Loos, 1915 (France and Flanders).

The 1ST Army launched the main British offensive of 1915 in September in the flat coal-mining district south of the La Bassée Canal. After initial gains, the attempt to breakthrough failed, as two untried divisions, only recently landed in France, proved unequal to the task. Much of the ground won was lost to German counter-attacks.

Following is part of the order published by the Commandant: "The Commandant wishes to thank all ranks of the regiment who were engaged in the action on the 25TH September for the services rendered by them on that day. He himself saw the gallant advance of the Sikh Company under Major Graham and their subsequent holding of the 2ND German lines to which they had penetrated and their stubborn retirement in the face of heavy bombing under Subedar Malook Singh."

2ND Punjab Regiment	(2ND Punjab Regiment, India)
Bengal Engineers	(Corps of Engineers, India)
8TH Punjab Regiment	(8TH Punjab Regiment, Pakistan)
13TH Frontier Force Rifles	(13TH Frontier Force Rifles, Pakistan)
15TH Punjab Regiment	(15TH Punjab Regiment, Pakistan)
16TH Punjab Regiment	(16TH Punjab Regiment, Pakistan)

Chronology of Sikh Battle Honours (cont.)

Somme, 1916 (France and Flanders).

The Battle of the Somme, also known as the Somme Offensive, fought from July to November 1916, was among the largest battles of the First World War. With more than 1.5 million casualties, it is also one of the bloodiest military operations recorded. The Allied forces attempted to break through the German lines along a 12-mile (19 km) front, north and south of the River Somme in northern France. One purpose of the battle was to draw German forces away from the Battle of Verdun. However, by its end, the losses on the Somme had exceeded those at Verdun. By the end of the war, the Allied losses proved replaceable. The official figure for the British casualties was 410,000.

Deccan Horse	(9TH Horse, India)
Scinde Horse	(14TH Horse, India)
18TH Cavalry	(18TH Cavalry, India)
4TH Horse	(4TH Horse, India)
Central India Horse	(Central India Horse, India)
19TH Lancers	(19TH Lancers, Pakistan)

Bazentin, 1916 (France and Flanders).

This attack was launched on 14TH July against Bazentin Ridge, with the object of exploiting the success in the southern sector. The troops advanced at dawn, following a five-minute intense bombardment. The German second line was overwhelmed all along its length, but the attack then bogged down and there was a nine-hour delay while the cavalry was brought forward. By the time the advance was resumed the chance of further progress had been missed.

Deccan Horse	(9TH Horse, India)
4TH Horse	(4TH Horse, India)
19TH Lancers	(19TH Lancers, Pakistan)

Delville Wood, 1916 (France and Flanders).

Delville Wood on the right flank of Bazentin was attacked on 15TH July 1916. There was continuous fighting in and around it for six weeks. It was not until the end of August that the Delville Wood was finally cleared.

Deccan Horse	(9TH Horse, India)

Flers-Courcelettes, 1916 (France and Flanders).

There was heavy fighting around the villages of Flers and Courcelettes, tanks being used for the first time. Courcelettes fell to the Canadians and Flers fell to the New Zealanders, but no breakthrough was achieved.

Deccan Horse	(9TH Horse, India)
4TH Horse	(4TH Horse, India)
19TH Lancers	(19TH Lancers, Pakistan)

Morval, 1916 (France and Flanders).

As soon the Flers-Courcelettes operations died down the British effort was switched to the right of Delville Wood against the Morval sector. The village was taken on 25TH September.

Scinde Horse	(14TH Horse, India)
18TH Cavalry	(18TH Cavalry, India)
Central India Horse	(Central India Horse, India)
19TH Lancers	(19TH Lancers, Pakistan)

Cambrai, 1917 (France and Flanders).

On 30TH November the Germans launched an offensive and created a large gap in the southern side of the salient, which the British had driven into their lines. Despite the resistance of the Guards Division, the British were eventually forced back and lost most of the ground they had gained.

Deccan Horse	(9TH Horse, India)
Scinde Horse	(14TH Horse, India)
18TH Cavalry	(18TH Cavalry, India)
4TH Horse	(4TH Horse, India)
Central India Horse	(Central India Horse, India)
19TH Lancers	(19TH Lancers, Pakistan)

Egypt, 1915-1917. (Campaign Honour)

When the Turks entered the war it was obvious that they would try to seize the Suez Canal. This they did in February 1915. They were repulsed and the British then moved forward from the Suez Canal into Sinai, whence they advanced into Palestine. The British also had to cope with a rising of the pro-Turkish Senussi tribe near the Libyan border. Full Campaign Honour was awarded to Indian regiments, including regiments belonging to the Indian Princely States.

Sikh Pioneers	(The Sikh Light Infantry, India)
11TH Sikh Regiment	(11TH Sikh Regiment, India)
1ST Patiala Infantry	15TH Battalion, Punjab Regiment, India)
Patiala Lancers	(61ST Cavalry, India)
2ND Punjab Regiment	(2ND Punjab Regiment, India)
1ST Punjab Regiment	(1ST Punjab Regiment, Pakistan)
8TH Punjab Regiment	(8TH Punjab Regiment, Pakistan)
12TH Frontier Force Regiment	(12TH Frontier Force Regiment, Pakistan)
13TH Frontier Force Rifles	(13TH Frontier Force Rifles, Pakistan)
14TH Punjab Regiment	(14TH Punjab Regiment, Pakistan)
15TH Punjab Regiment	(15TH Punjab Regiment, Pakistan)
16TH Punjab Regiment	(16TH Punjab Regiment, Pakistan)
1ST Mountain Battery	(1ST Mountain Battery, Pakistan)
6TH Mountain Battery	(6TH Mountain Battery, Pakistan)

Chronology of Sikh Battle Honours (cont.)

Suez Canal, 1915 (Egypt).

This Battle Honour was awarded for the repulse, with heavy loss, of the Turkish attack on the Suez Canal. The Honour was also awarded to cavalry and infantry units belonging to the Sikh Princely state of Patiala. These units defended the portion of the Suez Canal from Tinch to Port Said during the Turkish attacks between January and February 1915. Havildar Suba Singh was in command of a patrol of nine men of 13TH Frontier Force Rifles on the Suez Canal on the 22ND March 1915. He surprised and engaged a strong raiding party of Turks estimated at 400, under German officers, and in the fight that ensued he showed determined front and fought with great gallantry. Although severely wounded, Havildar, Suba Singh continued to lead and encourage his men and extricated his patrol from a very difficult situation with the loss of two killed and three wounded, whilst the losses to the enemy were estimated at 12 killed and 15 wounded.

Sikh Pioneers (The Sikh Light Infantry, India)
11TH Sikh Regiment (11TH Sikh Regiment, India)
1ST Patiala Infantry (15TH Battalion, Punjab Regiment, India)
Patiala Lancers (61ST Cavalry, India)
2ND Punjab Regiment (2ND Punjab Regiment, India)
1ST Punjab Regiment (1ST Punjab Regiment, Pakistan)
8TH Punjab Regiment (8TH Punjab Regiment, Pakistan)
12TH Frontier Force Regiment (12TH Frontier Force Regiment, Pakistan)
13TH Frontier Force Rifles (13TH Frontier Force Rifles, Pakistan)
14TH Punjab Regiment (14TH Punjab Regiment, Pakistan)
15TH Punjab Regiment (15TH Punjab Regiment, Pakistan)
16TH Punjab Regiment (16TH Punjab Regiment, Pakistan)
1ST Mountain Battery (1ST Mountain Battery, Pakistan)
6TH Mountain Battery (6TH Mountain Battery, Pakistan)

Palestine, 1917-1918. (Campaign Honour)

The first advance into Palestine was made in March 1917. After initial checks at the first and second battles of Gaza, the British broke through in October and advanced to Jaffa and Jerusalem, which fell in December. In September 1918, General Allenby won the decisive victory of Megiddo and the Turkish armies in Palestine disintegrated. During its final offensive from 19TH September to 26TH October, when Aleppo was entered, Allenby's force had destroyed three Turkish Armies and taken 83,000 prisoners The majority of the troops in the corps were Indian and although there is no desire to decry the contribution of other troops, the fact that the backbone of the corps was composed of the Indian troops must not be forgotten. It was a brilliant feat of arms by the Indian Army.

Palestine, 1917-1918. (cont.)

11TH Sikh Regiment	(11TH Sikh Regiment, India)
Sikh Pioneers	(The Sikh Light Infantry, India)
1ST Patiala Infantry	(15TH Battalion, Punjab Regiment, India)
2ND Lancers	(2ND Lancers, India)
Deccan Horse	(9TH Horse, India)
Scinde Horse	(14TH Horse, India)
4TH Horse	(4TH Horse, India)
Central India Horse	(Central India Horse, India)
9TH Mountain Battery	(9TH Mountain Battery, India)
12TH Mountain Battery	(12TH Mountain Battery, India)
Bengal Engineers	(Corps of Engineers, India)
Bombay Engineers	(Corps of Engineers, India)
2ND Punjab Regiment	(2ND Punjab Regiment, India)
19TH Lancers	(19TH Lancers, Pakistan)
8TH Punjab Regiment	(8TH Punjab Regiment, Pakistan)
13TH Frontier Force Rifles	(13TH Frontier Force Rifles, Pakistan)
12TH Frontier Force Regiment	(12TH Frontier Force Regiment, Pakistan)
14TH Punjab Regiment	(14TH Punjab Regiment, Pakistan)
15TH Punjab Regiment	(15TH Punjab Regiment, Pakistan)
16TH Punjab Regiment	(16TH Punjab Regiment, Pakistan)

Gaza, 1917 (Palestine).

The main Turkish defence line in Palestine ran from Gaza to Beersheba. Allenby made a wide sweep to seize Beersheba on the Turkish left with 20TH Corps, while the 21ST Corps made a holding attack on the Gaza defences. The main problem was the water supply, especially for the horses, but, following a night approach march, the 4TH Australian Light Horse Brigade galloped into Beersheba and secured the wells. The Turkish defences were then rolled up from that side in a week after the inception of the offensive. The Turks were forced in full retreat.

1ST Patiala Infantry	(15TH Battalion, Punjab Regiment, India)
23RD Sikh Pioneers	(The Sikh Light Infantry, India)
Jind Infantry	(13TH (Jind) Punjab Regiment, India)
13TH Frontier Force Rifles	(13TH Frontier Force Rifles, Pakistan)

El Mughar, 1917 (Palestine).

El Mughar was the scene of an action on 13TH November, which resulted in the capture of Junction Station and the cutting of communications between Jerusalem and Jaffa. El Mughar itself fell to the 52ND (Lowland) Division. Jaffa was occupied shortly afterwards.

13TH Frontier Force Rifles	(13TH Frontier Force Rifles, Pakistan)

Nebi Samwil, 1917 (Palestine).

This Battle Honour covers the capture of Nebi Samwil Ridge. This Ridge, traditional burial place of Prophet Samuel, dominated the approaches to Jerusalem. It fell to the recently formed 75TH Division and opened the advance to Jerusalem.

13TH Frontier Force Rifles	(13TH Frontier Force Rifles, Pakistan)

Jerusalem, 1917 (Palestine).

This Battle Honour commemorates the Turkish attempts to retake the city, which were repulsed after five days heavy fighting. The Turks pressed their attacks hard, but made no real progress and the British counter-attacks drove them back, about seven miles in some places.

13TH Frontier Force Rifles	(13TH Frontier Force Rifles, Pakistan)

Megiddo, 1918 (Palestine).

This Battle Honour covers the offensive, which finally smashed the Turkish armies in Palestine. The main thrust was on the coastal plain, where the British had quietly concentrated greatly superior numbers. The infantry attack broke straight through the Turkish defences. The cavalry followed up at once. Headed by the cavalry, the British left wing drove round behind the Seventh and Eighth Turkish Armies, cutting across their communications, while the British formations further inland attacked northwards.

Deccan Horse	(9TH Horse, India)
Scinde Horse	(14TH Horse, India)
18TH Cavalry	(18TH Cavalry, India)
4TH Horse	(4TH Horse, India)
Central India Horse	(Central India Horse, India)
9TH Mountain Battery	(9TH Mountain Battery, India)
12TH Mountain Battery	(12TH Mountain Battery, India)
Bengal Engineers	(Corps of Engineers, India)
Bombay Engineers	(Corps of Engineers, India)
2ND Punjab Regiment	(2ND Punjab Regiment, India)
11TH Sikh Regiment	(11TH Sikh Regiment, India)
Sikh Pioneers	(The Sikh Light Infantry, India)
19TH Lancers	(19TH Lancers, Pakistan)
8TH Punjab Regiment	(8TH Punjab Regiment, Pakistan)
12TH Frontier Force Regiment	(12TH Frontier Force Regiment, Pakistan)
13TH Frontier Force Rifles	(13TH Frontier Force Rifles, Pakistan)
14TH Punjab Regiment	(14TH Punjab Regiment, Pakistan)
15TH Punjab Regiment	(15TH Punjab Regiment, Pakistan)
16TH Punjab Regiment	(16TH Punjab Regiment, Pakistan)

Chronology of Sikh Battle Honours (cont.)

Sharon, 1918 (Palestine).

This Battle Honour covers the main break-through in the coastal sector and the subsequent exploitation into the Plains of Sharon behind the Turkish armies. Gardner's Horse, sent forward to seize the important Musmus Pass, charged a Turkish battalion sent to defend it and captured the lot for the loss of one man wounded.

Gardner's Horse	(2ND Lancers, India)
Deccan Horse	(9TH Horse, India)
Scinde Horse	(14TH Horse, India)
18TH Cavalry	(18TH Cavalry, India)
4TH Horse	(4TH Horse, India)
Central India Horse	(Central India Horse, India)
9TH Mountain Battery	(9TH Mountain Battery, India)
12TH Mountain Battery	(12TH Mountain Battery, India)
Bengal Engineers	(Corps of Engineers, India)
Bombay Engineers	(Corps of Engineers, India)
2ND Punjab Regiment	(2ND Punjab Regiment, India)
11TH Sikh Regiment	(11TH Sikh Regiment, India)
Sikh Pioneers	(The Sikh Light Infantry, India)
19TH Lancers	(19TH Lancers, Pakistan)
8TH Punjab Regiment	(8TH Punjab Regiment, Pakistan)
12TH Frontier Force Regiment	(12TH Frontier Force Regiment, Pakistan)
13TH Frontier Force Rifles	(13TH Frontier Force Rifles, Pakistan)
14TH Punjab Regiment	(14TH Punjab Regiment, Pakistan)
15TH Punjab Regiment	(15TH Punjab Regiment, Pakistan)

Nablus, 1918 (Palestine).

This Battle Honour covers the break-through in the centre of the British front, resulting in the capture of Nablus.

9TH Mountain Battery	(9TH Mountain Battery, India)
12TH Mountain Battery	(12TH Mountain Battery, India)
Bombay Engineers	(Corps of Engineers, India)
2ND Punjab Regiment	(2ND Punjab Regiment, India)
Sikh Pioneers	(The Sikh Light Infantry, India)
12TH Frontier Force Regiment	(12TH Frontier Force Regiment, Pakistan)
14TH Punjab Regiment	(14TH Punjab Regiment, Pakistan)
16TH Punjab Regiment	(16TH Punjab Regiment, Pakistan)

Chronology of Sikh Battle Honours (cont.)

Damascus, 1918 (Palestine).

This Battle Honour covers the advance to Damascus after the victory of Megiddo. Damascus fell on 1ST October 1918. The Deccan Horse was vanguard to the Brigade. It reached Pilgrim's road and captured a motorcar, two officers and 68 men. The Brigade now followed the Turkish main force towards Damascus. Two squadrons of the Deccan Horse received orders to seize a hill held by a few Turkish parties. The squadrons galloped the hill and cleared it of the enemy. Another squadron went through a village to get to their objective and found in the village the headquarters of a Turkish cavalry regiment. The Turks, including a cavalry divisional commander, 34 officers and 68 men surrendered. The leading troop of the Deccan Horse entered Damascus but was peremptorily ordered not to do so; it had apparently been decided to reserve the honour of entering Damascus for the Arabs under Lawrence who did so the next day, 1ST October. The fact however, remains that the 'B' squadron the Deccan Horse was the first to enter Damascus proper at about 5 p.m. on 30TH September.

Deccan Horse	(9TH Horse, India)
Scinde Horse	(14TH Horse, India)
18TH Cavalry	(18TH Cavalry, India)
4TH Horse	(4TH Horse, India)
Central India Horse	(Central India Horse, India)
Bengal Engineers	(Corps of Engineers, India)
Bombay Engineers	(Corps of Engineers, India)
2ND Punjab Regiment	(2ND Punjab Regiment, India)
Sikh Pioneers	(The Sikh Light Infantry, India)
12TH Frontier Force Regiment	(12TH Frontier Force Regiment, Pakistan)
14TH Punjab Regiment	(14TH Punjab Regiment, Pakistan)
16TH Punjab Regiment	(16TH Punjab Regiment, Pakistan)

Mesopotamia, 1914 – 18 (Campaign Honour)

Soon after Turkey entered the war a brigade was sent from India to ensure the protection of the oilfields of the Persian Gulf area. In Mesopotamia it captured the port of Basra on the Shatt el Arab. In 1915 operations were undertaken to reach Baghdad. After the battle of Ctesiphon the force had to fall back to Kut al Amara. After a Turkish siege lasting five months, the force surrendered to the Turks in April 1916. British resumed offensive and captured Baghdad in March 1917. After the fall of Baghdad the British were mainly concerned in consolidating their gains until the final months of war.

11TH Sikh Regiment	(11TH Sikh Regiment, India)
Sikh Pioneers	(The Sikh Light Infantry, India)
Patiala Lancers	(61ST Cavalry, India)
2ND Punjab Regiment	(2ND Punjab Regiment, India)

Mesopotamia, 1914 – 18 (cont.)

Regiment	Successor
Bombay Engineers	(Corps of Engineers, India)
Bengal Engineers	(Corps of Engineers, India)
2ND Lancers	(2ND Lancers, India)
4TH Horse	(4TH Horse, India)
12TH Cavalry	(12TH Cavalry, India)
18TH Cavalry	(18TH Cavalry, India)
20TH Lancers	(Training Regiment, India)
5TH Horse	(5TH Horse, Pakistan)
6TH Lancers	(6TH Lancers, Pakistan)
11TH Cavalry	(11TH Cavalry, Pakistan)
13TH Lancers	(13TH Lancers, Pakistan)
1ST Mountain Battery	(1ST Mountain Battery, Pakistan)
6TH Mountain Battery	(6TH Mountain Battery, Pakistan)
1ST Punjab Regiment	(1ST Punjab Regiment, Pakistan)
8TH Punjab Regiment	(8TH Punjab Regiment, Pakistan)
12TH Frontier Force Regiment	(12TH Frontier Force Regiment, Pakistan)
13TH Frontier Force Rifles	(13TH Frontier Force Rifles, Pakistan)
15TH Punjab Regiment	(15TH Punjab Regiment, Pakistan)
16TH Punjab Regiment	(16TH Punjab Regiment, Pakistan)

Basra, 1914 (Mesopotamia).

The British ordered 6TH Indian Division troops to march and capture Basra. The Ottomans sent cavalry to stop the Indian advance and there were many battles between the Indian infantry and the Turkish cavalry. Despite this, the Indians pushed on towards Basra. The Ottomans retreated from Basra, leaving only a few hundred troops to guard the city. The Indians attacked Basra and within an hour the remaining Turkish troops were defeated. The British went on to occupy Basra on 22ND November, 1914.

Regiment	Successor
Bombay Engineers	(Corps of Engineers, India)
3RD Mountain Battery	(3RD Mountain Battery, Pakistan)
14TH Punjab Regiment	(14TH Punjab Regiment, Pakistan)

Shaiba, 1915 (Mesopotamia).

This Battle Honour commemorates the three-day battle in April 1915, in which the Turkish offensive, designed to eject the British from the Persian Gulf area, was defeated. Shaiba was an entrenched camp about fifteen miles from Basra.

Regiment	Successor
18TH Cavalry	(18TH Cavalry, India)
Bombay Engineers	(Corps of Engineers, India)
6TH Lancers	(6TH Lancers, Pakistan)
1ST Punjab Regiment	(1ST Punjab Regiment, Pakistan)
14TH Punjab Regiment	(14TH Punjab Regiment, Pakistan)

Chronology of Sikh Battle Honours (cont.)

Kut al Amara, 1915 (Mesopotamia).

This Battle Honour covers the battle in which 6TH Indian Division had advanced up the River Tigris under General Townsend and had defeated the Turks at Kut al Amara. The British had outflanked the Turkish position by an eighteen-mile approach march across the desert, in which the Infantry had suffered badly from heat and lack of water. The Turks had retreated up the Tigris, having lost all their guns.

18TH Cavalry	(18TH Cavalry, India)

Ctesiphon, 1915 (Mesopotamia).

This Battle Honour commemorates the British capture of the Turkish first line at Ctesiphon. The British, who had suffered 4,000 casualties, were in no state to continue the advance and had to fall back to Kut al Amara pursued by the Turks.

18TH Cavalry	(18TH Cavalry, India)
Bengal Engineers	(Corps of Engineers, India)
Bombay Engineers	(Corps of Engineers, India)
6TH Lancers	(6TH Lancers, Pakistan)
1ST Punjab Regiment	(1ST Punjab Regiment, Pakistan)
14TH Punjab Regiment	(14TH Punjab Regiment, Pakistan)

Defence of Kut al Amara, 1915-1916 (Mesopotamia).

The 6TH Division of the Indian Army, under Major-General Charles Townshend had fallen back to the town of Kut after retreating from Ctesiphon. They had suffered significant losses. General Townshend chose to stay and hold the position at Kut instead of continuing the march downriver towards Basra. The Turks immediately besieged them. Townsend's force held out for nearly five months until forced to surrender on 28TH April 1916, by which time the men of the garrison were dying of disease at the rate of twenty a day. The British and Indian prisoners were marched to Anatolia in Southern Turkey where most of them died of disease or at the hands of the Turkish guards during captivity. Townshend himself was taken to the island of Malki on the Sea of Marmara, to sit out the war in luxury.

Bengal Engineers	(Corps of Engineers, India)
Bombay Engineers	(Corps of Engineers, India)
2ND Punjab Regiment	(2ND Punjab Regiment, India)
1ST Punjab Regiment	(1ST Punjab Regiment, Pakistan)
14TH Punjab Regiment	(14TH Punjab Regiment, Pakistan)

Chronology of Sikh Battle Honours (cont.)

Tigris, 1916 (Mesopotamia).

This Battle Honour covers the abortive attempts to relieve Kut al Amara. Successive Turkish positions at Sheikh Saad and Hanna were carried, but the position at Sannaiyat proved difficult to overcome. By the time Kut al Amara surrendered the 'Tigris Corps' had suffered some 21,000 casualties.

Sikh Pioneers	(The Sikh Light Infantry, India)
18TH Cavalry	(18TH Cavalry, India)
Bengal Engineers	(Corps of Engineers, India)
Bombay Engineers	(Corps of Engineers, India)
11TH Sikh Regiment	(11TH Sikh Regiment, India)
6TH Lancers	(6TH Lancers, Pakistan)
1ST Punjab Regiment	(1ST Punjab Regiment, Pakistan)
8TH Punjab Regiment	(8TH Punjab Regiment, Pakistan)
12TH Frontier Force Regiment	(12TH Frontier Force Regiment, Pakistan)
13TH Frontier Force Rifles	(13TH Frontier Force Rifles, Pakistan)
15TH Punjab Regiment	(15TH Punjab Regiment, Pakistan)
16TH Punjab Regiment	(16TH Punjab Regiment, Pakistan)

Kut al Amara, 1917 (Mesopotamia).

This Battle Honour commemorates the offensive in January and February 1917 in which the British, having cleared the right bank of the River Tigris to beyond Kut al Amara, crossed the river at the Shumran Bend, behind the main Turkish defences. They then had to force the Turks out of a strong defensive line along the Hai River. Both the 36TH and 45TH Sikhs were in Mesopotamia and participated in the Battle of Hai River. About 1,200 Turks held this position in very well prepared entrenchments. Both the Sikh Regiments assaulted the entrenchments shoulder to shoulder in the face of heavy machine gun fire. Although the first three trench lines were captured, casualties were very heavy during the course of the day. At one time, the 45TH was more or less isolated as the Turks launched enveloping counter attacks. The fierceness of the fighting can be judged by the fact that, at end of the day, the 45TH was left with just three British and three Indian officers and 200 men. Of the 22 British and Indian officers who had become casualties, two thirds, including the commanding officer, were killed. The other battalion also suffered heavily and was led out of the action by the Subedar Major, the lone survivor of the British and Indian officers who had taken part in the battle. The British went on to capture the Sannaiyat position and proceeded to occupy Baghdad on 11TH March.

Sikh Pioneers	(The Sikh Light Infantry, India)
11TH Sikh Regiment	(11TH Sikh Regiment, India)
Bengal Engineers	(Corps of Engineers, India)
Bombay Engineers	(Corps of Engineers, India)
20TH Lancers	(Training Regiment, India)
12TH Cavalry	(12TH Cavalry, India)

Chronology of Sikh Battle Honours (cont.)

Kut al Amara, 1917 (Mesopotamia). (cont.)

Regiment	Present designation
11TH Cavalry	(11TH Cavalry, Pakistan)
13TH Lancers	(13TH Lancers, Pakistan)
8TH Punjab Regiment	(8TH Punjab Regiment, Pakistan)
12TH Frontier Force Regiment	(12TH Frontier Force Regiment, Pakistan)
13TH Frontier Force Rifles	(13TH Frontier Force Rifles, Pakistan)
15TH Punjab Regiment	(15TH Punjab Regiment, Pakistan)
16TH Punjab Regiment	(16TH Punjab Regiment, Pakistan)

Baghdad, 1917 (Mesopotamia).

After the capturing Kut al Amara the troops advanced on Baghdad. The cavalry and infantry attacked the Turkish positions frontally and Baghdad was occupied on 11TH March. This Battle Honour covers the operations in the six weeks after the fall of Baghdad; the British had pushed on about seventy-five miles along the Rivers Tigris, Euphrates and up the Diyala towards the Persian frontier.

Regiment	Present designation
Sikh Pioneers	(The Sikh Light Infantry, India)
Bengal Engineers	(Corps of Engineers, India)
Bombay Engineers	(Corps of Engineers, India)
11TH Sikh Regiment	(11TH Sikh Regiment, India)
6TH Lancers	(6TH Lancers, Pakistan)
11TH Cavalry	(11TH Cavalry, Pakistan)
13TH Lancers	(13TH Lancers, Pakistan)
8TH Punjab Regiment	(8TH Punjab Regiment, Pakistan)
12TH Frontier Force Regiment	(12TH Frontier Force Regiment, Pakistan)
13TH Frontier Force Rifles	(13TH Frontier Force Rifles, Pakistan)
14TH Punjab Regiment	(14TH Punjab Regiment, Pakistan)
15TH Punjab Regiment	(15TH Punjab Regiment, Pakistan)
16TH Punjab Regiment	(16TH Punjab Regiment, Pakistan)

Khan Baghdadi, 1918 (Mesopotamia).

This Battle Honour commemorates the Turkish defeat at Khan Baghdadi. Early in 1918 the Turks advanced against Baghdad down the River Euphrates. They were driven back and the British, following up, inflicted a complete defeat on them at Khan Baghdadi.

Regiment	Present designation
Sikh Pioneers	(The Sikh Light Infantry, India)
4TH Horse	(4TH Horse, India)
Bengal Engineers	(Corps of Engineers, India)
10TH Guides Cavalry	(10TH Guides Cavalry, Pakistan)
11TH Cavalry	(11TH Cavalry, Pakistan)
13TH Lancers	(13TH Lancers, Pakistan)
8TH Punjab Regiment	(8TH Punjab Regiment, Pakistan)
14TH Punjab Regiment	(14TH Punjab Regiment, Pakistan)

Chronology of Sikh Battle Honours (cont.)

Sharqat, 1918 (Mesopotamia).

This Battle Honour commemorates the scene of the defeat of the main Turkish force at the River Tigris during the final British advance to Mosul in October 1918. On evacuation from Gallipoli, 14TH Ferozepore Sikhs were in Bushire, in the Persian Gulf region, and they witnessed some fiercer fighting on the Tigris River in October 1918, where they suffered 322 casualties, the heaviest amongst the units of 17TH Division.

11TH Sikh Regiment	(11TH Sikh Regiment, India)
Sikh Pioneers	(The Sikh Light Infantry, India)
Bengal Engineers	(Corps of Engineers, India)
5TH Mountain Battery	(5TH Mountain Battery, India)
6TH Lancers	(6TH Lancers, Pakistan)
10TH Guides Cavalry	(10TH Guides Cavalry, Pakistan)
11TH Cavalry	(11TH Cavalry, Pakistan)
13TH Lancers	(13TH Lancers, Pakistan)
12TH Frontier Force Regiment	(12TH Frontier Force Regiment, Pakistan)

Persia, 1915-1919. (Campaign Honour)

This Campaign Honour was awarded to all of the regiments that had served in Persia during the First World War. During this war Persia declared strict neutrality but was powerless to prevent the two warring sides from operating on their land. Both Germany and Turkey tried to force Persia into the war on their side. To check the spread of hostile influences and to secure the Abidjan oilfields, the British and the Russians decided to establish a cordon in East Persia. The Russians did so in the northern provinces and the British in the south. After the Russian revolution the British effort was extended northwards and they clashed with the Bolsheviks. They entered Russian territory, both from Northwest and North-East Persia. The most outstanding regiments in the operations in Persia were three regiments of Burma Mounted Rifles with a composition of Sikhs and Punjabi Mussulmans in equal numbers.

11TH Sikh Regiment	(11TH Sikh Regiment, India)
7TH Cavalry	(7TH Cavalry, India)
20TH Lancers	(Training Regiment, India)
Bengal Engineers	(Corps of Engineers, India)
Bombay Engineers	(Corps of Engineers, India)
1ST Mountain Battery	(1ST Mountain Battery, Pakistan)
6TH Mountain Battery	(6TH Mountain Battery, Pakistan)
15TH Punjab Regiment	(15TH Punjab Regiment, Pakistan)
Burma Mounted Rifles	(Burma Mounted Rifles, Burma)

Chronology of Sikh Battle Honours (cont.)

Merv, 1918-1919 (Russia).

This Battle Honour covers the British occupation of Merv in Russia. In 1918, while guarding Abidjan oilfields in Persia, the British troops confronted and clashed with the Bolshevik troops on Persia's borders with Russia. The British pursued the Bolsheviks into Russian territory and occupied Merv. It was in the advance to Merv that they fought several actions, earning that unusual battle honour.

7TH Cavalry	(7TH Cavalry. India)
14TH Punjab Regiment	(14TH Punjab Regiment, Pakistan)

Gallipoli, 1915-1916 (Turkey). (Campaign Honour)

The assault on the Gallipoli Peninsula in Turkey was an attempt to force a way through the Dardanelles and open up communications with Russia. British forces landed on either side of Cape Helles at the western extremity, while Australians and New Zealanders went ashore at 'Anzac' further along the northern coast.

They could not progress inland due to the Turkish defences and in an attempt to break the deadlock; a fresh landing was made at Suvla beyond Anzac in August. It was planned to link this up with a drive from Anzac and across the peninsula to the straits, but these operations again failed to break the Turkish defences. It was finally decided to abandon the whole enterprise after ten months and more than 200,000 casualties. Suvla and Anzac were evacuated on the night of 19TH–20TH December and Helles twenty nights later, in both cases without loss. The Sikh regiment lost heavily in this campaign and was reinforced by the detachments from the Sikh Princely State regiment of Patiala Infantry, based in Egypt.

Helles, 1915 (Turkey).

This Battle Honour covers the operations based on Cape Helles on the Asiatic side of the Dardanelles straits.

11TH Sikh Regiment	(11TH Sikh Regiment, India)
2ND Punjab Regiment	(2ND Punjab Regiment, India)
8TH Punjab Regiment	(8TH Punjab Regiment, Pakistan)

Anzac - Landing at Anzac - Defence of Anzac, 1915 (Turkey).

These three Battle Honours cover the operations in the Anzac sector, including its defence against the determined Turkish attempts to eliminate it. The fighting there involved Australian and New Zealand troops, but they were supported by the Kohat and Jacob's Mountain Batteries of the Indian Army, both of which were awarded these three Honours.

1ST Mountain Battery	(1ST Mountain Battery, Pakistan)
6TH Mountain Battery	(6TH Mountain Battery, Pakistan)

Chronology of Sikh Battle Honours (cont.)

Krithia, 1915 (Turkey).

This Battle Honour commemorates the British attempts to extend the beachhead to secure the village of Krithia on 12TH May. The Sikhs with no time to familiarise with their new surroundings were thrown into battle near Krithia. The battle of Krithia was a traumatic experience for the Sikhs, in which they suffered about 400 casualties in two days. In spite of these tremendous losses Sir Ian Hamilton wrote to the commander-in-chief in India: " . . . there was not a sign of wavering all day. Not an inch of the ground was given up and not a single straggler came back. The end of the enemy's trenches were found be blocked with the bodies of the Sikhs and the enemy who died fighting in close quarters, and the glacis slope is thickly dotted with the bodies of these fine soldiers, all lying on their faces as they fell in their steady advance on the enemy. The history of the Sikhs affords many instances of their value as soldiers, but it may be safely asserted that nothing finer than the grim valour and steady discipline displayed by them on the 4TH of June has ever been done by soldiers of the 'Khalsa'." They were in action again on the 4TH June in the attack on Turkish line toward Achi Baba, being highly praised for their gallantry and determination in a series of bitter hand-to-hand encounters.

11TH Sikh Regiment	(11TH Sikh Regiment, India)
2ND Punjab Regiment	(2ND Punjab Regiment, India)
8TH Punjab Regiment	(8TH Punjab Regiment, Pakistan)

Sari Bair, 1915 (Turkey).

This Battle Honour commemorates a series of attacks on the Sari Bair Ridge from the Anzac beachhead, which began on 6TH August 1915. Anticipating help from Suvla, which failed to materialize, success eluded the British attackers.

11TH Sikh Regiment	(11TH Sikh Regiment, India)
1ST Mountain Battery	(1ST Mountain Battery, Pakistan)
6TH Mountain Battery	(6TH Mountain Battery, Pakistan)

Lance Naik Karam Singh of the Mountain Battery was awarded the highest gallantry award for Indian soldiers, the 'Indian Order of Merit', for conspicuous gallantry on 19TH May during operations near Gaba Tepe. He continued to pass orders and so enabled the fire of his section to proceed without interruption, although he was rendered absolutely blind by a bullet, which had passed behind his eyes. He remained on duty until forcibly removed.

Suvla, 1915 (Turkey).

This Battle Honour covers the fighting in the Suvla sector. The main object of these operations was to seize the Sari Bair Ridge, which dominated the Dardanelles straits. The objective was not achieved.

11TH Sikh Regiment	(11TH Sikh Regiment, India)
1ST Mountain Battery	(1ST Mountain Battery, Pakistan)

Chronology of Sikh Battle Honours (cont.)

Macedonia, 1915-1918. (Campaign Honour)

This Campaign Honour was awarded to the regiments that had participated in the Salonika Campaign. This campaign started in October 1915, when British and French troops landed at Salonika with the object of giving help to the hard-pressed Serbs fighting the Bulgars. The Allies established themselves on a line along the River Struma and the northern Greek frontier. They went over to the offensive in April 1917, but without achieving much success. Operations were thereafter of local nature until September 1918, when a final Allied offensive drove back the Bulgars, who asked for armistice on the 30TH September 1918. The troops involved in the campaign suffered badly from malaria, which particularly affected the Struma Valley.

8TH Punjab Regiment (8TH Punjab Regiment, Pakistan)
14TH Punjab Regiment (14TH Punjab Regiment, Pakistan)
16TH Punjab Regiment (16TH Punjab Regiment, Pakistan)

Aden, 1915-1918. (Campaign Honour)

This Campaign Honour commemorates fighting against the Turks in the Aden colony. From the middle of 1915, when the Turks closed in on Aden, until the end of the war, the British of the Aden Troop were on the defensive. On June 1915 the Sikh Pioneers fought off an attempt by Turks to land on the island of Perim. During July and August the Turks were attacked and routed at Sheikh Othman, Fiyush, and What. During 1916 the Aden Troop was in continuous action. Turkish outposts at Jabir, Mahat, Subar, and Imad were attacked and 200 casualties inflicted. On 5TH January 1917, Hatum and Jabir were occupied and a Turkish counter attack successfully repulsed. The port of Aden was never seriously threatened by the enemy, which simply could not pierce its defensive cordon. The Sikhs of the Malay States Guides were most prominent in the Aden Troop. The Guides had three Indian officers, 54 gunners, 50 drivers and followers, and the infantry numbered 788 all ranks. They were almost continuously in contact with the Turks, with frequent engagements and a great deal of marching under very hot sun.

Sikh Pioneers (The Sikh Light Infantry, India)
Bengal Engineers (Corps of Engineers, India)
Bombay Engineers (Corps of Engineers, India)
1ST Punjab Regiment (1ST Punjab Regiment, Pakistan)
12TH Frontier Force Regiment (12TH Frontier Force Regiment, Pakistan)
13TH Frontier Force Rifles (13TH Frontier Force Rifles, Pakistan)
16TH Punjab Regiment (16TH Punjab Regiment, Pakistan)
Malay States Guides Disbanded 1920

Chronology of Sikh Battle Honours (cont.)

Tsingtao, 1914 (China).

When Japan entered the war she undertook the destruction of this German-owned port in North China. A small British contingent was sent to help the Japanese in these operations. It took place between 31ST October and 7TH November 1914 and was fought by Imperial Japan and the United Kingdom against Germany. It was the first encounter between Japanese and German forces and the first British-Japanese operation in the First World War. The Germans surrendered on 7TH November. The South Wales Borderers and the Sikh Regiment were the only two Allied regiments awarded this Honour.

11TH Sikh Regiment (11TH Sikh Regiment, India)

East Africa, 1914-1918. (Campaign Honour)

This Theatre Honour was awarded to all the regiments that had served in East Africa. The campaign in German East Africa (Tanganyika) started in 1914 with an unsuccessful attempt by the British to capture the port of Tanga. Until March 1916 there had been inconclusive fighting along the border with British East Africa (Kenya). In that month, reinforced by South African troops, the British launched an offensive, forcing the Germans to retire southwards. From then on it was a case of the British trying to envelop the less numerous German forces. They eventually followed them into Portuguese East Africa (Mozambique) where, in August 1918, the Germans turned north and actually entered Northern Rhodesia. The German commander, General Von Lettow-Vorbeck, finally surrendered at Abecorn a fortnight after the Armistice had been signed in Europe. The Sikh Princely States regiment, the Faridkot Sappers and Miners, was especially singled out for commendation. Another Sikh Princely States regiment, Jind Infantry, having only landed on 3RD October 1914, defended Gazi against strong German attack, thereby becoming the first of the Indian State Forces to see action during the Great War.

2ND Mountain Battery (2ND Mountain Battery, India)
4TH Mountain Battery (4TH Mountain Battery, India)
7TH Mountain Battery (7TH Mountain Battery, India)
Bombay Engineers (Corps of Engineers, India)
Faridkot Sappers (94TH (Faridkot) Bengal Group, India)
Jind Infantry (13TH (Jind) Punjab Regiment, India)
Kapurthala Infantry Disbanded
13TH Frontier Force Rifles (13TH Frontier Force Rifles, Pakistan)
14TH Punjab Regiment (14TH Punjab Regiment, Pakistan)
15TH Punjab Regiment (15TH Punjab Regiment, Pakistan)
16TH Punjab Regiment (16TH Punjab Regiment, Pakistan)
8TH Mountain Battery (8TH Mountain Battery, Pakistan)
12TH Cavalry (12TH Cavalry, Pakistan)

Kilimanjaro, 1916 (East Africa).

This Battle Honour represents the British offensive launched in the Mount Kilimanjaro area of East Africa in March 1916, which resulted later in the year in the occupation of the German capital of Dar es Salaam.

7TH Mountain Battery	(7TH Mountain Battery, India)
Bombay Engineers	(Corps of Engineers, India)
Faridkot Sappers	(94TH (Faridkot) Bengal Group, India)
15TH Punjab Regiment	(15TH Punjab Regiment, Pakistan)
8TH Mountain Battery	(8TH Mountain Battery, Pakistan)

Beho Beho, 1917 (East Africa).

This Battle Honour commemorates an action in January 1917, when the British nearly surrounded the German forces at Beho Beho before Von Lettow got away across the Rufiji River.

Faridkot Sappers	(94TH (Faridkot) Bengal Group, India)
16TH Punjab Regiment	(16TH Punjab Regiment, Pakistan)

Narugombe, 1917 (East Africa).

This Battle Honour covers an action fought by the British at Narugombe to gain possession of some vital water holes.

2ND Mountain Battery	(2ND Mountain Battery, India)
7TH Mountain Battery	(7TH Mountain Battery, India)
14TH Punjab Regiment	(14TH Punjab Regiment, Pakistan)
16TH Punjab Regiment	(16TH Punjab Regiment, Pakistan)

Nyangao, 1917 (East Africa).

This Battle Honour commemorates the last major battle to take place in German East Africa. The Germans inflicted nearly fifty percent casualties on the British before they slipped away to the Portuguese territory of Mozambique.

7TH Mountain Battery	(7TH Mountain Battery, India)
16TH Punjab Regiment	(16TH Punjab Regiment, Pakistan)

The Jind Infantry was in Africa from October 1914 to December 1917. They earned the highest opinions from all the generals under whom they served, especially for their fighting at Jasin. Jasin was a frontier town on the coast north of Tanga, taken from the Germans in January 1915. The Jind Infantry garrisoned the town, which was attacked and retaken by a German force of 2,000 on 18TH January.

Subedar Harnam Singh, Jind Infantry, was awarded the 'Indian Order of Merit' for his gallant conduct at Jasin. He rallied a small party to cover a retirement and held the enemy in check until his party was killed and he himself severely wounded and taken prisoner.

Chronology of Sikh Battle Honours (cont.)

N.W. Frontier, India 1914-15, 1916-17. (Campaign Honour)

When Turkey entered the war there was concern in India that the Pathan tribes on the North West Frontier might rise to support their Muslim co-religionists. A number of regular units were therefore retained to deal with such an eventuality. In 1914-15 there was trouble in the Tochi area. Operations were carried out against the Bunerwals and Swatis in 1915, and against Mohmands and Mahsuds in 1917.

11TH Sikh Regiment	(11TH Sikh Regiment, India)
2ND Punjab Regiment	(2ND Punjab Regiment, India)
5TH Mountain Battery	(5TH Mountain Battery, India)
9TH Mountain Battery	(9TH Mountain Battery, India)
12TH Cavalry	(12TH Cavalry, India)
Bengal Engineers	(Corps of Engineers, India)
Bombay Engineers	(Corps of Engineers, India)
20TH Lancers	(Training Regiment, India)
6TH Lancers	(6TH Lancers, Pakistan)
10TH Guides Cavalry	(10TH Guides Cavalry, Pakistan)
13TH Lancers	(13TH Lancers, Pakistan)
1ST Punjab Regiment	(1ST Punjab Regiment, Pakistan)
14TH Punjab Regiment	(14TH Punjab Regiment, Pakistan)
15TH Punjab Regiment	(15TH Punjab Regiment, Pakistan)
16TH Punjab Regiment	(16TH Punjab Regiment, Pakistan)
12TH Frontier Force Regiment	(12TH Frontier Force Regiment, Pakistan)
13TH Frontier Force Rifles	(13TH Frontier Force Rifles, Pakistan)

Baluchistan, 1915-1916 and **1918**. (Campaign Honour)

To the south of the North-West Frontier there were disturbances in the Kalat district of Baluchistan in 1915-16, while in 1918 the Merri and Khetran tribes caused more trouble.

Bengal Engineers	(Corps of Engineers, India)
Bombay Engineers	(Corps of Engineers, India)
3RD Mountain Battery	(3RD Mountain Battery Pakistan)
13TH Frontier Force Rifles	(13TH Frontier Force Rifles, Pakistan)

Chronology of Sikh Battle Honours (cont.)

Afghanistan, 1919. (Campaign Honour)

The Third Afghan War was launched by Amir Amanullah, who had been placed on the Afghan throne in February 1919 by the army, after the murder of his father. He proclaimed a Jihad against Britain, and on 3RD May 1919, Afghan troops crossed the Indian border and occupied Bagh. British Indian troops recaptured Bagh on 11TH May and pushed on into Afghanistan. Operations ranged along much of the border area. Fighting occurred in Chitral, in the Khyber Pass, through the Kurram Valley, in the Tochi Valley, in Waziristan and in Baluchistan. Amanullah sued for peace on 31ST May and peace was restored by the treaty of Rawalpindi on the 8TH August 1919.

"At no time in their history had the Mahsuds and Wazirs been so well armed as at this junture, since in additon to their normal armament, considerable quantities of government rifles and ammunition had fallen recently into their hands. To supplement their stocks the tribesmen had received large supplies of ammunition through the agency of anti-British Afghan officials in Khost. These tribesmen have long been remarkable for their courage, activity and hardihood and when the mountanious and difficult nature of their country is considered, together with the fact that their numbners included about 1,800 deserters and others highly trained in our tactics and methods of fighting, it will be realized that they constituted a formidable enemy."

Sikh Pioneers	(The Sikh Light Infantry, India)
11TH Sikh Regiment	(11TH Sikh Regiment, India)
2ND Punjab Regiment	(2ND Punjab Regiment, India)
Bengal Engineers	(Corps of Engineers, India)
Bombay Engineers	(Corps of Engineers, India)
2ND Lancers	(2ND Lancers, India)
7TH Cavalry	(7TH Cavalry, India)
8TH Cavalry	(8TH Cavalry, India)
12TH Cavalry	(12TH Cavalry, India)
15TH Lancers	(15TH Lancers, India)
7TH Mountain Battery	(7TH Mountain Battery, India)
1ST Punjab Regiment	(1ST Punjab Regiment, Pakistan)
8TH Punjab Regiment	(8TH Punjab Regiment, Pakistan)
12TH Frontier Force Regiment	(12TH Frontier Force Regiment, Pakistan)
13TH Frontier Force Rifles	(13TH Frontier Force Rifles, Pakistan)
14TH Punjab Regiment	(14TH Punjab Regiment, Pakistan)
16TH Punjab Regiment	(16TH Punjab Regiment, Pakistan)
6TH Lancers	(6TH Lancers, Pakistan)
11TH Cavalry	(11TH Cavalry, Pakistan)
13TH Lancers	(13TH Lancers, Pakistan)
3RD Mountain Battery	(3RD Mountain Battery, Pakistan)
8TH Mountain Battery	(8TH Mountain Battery, Pakistan)

Chronology of Sikh Battle Honours (cont.)

SECOND WORLD WAR 1939-1945

When World War II began in 1939, Germany was the aggressor; it was later joined in June 1940 by Italy, and Japan in December 1941. On the morning of September 1ST 1939, the world was forever changed as Germany invaded Poland and executed its first "Blitzkrieg" or "Lightning attack", quickly crushing Polish resistance. From 1939 to 1945 Germany's military machine struck out and conquered most of Western Europe, swept into deserts of North Africa and drove deep into the hinterlands of Russia. In time, however, the Allies gathered strength and eventually crushed the German Army and Axis powers with a display of brute force that has remained unmatched to this day. Allied to Britain, India automatically got involved in the war and its forces fought in Africa, the Middle East, Malaya, Italy and Burma. At the outbreak of World War II, the Indian Army numbered only 205,000 men. Later during the War, it became the largest all-volunteer force in history, rising to over 2.5 million men in size - which included tank, artillery and airborne forces. More than 87,000 Indian soldiers lost their lives during this conflict. Particularly notable contributions of the Indian Army during this conflict include the Battle of Kohima and the Battle of Imphal (both in Burma), the First and Second Battles of El Alamein (North Africa) and the Battle of Monte Cassino (Italy).

British Somaliland, 1941. (Campaign Honour)

This Campaign Honour covers the operations in British Somaliland. The Italians invaded British Somaliland and the small British garrison was compelled to withdraw in the face of much superior forces. However, a British task force from Aden recaptured the capital, Berbera, in March 1941.

2ND Punjab Regiment	(2ND Punjab Regiment, India)
15TH Punjab Regiment	(15TH Punjab Regiment, Pakistan)

Abyssinia, 1940-1941. (Campaign Honour)

This Campaign Honour was awarded to all the regiments that had served in Abyssinia during 1940-1941. During 1940 British troops in Abyssinia, Sudan and Kenya were on the defensive and the Italians were able to make some small gains. However the 4TH and the 5TH Indian Divisions ejected the invaders from Sudan and advanced into Eritrea. After a tough struggle at Keren they captured Asmara and Massawa and followed up the retreating Italians into Abyssinia to Amba Alagi, where General Cunningham's forces closed in from the south. The main Italian Army surrendered in mid-May.

4TH Battalion, 11TH Sikh Regiment	(4TH Battalion, 11TH Sikh Regiment, India)
1ST Punjab Regiment	(1ST Punjab Regiment, Pakistan)
2ND Punjab Regiment	(1ST Punjab Regiment, India)
12TH Frontier Force Regiment	(12TH Frontier Force Regiment, Pakistan)
13TH Frontier Force Rifles	(13TH Frontier Force Rifles, Pakistan)

Chronology of Sikh Battle Honours (cont.)

Abyssinia, 1940-1941. (cont.)

14TH Punjab Regiment (14TH Punjab Regiment, Pakistan)
15TH Punjab Regiment (15TH Punjab Regiment, Pakistan)
16TH Punjab Regiment (16TH Punjab Regiment, Pakistan)

Gallabat 1941 (British Somaliland).

The opening Italian moves were to occupy a number of Sudan border posts such as Gallabat and Kassala and to occupy British Somaliland. Gallabat was recaptured by the 5TH Indian Division in 1941. The pursuit of the Italians was impeded by their destruction of long stretches of the road, which they mined and destroyed. It was for his outstanding courage and endurance in clearing a way through these mines that 2ND Lieutenant P.S. Bhagat Singh was awarded the Victoria Cross, the first awarded to the Indian Army in this war.

Bombay Engineers (Corps of Engineers, India)
12TH Frontier Force Regiment (12TH Frontier Force Regiment, Pakistan)

Agordat, 1941 (Abyssinia).

This Battle Honour commemorates the conquest of Agordat in 1941. The 4TH Indian Division, in a frontal attack, captured the four hills astride the road just outside the town, which were fortified with concrete emplacements, trenches and wire. Resistance died away in the face of this attack and the Italians bolted away before they were captured. Next day the Division went into Agordat, which was found to be abandoned and the enemy had slipped away, leaving his guns, vehicles, and huge quantities of stores. About a thousand prisoners had been taken and this number was doubled when the pursuing forces overtook stragglers.

4TH Battalion, 11TH Sikh Regiment (4TH Battalion, 11TH Sikh Regiment, India)
1ST Punjab Regiment (1ST Punjab Regiment, Pakistan)
2ND Punjab Regiment (2ND Punjab Regiment, India)
12TH Frontier Force Regiment (12TH Frontier Force Regiment, Pakistan)
14TH Punjab Regiment (14TH Punjab Regiment, Pakistan)

Barentu, 1941 (Abyssinia).

Fighting round Barentu was a grim soldier's battle in which the better men won by sheer fighting ability. The commanding heights and the lower features were well held by the enemy. On subsequent days of stiff fighting the enemy would be cleared from one feature, but there were always other positions in this hilly intricate country. On the morning of February 2ND the Italians abandoned their defences and Barentu fell. The Bombay Engineers worked like heroes at many roadblocks, frequently under fire.

Bombay Engineers (Corps of Engineers, India)
12TH Frontier Force Regiment (12TH Frontier Force Regiment, Pakistan)
13TH Frontier Force Rifles (13TH Frontier Force Rifles, Pakistan)

Chronology of Sikh Battle Honours (cont.)

Keren, 1941 (Abyssinia).

This Battle Honour commemorates the conquest of Eritrea in 1941. Keren was the decisive battle of the northern advance into Abyssinia. The struggle lasted from 3RD February to 31ST March 1941, with repeated unsuccessful attempts to capture the position. Finally two divisions, the 4TH Division and the 5TH Indian Division, in a night attack, smashed the Italian defensive position. The final victory led to the conquest of Eritrea.

4TH Battalion, 11TH Sikh Regiment	(4TH Battalion, 11TH Sikh Regiment, India)
1ST Punjab Regiment	(1ST Punjab Regiment, Pakistan)
2ND Punjab Regiment	(2ND Punjab Regiment, India)
12TH Frontier Force Regiment	(12TH Frontier Force Regiment, Pakistan)
13TH Frontier Force Rifles	(13TH Frontier Force Rifles, Pakistan)
14TH Punjab Regiment	(14TH Punjab Regiment, Pakistan)

Ad Teclesan, 1941 (Abyssinia).

This Battle Honour commemorates the capture of Ad Teclesan. There was some hard fighting along the road in which the troops particularly distinguished themselves, some of them carried out a brilliant march, which placed them in the rear of the enemy's position. The Italians were however very disorganized and their morale shattered. In the face of these determined attacks they gave away easily.

23RD Mountain Regiment	(23RD Mountain Regiment, India)
2ND Punjab Regiment	(2ND Punjab Regiment, India)
12TH Frontier Force Regiment	(12TH Frontier Force Regiment, Pakistan)
13TH Frontier Force Rifles	(13TH Frontier Force Rifles, Pakistan)

Massawa, 1941 (Abyssinia).

As the British advanced toward Eritrea, Mario Bonetti, the Italian commander of the Red Sea Flotilla based at Massawa, realized that his harbor was going to be overrun by the enemy. In the first week of April, 1941, he began to destroy the harbor's facilities and ruin its usefulness to the British. The enemy's resistance increased and was shattered as the 4TH Indian Division charged towards Massawa. It then became a race for who should be first into town; a race that was won by the 16TH Punjab Regiment. Over 400 officers, including admirals and generals were captured.

16TH Punjab Regiment	(16TH Punjab Regiment, Pakistan)

Amba Alagi, 1941 (Abyssinia).

This Battle Honour commemorates the surrender of the Italian Army on 19TH May 1941. On retreating from Eritrea, the Italians fell back on Amba Alagi in Abyssinia. They ceremonially surrendered to the British on 19TH May 1941.

12TH Frontier Force Regiment	(12TH Frontier Force Regiment, Pakistan)

Chronology of Sikh Battle Honours (cont.)

Berbera 1941, (British Somaliland).

A British force from Aden recaptured Berbera in March 1941, in a combined operation with the Royal Navy, the Royal Indian Navy and the Royal Air Force. The main landing was carried out by the 2ND Punjab Regiment and 15TH Punjab Regiment supported by naval vessels, which bombarded the enemy positions from the sea. Berbera was soon occupied; the enemy fleeing away towards Hargeisa. About 120 prisoners with ten guns were captured, while Indian casualty was one man wounded.

2ND Punjab Regiment	(2ND Punjab Regiment, India)
15TH Punjab Regiment	(15TH Punjab Regiment, Pakistan)

Iraq, 1941. (Campaign Honour)

This Campaign Honour was awarded to all of the regiments that had served in Iraq during 1941. In order to protect British interests, the 8TH Indian Division was landed at Basra. In May Iraqis attacked the Royal Air Force base at Habbaniya near Baghdad. The 8TH Indian Division occupied Baghdad and, in conjunction with a column from Palestine, relieved Habbaniya.

3RD Battalion, 11TH Sikh Regiment	(3RD Battalion, 11TH Sikh Regiment, India)

Syria, 1941. (Campaign Honour)

This Campaign Honour was awarded to all of the regiments that had served in Syria during 1941. German forces had infiltrated Syria and posed a serious threat to the Allied interests. Early in June, British forces began to advance into Syria and the Lebanon from Palestine. The Indian force engaged was a brigade of the 4TH Indian Division. Vichy French sued for peace on 12TH July.

1ST Punjab Regiment	(1ST Punjab Regiment, Pakistan)
13TH Frontier Force Rifles	(13TH Frontier Force Rifles, Pakistan)

North Africa, 1940-1943. (Campaign Honour)

When Italy entered the war in June 1940, the main Allied problem was the defence of Egypt against the vastly superior Italian force assembled in Libya. The Italians duly invaded Egypt, but only progressed as far as Sidi Barrani. In December the British Army went over to the offensive, won a decisive victory, and drove the Italians right back through Cyrenaica to the area of El Agheila. Meanwhile a German contingent, the nucleus of the 'Africa Corps', had landed in Tripoli under General Rommel. In March 1941 Rommel struck at the British and forced them back across the Egyptian frontier, although Tobruk still held out. Early in December Tobruk was relieved and the enemy was compelled to evacuate Cyrenaica. In January 1942 Rommel struck again, and the British had to withdraw to a defensive position at Gazala. The Axis forces attacked them there in May and won a complete victory - the British being driven back into Egypt with the loss of Tobruk.

North Africa, 1940-1943. (cont.)

The enemy advance was finally halted at the First Battle of El Alamein. Rommel made one more serious attempt to break through, in the battle of Alam Halfa at the end of August, but he was repulsed. In October General Montgomery launched an offensive, won the decisive Battle of Al Alamein and the British advance continued until the enemy had been driven out of Libya into Tunisia. Here the Axis forces made a stand on the Mareth line, but were forced back. Montgomery's Eighth Army joined up with the Anglo-American forces that had advanced from Algeria, to participate in the final elimination of the Axis armies in North Africa.

11TH Sikh Regiment (11TH Sikh Regiment, India)
1ST Punjab Regiment (1ST Punjab Regiment, Pakistan)
2ND Punjab Regiment (2ND Punjab Regiment, India)
12TH Frontier Force Regiment (12TH Frontier Force Regiment, Pakistan)
13TH Frontier Force Rifles (13TH Frontier Force Rifles, Pakistan)
14TH Punjab Regiment (14TH Punjab Regiment, Pakistan)
16TH Punjab Regiment (16TH Punjab Regiment, Pakistan)
18TH Cavalry (18TH Cavalry, India)
PAVO Cavalry (PAVO Cavalry, Pakistan)
Bengal Engineers (Corps of Engineers, India)
Bombay Engineers (Corps of Engineers, India)

Sidi Barani, 1940 (Libya).

Sidi Barani commemorates the decisive British victory over the Italians. The British achieved complete surprise after advancing across the desert for seventy miles during two nights. Five Italian divisions were put out of action and 39,000 prisoners taken. The Italians were forced into retreat which took them back right across Cyrenaica. In three days the 4TH Indian Division had taken over 20,000 prisoners, with many guns, tanks and stores. Three enemy divisions had been utterly routed. After the Battle the 4TH Indian Division was sent to the Kassala front in the Sudan.

1ST Punjab Regiment (1ST Punjab Regiment, Pakistan)
16TH Punjab Regiment (16TH Punjab Regiment, Pakistan)

El Mechili, 1941 (Libya).

This Battle Honour commemorates the desperate efforts to hold El Mechili, located to the west of Tobruk. The 3RD Indian Motor Brigade was asked to hold this position as it had a big petrol dump and was the only place on that route to have water. The Germans surrounded the force for four days and eventually some soldiers broke out and the remainder surrendered.

18TH Cavalry (18TH Cavalry, India)
PAVO Cavalry (PAVO Cavalry, Pakistan)

Chronology of Sikh Battle Honours (cont.)

Defence of Tobruk, 1941 (Libya).

This Battle Honour commemorates the defence of Tobruk Garrison when the British withdrew into Egypt. The 9TH Australian Division and some British and Indian troops successfully defended this garrison. The holding of Tobruk made it impossible for Rommel to mount his projected invasion of Egypt.

18TH Cavalry	(18TH Cavalry, India)

Omars, 1941 (Libya).

This Battle Honour covers the reduction of the enemy-defended localities on the frontier; known as the Omars, by the 4TH Indian Division during the period 22ND November to 2ND December 1941. This would deprive Rommel of a base for operations across the rear of the Eighth Army. During this battle platoons of the Sikh Regiment started off across the open plain to capture an Italian garrison at Qineiqina. Artillery, mortars, machine guns, and anti-tank guns pinned the platoons to the ground. There was a minefield around the post and the Sikhs had no supporting fire whatsoever. Their ammunition would not last all day and when it was finished the Italians would be able to pick off the prone attackers one by one. It looked as if two platoons would be wiped out. The only way out of the difficulty was to go forward. If they had to die, how much better to die trying to kill the enemy rather than lying waiting for the end. With a roar of "Wah Guru ji Ki Fateh" they swept up to the position and within minutes all was over. The Sikhs captured all the heavy guns and accounted for twenty-five of the enemy.

4TH Battalion, 11TH Sikh Regiment	(11TH Sikh Regiment, India)
1ST Punjab Regiment	(1ST Punjab Regiment, Pakistan)
16TH Punjab Regiment	(16TH Punjab Regiment, Pakistan)

Alem Hamza, 1941 (Libya).

Alem Hamza covers the attempt by 4TH Indian Division to cut off the enemy retiring to the Gazala position. The enemy defences at Alem Hamza were well prepared and cleverly sited. Part of the Alem Hamza feature was captured but the other attacks failed and the Punjabis were awarded and elected to carry the Honour.

1ST Punjab Regiment	(1ST Punjab Regiment, Pakistan)

Gazala, 1942 (Libya).

This Battle Honour covers the period from the launching of the first German attacks on the British positions on the Gazala line on 26TH May 1942, until 21ST June. The British Armour had been shattered in a series of clashes in which its tanks had proved inferior to those of the Germans and the British had withdrawn over the Egyptian frontier, and Tobruk had fallen.

7TH Field Regiment	(7TH Field Regiment, India)
13TH Lancers	(13TH Lancers, Pakistan)

Chronology of Sikh Battle Honours (cont.)

Point 171, 1942 (Libya).

This Battle Honour commemorates the battle between tanks and field artillery at Point 171, in the vicinity of Bir Hacheim, on 27TH May 1942. This was the scene of a gun-to-gun battle between the German tanks and the 22 Pounder guns of 2ND Field Regiment, in which twenty-four German tanks were destroyed. The Battery Commander of 7TH Field Battery, Major (later General) P. P. Kumaramangalam, managed to extricate all but a few of his guns and was awarded the DSO. The British Premier Winston Churchill, on the floor of the House of Commons, praised the performance of this unit. "These gallant gunners fought right to the end. There was Havildar Mohan Singh who, wounded himself and with all the other members of the gun crew dead around him, kept his gun in action alone. Loading, laying and firing, he knocked out two tanks single-handedly before he himself fell dead across the gun he had served so faithfully."

2ND Field Indian Regiment (2ND Field Indian Regiment, India)

Cauldron, 1942 (Libya).

The Cauldron was actually the laagar formed by the German armoured forces when they originally broke through into the British positions. The British counter attack resulted in severe losses to the British Armour.

4TH Field Indian Regiment (4TH Field Indian Regiment, India)
12TH Frontier Force Regiment (12TH Frontier Force Regiment, Pakistan)

Mersa Matruh, 1942 (Libya).

This Battle Honour covers the action at Mersa Matruh in Libya. At the fall of Tobruk, a new defensive position at Mersa Matruh was occupied. The Germans attacked this position on 26TH June 1942, achieved a breakthrough in the middle, and then completely encircled the position. This compelled the British to withdraw to the El Alamein position.

2ND Battalion, 11TH Sikh Regiment (2ND Battalion, 11TH Sikh Regiment, India)
61ST Field Company (61ST Field Company, India)
13TH Frontier Force Rifles (13TH Frontier Force Rifles, Pakistan)

Deir el Shein, 1942 (Libya).

This Battle Honour commemorates the fighting at Deir el Shein in Libya. On IST July a day-long fight took place when the Germans attacked this position. The British counter-attacked and compelled the Germans to withdraw.

4TH Battalion, 11TH Sikh Regiment (4TH Battalion, 11TH Sikh Regiment, India)
10TH Guides Cavalry (10TH Guides Cavalry, Pakistan)

Chronology of Sikh Battle Honours (cont.)

Ruweisat Ridge, 1942 (Libya).

Ruweisat covers the first real British counter–attack during the period 2ND – 4TH July, involving some heavy fighting in which the enemy lost nearly 40 tanks and anti-tank guns to the newly introduced 6-pounder British anti-tank gun.

1ST Punjab Regiment	(1ST Punjab Regiment, Pakistan)

El Alamein, 1942 (Libya).

El Alamein covers the decisive victory of the British over the German–Italian forces in fighting which lasted for twelve days from 23RD October. By then the Germans had only thirty-five tanks left and were soon in full retreat, a retreat which was to end only when the Axis forces evacuated Libya and crossed the frontier into Tunisia.

1ST Punjab Regiment	(1ST Punjab Regiment, Pakistan)
16TH Punjab Regiment	(16TH Punjab Regiment, Pakistan)

Akarit, 1943 (Libya).

Akarit commemorates the defeat of the Axis forces endeavouring to stand on the line of Wadi Akarit on 6TH and 7TH April. The 4TH Indian Division broke the enemy positions in a completely successful night attack.

16TH Punjab Regiment	(16TH Punjab Regiment, Pakistan)

Italy, 1943-1945. (Campaign Honour)

This Campaign Honour was awarded to all of the regiments that served in Italy during 1943-1945. The initial landing was made on the 'toe' of Italy on 3RD September, 1943, by the troops of the 8TH Army. Subsequently the 8TH Army advanced up the east coast until contact was made with the German 'Gustav Line', which ran along the Rivers Garigliano and Rapido, its strongest point being Monte Cassino. The Allies were held up here. At this period the 8TH Army included the 4TH, the $8^{TH,}$ and the 10TH Indian Divisions including the Sikh State Forces regiment, the Nabha Akal Infantry. In the middle of May a breakthrough in the Cassino sector led to the occupation of Rome. The Germans fell back fighting to the 'Gothic Line', stretching across Italy just to the north of Florence, which the allies reached in August. They broke through at the end of September and pursued the Germans to the Po Valley. The German Army in Italy surrendered on 29TH April 1945.

1ST Punjab Regiment	(1ST Punjab Regiment, Pakistan)
2ND Punjab Regiment	(2ND Punjab Regiment, India)
8TH Punjab Regiment	(8TH Punjab Regiment, Pakistan)
11TH Sikh Regiment	(11TH Sikh Regiment, India)
12TH Frontier Force Regiment	(12TH Frontier Force Regiment, Pakistan)
13TH Frontier Force Rifles	(13TH Frontier Force Rifles, Pakistan)
15TH Punjab Regiment	(15TH Punjab Regiment, Pakistan)
Nabha Akal Infantry	(14TH (Nabha Akal) Punjab Regiment, India)

Italy, 1943-1945 (cont.)

Bombay Engineers	(Corps of Engineers, India)
Bengal Engineers	(Corps of Engineers, India)

Landing in Sicily, 1943 (Italy).

Landing in Sicily covers the actual landing by sea. The assault achieved complete surprise, largely because the defenders did not think it could be mounted in such bad weather. The ground forces seized the vital Ponte Grande, and secured the bridge.

12TH Frontier Force Regiment	(12TH Frontier Force Regiment, Pakistan)

Trigno, 1943 (Italy).

At Trigno the Eighth Indian Division was committed to its first action in Europe. Trigno commemorates the establishment of a bridgehead over that river as a result of heavy fighting during the periods 22ND October–5TH November. A decisive event was the capture of the enemy positions on the San Salvo Ridge, which dominated the area north of the river.

8TH Punjab Regiment	(8TH Punjab Regiment, Pakistan)
13TH Frontier Force Rifles	(13TH Frontier Force Rifles, Pakistan)

Tufillo, 1943 (Italy).

After crossing the Trigno the 13TH Frontier Force Rifles immediately prepared to seize Tufillo village and Monte Ferrano on the high ground. The Frontiersmen's assault was launched against typical 'hedgehog' position. All approaches were mined and booby-trapped. A curtain of mortar bombs covered the minefield. Every house held a sniper. Attempts to close were met with showers of Grenades. Quick savage sallies were flung against any ground won. The leading companies pushed through the barrage and up the hillside under murderous machine-gun fire from front and flanks. The 8TH Punjab Regiment joined the Frontiersmen in a new assault upon Tufillo. The recurrent assaults had their effect - the Germans were forced to retire to their main battle positions.

8TH Punjab Regiment	(8TH Punjab Regiment, Pakistan)
13TH Frontier Force Rifles	(13TH Frontier Force Rifles, Pakistan)

The Sangro, 1943 (Italy).

Sangro commemorates the fighting over the period 19TH November–3RD December, in which the Eighth Army forced the crossing of the river Sangro. After heavy fighting they captured Sangro ridge, which was occupied by the Germans. After holding the ridge against determined counter attacks, they proceeded against the villages of Fossacesia, San Maria, Mozzagrogna, Romagnoli and Andrioli. These scattered hamlets on the crest of the escarpment provided ideal sites for German defensive positions.

Chronology of Sikh Battle Honours (cont.)

The Sangro, 1943 (Italy). (cont.)

8TH Punjab Regiment	(8TH Punjab Regiment, Pakistan)
12TH Frontier Force Regiment	(12TH Frontier Force Regiment, Pakistan)
13TH Frontier Force Rifles	(13TH Frontier Force Rifles, Pakistan)
15TH Punjab Regiment.	(15TH Punjab Regiment, Pakistan)

Mozzagrogna, 1943 (Italy).

From Sangro the Eighth Indian Division advanced on the fortified village of Mozzagrogna. Corps artillery concentrated a terrific shoot on the village as 12TH Frontier Force moved forward to attack and capture the place. The bombardment held the enemy garrison in the dugouts and once it lifted the Germans rushed to their surface posts. The battle resolved into dozens of sudden deadly encounters in cellars, on rooftops, in alleys, and behind the angles of broken walls. In a crypt a number of Germans who had taken refuge in the wine vats were dispatched. With the arrival of the British Armour the defences of Mozzagrogna collapsed and essential crossroads to the northwest of Mozzagrogna were secured. An enemy force, which included flame–throwers, charged the consolidation groups and cut off the Dogra Company. At dawn the Sikh and Dogra companies of Frontiersmen hurled back the enemy in headlong flight and captured the disabled tanks. One thousand prisoners had been taken and a number of German units had been decimated.

12TH Frontier Force Regiment	(12TH Frontier Force Regiment, Pakistan)
15TH Punjab Regiment	(15TH Punjab Regiment, Pakistan)

Romagnoli, 1943 (Italy).

To sustain the momentum of the advance, 21ST Indian Brigade turned west from Mozzagrogna along the top of the ridge with Romagnoli. The next objective was a line of trenches concealed behind hedges on the outskirts of the village. Pinning down the defenders, the village was stormed. Three counter–attacks were shattered in quick succession, convinced the enemy that Romagnoli could not be regained.

12TH Frontier Force Regiment	(12TH Frontier Force Regiment, Pakistan)

"Impossible Bridge", 1943 (Italy).

The next objective was to take Caldari beyond the river Moro. The 8TH Indian Division was told to cross the river and capture Caldari as the other two divisions on the flanks failed to cross the river. It was impossible to build a bridge from the near bank, so it was decided to build it backwards from the enemy's bank. "The Impossible Bridge" over the River Moro came to be a legend in the annals of combat engineering when the Indian Engineers crossed over to the enemy side and built a bridge in reverse direction, to overcome the technical difficulty arising out of lack of construction space on the home bank."

Chronology of Sikh Battle Honours (cont.)

"Impossible Bridge", 1943 (Italy). (cont.)

The area surrounding the bridge site was extremely active with German fighting patrols and they reacted violently to this incursion. The Frontiersmen cleared the enemy patrols with the bayonet.

Bengal Engineers (Corps of Engineers, India)
12TH Frontier Force Regiment (12TH Frontier Force Regiment, Pakistan)
13TH Frontier Force Rifles (13TH Frontier Force Rifles, Pakistan)

Caldari, 1943 (Italy).

At the opening of the "Impossible Bridge" the 8TH Indian Division advanced against Caldari. The 12TH Frontier Force Regiment stormed the village after some fierce fighting and seized positions along the road, which ran parallel to the Moro. An enemy tank force, which included flame-throwers, charged the consolidation group and cut off the Dogra Company. British tanks hurried up. At dawn the Sikh companies of Frontiersmen hurled back the enemy in headlong flight and captured two disabled tanks. The 15TH Punjabis joined the fray and seized fresh positions along the lateral road. The Indians were now firmly embedded in the main German defences.

12TH Frontier Force Regiment (12TH Frontier Force Regiment, Pakistan)
15TH Punjab Regiment (15TH Punjab Regiment, Pakistan)

Villa Grande, 1943 (Italy).

Villa Grande commemorates a series of fierce actions fought from 22ND to 28TH December on the outskirts of the village. Enemy machine gunners that had occupied weapon-pits and dugouts opened heavy fire. Without hesitation the leading Punjabi company changed direction and swept to flank to deal with this menace. There was particularly fierce fighting involving 8TH Punjab Regiment, within the village of Villa Grande itself. The ground had dried and the British tanks were able to come forward. Riding on the outside of the leading tank, Major Gardhari Singh pointed out enemy posts. As high explosive and Armour-piercing shells crashed into the emplacements, the Germans bolted into the open. As they ran, machine-guns brought them down. On the northern fringe of the village a few last-stand parties stuck it out until mopped up. Otherwise the battle for Villa Grande was over.

8TH Punjab Regiment (8TH Punjab Regiment, Pakistan)
13TH Frontier Force Rifles (13TH Frontier Force Rifles, Pakistan)

Sikh soldier of the 4th Division (the Red Eagles) holding a captured swastika after the surrender of German forces in Italy, May 1945.

Chronology of Sikh Battle Honours (cont.)

Cassino 1, 1944 (Italy).

Cassino 1 represents three attempts by the Americans, the New Zealanders and the 4TH Indian Division to capture Monte Cassino, the dominant height crowned by its monastery, which covered the entrance to the Liri Valley and was the linchpin of the Gustav Line, over the period 20TH January- 25TH March. The Monastery remained out of reach in one of the hardest fought battles of the war in which 4TH Indian Division lost 4,000 men. A gunner officer expressed the characteristic view: "There is fierce chagrin that the two best divisions in the British Army, the New Zealanders and the 4TH Indian Division, forming a corps that seemed a perfect combination, should have achieved nothing."

16TH Punjab Regiment (16TH Punjab Regiment, Pakistan)

Cassino 11, 1944 (Italy).

This Battle Honour covers the fighting over the period 11TH to 18TH May 1944. The 8TH Indian Division and the Polish Corps were brought over from the Adriatic to breach the Gustav Line to enable British divisions to pass through. This they did on 15TH May and the armour poured through the gap resulting in the final capture of Monte Cassino itself. The 8TH Indian Division cleared the town of Cassino, while the Poles took the Monastery from the north.

Bengal Engineers (Corps of Engineers, India)
6TH Lancers (6TH Lancers, Pakistan)
12TH Frontier Force Regiment (12TH Frontier Force Regiment, Pakistan)
13TH Frontier Force Rifles (13TH Frontier Force Rifles, Pakistan)
15TH Punjab Regiment (15TH Punjab Regiment, Pakistan)

Liri Valley, 1944 (Italy).

Liri Valley covers the exploitation towards Rome after the capture of Cassino. As the 8TH Indian Division prepared to attack, 15TH Panzer Grenadier Division held the Liri Valley and provided garrisons for the fortifications both of Gustav and Adolf Hitler Lines. As the Frontiersmen pushed ahead the German posts, undetected under the blanket of fog, lay doggo in the midst of the Indians, opening fire from the rear and fighting to the last. Sikhs of the 8TH Punjab Regiment, locating their first objective charged in line abreast. A few yards short of the position a belt of wire halted them, and four covering machine-guns opened at point-blank range. Major Sujan Singh, who had led the charge, fell dead. One platoon, which by impetus of its rush had penetrated the position, was wiped out to a man. They were afterwards found lying under the muzzles of the machine-guns. Major Amar Singh, who had led his company in many gallant actions in Italy, was also killed. The 8TH Indian Division relentlessly pushed forward towards Rome. On the day Frontiersmen attacked Monte Pavone, a commanding feature which covered the approach to Acre, one-and-a-half companies of German paratroopers occupied the peak.

Liri Valley, 1944 (Italy). (cont.)

As Subedar Sadhu Singh's Sikhs closed in, the Germans perceived the Indians to be comparatively few in numbers. They sprang to their feet and charged. The Sikhs were for an instant astounded by such foolhardiness; as one man they rose with their war cry of "Sat Siri Akal!" and leapt to meet the assailants. It was bayonet to bayonet and the paratroopers were outmatched. They broke and ran. The Sikhs swept forward to seize the enemy positions, capturing a number of prisoners, including a German officer.

8TH Punjab Regiment	(8TH Punjab Regiment, Pakistan)
12TH Frontier Force Regiment	(12TH Frontier Force Regiment, Pakistan)

San Angelo, 1944 (Italy).

As the 8TH Army pushed forward, their pressing need was to clean up San Angelo. This stubborn knuckle of resistance blocked further advance on 17TH Brigade's front. At noon on May 13TH, seven field regiments crashed a vicious shoot on the village. After five minutes of bombardment the infantry dashed in. Sixty minutes of deadly fighting followed. No German asked quarter – none was given. In the deep shelters the last fanatical defenders were exterminated. The capture of San Angelo alarmed the German garrison, who had watched the progress of the attack and the deployment of tanks in the open ground beyond the village. Without further resistance this strong point hung out white flags and surrendered in most un-German fashion.

8TH Punjab Regiment	(8TH Punjab Regiment, Pakistan)
13TH Frontier Force Rifles	(13TH Frontier Force Rifles, Pakistan)

Pignataro, 1944 (Italy).

To the south of San Angelo, 13TH Frontier Force Rifles with tank support was to advance up the valley. As Jemadar Thakur Singh led his platoon forward, his men spotted four self-propelled German guns concealed under the foliage of trees. A burst of tracer gave the tank escorts ot the Frontiersmen the clue. The tanks plastered the site with Armour piercing shells as they closed in for the kill. Similarly when German armoured vehicles sallied out to deal with the Indian skirmishers, the tank men saw them first and smashed them. Their wreckage sign-posted the line of advance. The enemy was unable to frustrate such efficient teamwork, and Panaccioni fell to the Frontier Force Rifles at 1400 hours on the afternoon of May 13TH. The Frontier Force Rifles with tank support attacked Pignataro at twilight. The defenders fought fanatically but by dawn Pignataro was cleared of the enemy. In the four days of fierce fighting, approximately 1,000 Germans had been killed, and the San Angelo - Pignataro - Panaccioni Horseshoe had been captured.

13TH Frontier Force Rifles	(13TH Frontier Force Rifles, Pakistan)

Montone, 1944 (Italy).

Montone, a strong position in the Tiber Valley in the 8TH Army sector, was captured by the 25TH Indian Brigade in fighting over the period 5TH - 7TH July. On July 6TH the Punjabis pushed on and established contact with the enemy. Throughout the burning heat of the afternoon Sikhs and Mussulman companies battled their way forward across the open countryside. The Germans, in a characteristic fashion, stuck it out obstinately and several hours of street fighting ensued before Montone was cleared and held.

1ST Punjab Regiment (1ST Punjab Regiment, Pakistan)

Advance to Florence, 1944 (Italy).

On August 1ST as the 8TH Indian Division advanced on Florence, the leading Indian Brigades brushed aside light opposition and occupied commanding ground within nine miles of Florence. When the sun rose in the morning the Indians caught their first glimpse of one of the most beautiful cities in the world. Both brigades approached the Arno on the reach where it loops through the heavily populated countryside to the south-west of the city. Bit by bit the great city was brought under control, the last enemies extirpated and public services restored.

12TH Frontier Force Regiment (12TH Frontier Force Regiment, Pakistan)
13TH Frontier Force Rifles (13TH Frontier Force Rifles, Pakistan)

Il Castello, 1944 (Italy).

This Battle Honour commemorates the heavy fighting at Il Castello in August 1944. The 8TH Indian Division captured Il Castello after heavy fighting from 3RD to 8TH August. By mid-August the 8TH Division had reached Florence.

8TH Punjab Regiment (8TH Punjab Regiment, Pakistan)

Gothic Line, 1944 (Italy).

This Battle Honour commemorates the breaching of the German defensive Gothic Line stretching from Pisa to Rimini, between 25TH August and 22ND September 1944, when the Eighth Army breached the line in the east and captured Rimini. All of the Indian Divisions; the 4TH Indian Division, the 8TH Indian Division, and the 10TH Indian Division, were destined to fight in the forthcoming battles.

11TH Sikh Regiment (4TH Battalion, 11TH Sikh Regiment, India)
1ST Punjab Regiment (1ST Punjab Regiment, Pakistan)
12TH Frontier Force Regiment (12TH Frontier Force Regiment, Pakistan)
13TH Frontier Force Rifles (13TH Frontier Force Rifles, Pakistan)
15TH Punjab Regiment (15TH Punjab Regiment, Pakistan)

Monte Calvo, 1944 (Italy).

This Battle Honour commemorates the capture of Monte Calvo in August 1944. This was to secure a firm base for the main assault on the Gothic Line. The 4TH Indian Division captured Monte Calvo between 29TH and 31ST August.

4TH Battalion, 11TH Sikh Regiment	(4TH Battalion, 11TH Sikh Regiment, India)

Pratelle Pass, 1944 (Italy).

This Battle Honour commemorates the breaching of the Gothic Line by the Indian Division. The 8TH Indian Division breached a part of the Gothic Line in the centre and secured Pratelle Pass.

2ND Punjab Regiment	(2ND Punjab Regiment, India)

Coriano, 1944 (Italy).

This Battle Honour commemorates the fighting for the Coriano Ridge. The first attacks were repulsed with heavy casualties, but eventually the 4TH Indian Division captured the ridge, though with heavy casualties.

2ND Battalion. 11TH Sikh Regiment	(2ND Battalion, 11TH Sikh Regiment, India)
12TH Frontier Force Regiment	(12TH Frontier Force Regiment, Pakistan)

San Giovanni, 1944 (Italy).

This Battle Honour commemorates the capture of Poggio San Giovanni, which was attacked by the 4TH Indian Division simultaneously with Coriano, and captured on the 5TH September 1944.

2ND Battalion, 11TH Sikh Regiment	(2ND Battalion, 11TH Sikh Regiment, India)

San Marino, 1944 (Italy).

This Battle Honour commemorates the capture of San Marino in September 1944. The 4TH Indian Division captured this small Independent Republic within Italy on 20TH September 1943.

4TH Battalion, 11TH Sikh Regiment	(4TH Battalion, 11TH Sikh Regiment, India)

San Martino Sogliano and Monte Farneto, 1944 (Italy).

This Battle Honour commemorates the capture of San Martino Sogliano and Monte Farneto. by the 10TH Indian Division, on 4TH - 5TH October 1944.

2ND Punjab Regiment	(2ND Punjab Regiment, India)

Casa Bettini, 1944 (Italy).

This Battle Honour covers the capture of Casa Bettini. Following continuous attacks from 24TH November 1944, Casa Bettini was captured on 1ST December 1944.

2ND Punjab Regiment	(2ND Punjab Regiment, India)

Chronology of Sikh Battle Honours (cont.)

The Senio, 1945 (Italy).

The Senio covers the operations to force a crossing over that river and the Santerno during the period 9TH – 12TH April. The Germans suffered very heavy casualties and 2,500 prisoners were taken.

8TH Punjab Regiment	(8TH Punjab Regiment, Pakistan)
12TH Frontier Force Regiment	(12TH Frontier Force Regiment, Pakistan)
13TH Frontier Force Rifles	(13TH Frontier Force Rifles, Pakistan)

Santerno Crossing, 1945 (Italy).

Santerno Crossing was a subsidiary Honour for the battle of Senio. In the face of strong enemy opposition and continuous counter-attacks, the 8th Indian Division established and consolidated shallow bridgeheads over the Santerno River on an eight-mile front on April 12TH.

12TH Frontier Force Regiment	(12TH Frontier Force Regiment, Pakistan)

Idice Bridgehead, 1945 (Italy).

The river Idice was crossed by the 10TH Indian Division on 20TH April after fierce fighting.

2ND Punjab Regiment	(2ND Punjab Regiment, India)

Bologna, 1945 (Italy).

Bologna was captured on 21ST April, and here the Poles destroyed the renowned Parachute Division. Axis forces attempted in vain to prevent the juncture of the Fifth and Eighth Armies, desperately trying to buy time for small detachments of their comrades to escape. But the Allied onslaught, now moving at full speed, quickly swept aside the hasty defences, overwhelming and annihilating numerous Axis rear-guard detachments in the process. Ultimately, over 100,000 Axis troops were forced to surrender in the areas south of the river. The war in this theatre ended on 29TH April with the German command signing the instrument of surrender.

13TH Frontier Force Rifles	(13TH Frontier Force Rifles, Pakistan)

Greece, 1944-1945. (Campaign Honour)

This Campaign Honour was awarded to the regiments that operated in Greece in 1944-1945. British troops were landed in Greece to prevent chaos and communist take-over after the German withdrawal. As the civil war broke out, the 4TH Indian Division was sent there from Italy and was engaged against the communist rebels until mid-January.

2ND Battalion, 11TH Sikh Regiment	(2ND Battalion, 11TH Sikh Regiment, India)
Bombay Engineers	(Corps of Engineers, India)

South East Asia, 1941. (Campaign Honour)

'South East Asia 1941', covers the fighting in Hong Kong and in British North Borneo.

14TH Punjab Regiment	(14TH Punjab Regiment, Pakistan)
15TH Punjab Regiment	(15TH Punjab Regiment, Pakistan)

Hong Kong, 1941

Hong Kong commemorates the defence of the Colony against greatly superior Japanese forces from 8TH to 25TH December 1941. The Japanese attack began shortly after 8 am on 8TH December 1941. Eighteen days after the battle began, after suffering heavy casualties, British colonial officials headed in person by the Governor of Hong Kong, Sir Mark Aitchison Young, surrendered on 25TH December 1941 at the Japanese headquarters. The Sikh gunners of the Hong Kong and Singapore Royal Artillery made a gallant stand against the Japanese. However, 20 gunners were massacred at the San Wai Battery after they had surrendered.

14TH Punjab Regiment	(14TH Punjab Regiment, Pakistan)
Hong Kong & Singapore Artillery	Singapore

Malaya 1941 – 42. (Campaign Honour)

This Theatre Honour was awarded to all the regiments that had served in Malaya during 1941-1942. The Japanese invasion of Malaya started with landings on the east coast and a simultaneous advance from Thailand. As the invaders advanced down the peninsula, the British troops withdrew to Singapore Island. The Japanese attacked and captured Singapore on the 15TH February 1942.

5TH Battalion, 11TH Sikh Regiment	(5TH Battalion, 11TH Sikh Regiment, India)
2ND Punjab Regiment	(2ND Punjab Regiment, India)
3RD Cavalry	(3RD Cavalry, India)
8TH Punjab Regiment	(8TH Punjab Regiment, Pakistan)
16TH Punjab Regiment	(16TH Punjab Regiment, Pakistan)
Bengal Engineers	(Corps of Engineers, India)
Bombay Engineers	(Corps of Engineers, India)

Northern Malaya, 1941. (Campaign Honour)

This Campaign Honour covers the early stages of the campaign in Northern Malaya from 8TH to 23TH December 1941. In December 1941, Japanese troops landed in northern Malaya as part of their rapid advance into the resource-rich British and Dutch colonies of the South Seas. For the next two months they fought their way down the Malayan peninsula, steadily pushing back the British, Indian, Australian and Malay troops who opposed them.

Chronology of Sikh Battle Honours (cont.)

Northern Malaya, 1941. (cont.)

3RD Cavalry	(3RD Cavalry, India)
8TH Punjab Regiment	(8TH Punjab Regiment, Pakistan)
12TH Frontier Force Regiment	(12TH Frontier Force Regiment, Pakistan)
13TH Frontier Force Rifles	(13TH Frontier Force Rifles, Pakistan)

Kota Bahru, 1941 (Malaya).

The war in Malaya began with the Japanese landings at Kota Bahru, on Malaya's north-eastern coast. The Japanese objective was to seize the three airfields in the vicinity of Kota Bahru. The defence of Kota Bahru was assigned to the 8TH Indian Brigade of the 9TH Division, composed of 4 Indian infantry battalions. The Japanese landed the 56TH Infantry Regiment, which were 3 battalions strong. The landings were costly to the Japanese. Japanese casualties were heavy at around 30%. However, they managed to secure a beachhead. Despite attempting a counterattack with their reserve, the British were unable to dislodge the Japanese beachhead.

12TH Frontier Force Regiment	(12TH Frontier Force Regiment, Pakistan)
13TH Frontier Force Rifles	(13TH Frontier Force Rifles, Pakistan)
21ST Mountain Battery	(21ST Mountain Battery, Pakistan)
73RD Field Battery	(73RD Field Battery, Pakistan)

Jitra, 1941 (Malaya).

This Battle Honour commemorates the fighting in the north west of Malaya around Jitra. The Battle of Jitra was the first major engagement fought between the invading Japanese and British forces in Malaya. The actual battle was fought from 11TH–12TH December 1941. On 11TH December the 1ST Battalion, 14TH Punjab Regiment at Changlun was directed to occupy and intermediate position before Asun. Now came catastrophe. As the Punjabis were assembling to occupy their new position, a Japanese mechanized force headed by medium tanks broke through the rearguard, caught the anti-tank guns limbering up, destroyed them and smashed through and swarmed right through the battalion. By evening the 14TH Punjab Regiment had ceased to exist as a fighting formation. The 16TH Punjab Regiment with Major Brown's Sikhs withdrew and took part in the confused fighting at Anak Bukit and formed part of the rear guard at Simpang Ampat.

8TH Punjab Regiment	(8TH Punjab Regiment, Pakistan)
14TH Punjab Regiment	(14TH Punjab Regiment, Pakistan)
16TH Punjab Regiment	(16TH Punjab Regiment, Pakistan)

Chronology of Sikh Battle Honours (cont.)

Central Malaya, 1941. (Campaign Honour)

This Campaign Honour covers the operations over the period 26TH December to 10TH January 1941. At the beginning of January 1942, the British fell back to the Slim River and the approaches to the southern airfields near Kuala Lumpur. On the night of 7TH January, Japanese tanks cut through these positions and advanced another 30 km (18 miles), cutting off around 4,000 British troops. The Allies abandoned central Malaya, hastening the Japanese advance on Singapore before sufficient reinforcements could arrive. Kuala Lumpur was abandoned and the Allied defence moved back to Johore, but this enabled the Japanese to use better roads and so advance two divisions at once, intensifying the attack and accelerating the Allied retreat.

3RD Cavalry (3RD Cavalry, India)
2ND Punjab Regiment (2ND Punjab Regiment, India)
12TH Frontier Force Regiment (12TH Frontier Force Regiment, Pakistan)

Ipoh, 1941 (Malaya).

This Battle Honour commemorates the fighting at Ipoh from 26TH to 29TH December 1941.

2ND Punjab Regiment (2ND Punjab Regiment, India)
16TH Punjab Regiment (16TH Punjab Regiment, Pakistan)

Kuantan, 1942 (Malaya).

The Japanese forces that had landed at Kota Bahru, had their eyes firmly fixed on Kuantan, a small, isolated coastal town in Pahang state, connected with the railway at Jarantut by a single road running through a hundred miles of jungle. The 22ND Indian Brigade held Kuantan town and aerodrome. On the night of 3RD - 4TH January, as the Japanese advanced, the 22ND Brigade were ordered to retire. As they retreated to the railway at Jarantut, they fought some sharp actions against the Japanese. The fighting had reduced the 12TH Frontier Force Regiment to 220 officers and men.

5TH Battalion, 11TH Sikh Regiment (5TH Battalion, 11TH Sikh Regiment, India)
12TH Frontier Force Regiment (12TH Frontier Force Regiment, Pakistan)

Kampar, 1941 (Malaya).

The Kampar position was one of the strongest in Malaya. The 28TH Brigade held the hill when the Japanese attacked on 31ST December. There, in a four-day battle, the Japanese suffered heavy casualties and the Sikhs carried out bayonet charges through machine-gun and mortar fire. By January 2ND, as the Indian 11TH Infantry Division was out flanked and cut off from the road to Singapore, they withdrew to some prepared positions at Trolak five miles north of the Slim River.

Chronology of Sikh Battle Honours (cont.)

Kampar 1941 (Malaya). (cont.)

5TH Battalion, 11TH Sikh Regiment (5TH Battalion, 11TH Sikh Regiment, India)
16TH Punjab Regiment (16TH Punjab Regiment, Pakistan)

Slim River, 1942 (Malaya).

On 7TH January 1942 the two Indian Brigades of the British Army were overrun at Slim River leaving the Japanese with a straight run through to Kuala Lumpur, the Malayan capital. By the 9TH January the British situation was extreme and General Wavell (Commanding) decided to withdraw the entire British Army to north Johore leaving Kuala Lumpur free for occupation, which the Japanese did on the 13th January.

5TH Battalion, 11TH Sikh Regiment (5TH Battalion, 11TH Sikh Regiment, India)
13TH Frontier Force Rifles (13TH Frontier Force Rifles, Pakistan)
16TH Punjab Regiment (16TH Punjab Regiment, Pakistan)

The Muar, 1942 (Malaya).

The Battle of Muar was the last major battle of the Malayan campaign. It took place from 14TH to 22ND January 1942, around Gemensah Bridge and on the Muar River. Allied soldiers, under the command of Major General Gordon Bennett, inflicted severe losses on Japanese forces. By late afternoon the Japanese, who had already made the crossing higher up, stormed into Muar Town and captured the garrison headquarters, killing all the officers. By nightfall of 16TH January, Muar Town and the harbour had fallen into Japanese hands. The remnants of the garrison retreated down the coast several miles as far as Parit Jawa. Japanese ambushes were soon deployed to repel any Allied counter-attacks.

13TH Frontier Force Rifles (13TH Frontier Force Rifles, Pakistan)

Niyor, 1942 (Malaya).

This Battle Honour commemorates the action at Niyor 1942, the last engagement fought in Malaya. Thereafter the retreating troops destroyed the causeway connecting the peninsula to Singapore Island.

5TH Battalion, 11TH Sikh Regiment (5TH Battalion, 11TH Sikh Regiment, India)

Sikh Mounted Cavalry Malaya 1894

Chronology of Sikh Battle Honours (cont.)

Singapore Island, 1942.

This Battle Honour covers the defence of Singapore in the week beginning 8TH February 1942. This culminated in the greatest single disaster in British military history in the East, when the supposedly impregnable "Bastion of the Empire" surrendered to the Japanese. On the night of 8TH February, two divisions of the Japanese invasion force crossed the straits and landed on Singapore Island. Singapore's defence was ineffective; by morning, around 13,000 Japanese soldiers had landed and the British defenders had retreated to inland positions. By the end of the day there were over 30,000 Japanese troops on Singapore and they had established a stronghold on the north-western part of the island. The Japanese advance continued and by 15TH February the defenders had been driven back to the suburbs of Singapore city on the south coast of the island. Food and water supplies were low and that evening General Percival surrendered to the Japanese.

3RD Cavalry	(3RD Cavalry, India)
1ST Punjab Regiment	(1ST Punjab Regiment, Pakistan)
2ND Punjab Regiment	(2ND Punjab Regiment, India)
12TH Frontier Force Regiment	(12TH Frontier Force Regiment, Pakistan)
13TH Frontier Force Rifles	(13TH Frontier Force Rifles, Pakistan)
14TH Punjab Regiment	(14TH Punjab Regiment, Pakistan)
16TH Punjab Regiment	(16TH Punjab Regiment, Pakistan)

Burma, 1942. (Campaign Honour)

This Theatre Honour was awarded to all of the regiments that had served in Burma during 1942. After severe fighting in January 1942, the Japanese offensive forced the British to retreat across the River Chindwin into India. By the end of the year the Japanese had virtually occupied all of Burma.

1ST Battalion, 11TH Sikh Regiment	(1ST Battalion, 11TH Sikh Regiment, India)
2ND Mountain Battery	(2ND Mountain Battery, Pakistan)
5TH Mountain Battery	(5TH Mountain Battery, India)
12TH Mountain Battery	(12TH Mountain Battery, Pakistan)
23RD Mountain Battery	(23RD Mountain Battery, Pakistan)
27TH Mountain Regiment	(27TH Mountain Regiment, Pakistan)
1ST Punjab Regiment	(1ST Punjab Regiment, Pakistan)
12TH Frontier Force Rifles	(12TH Frontier Force Regiment, Pakistan)
Burma Rifles	(Burma Rifles, Burma)
Burma Frontier Force	Disbanded
Burma Military Police Battalions	Disbanded

Chronology of Sikh Battle Honours (cont.)

Sittang, 1942 (Burma).

This Battle Honour covers the attempts by the 17TH Indian Division to hold the initial Japanese invasion along the rivers Bilin and Sittang. Unfortunately the bridge over the Sittang was prematurely destroyed while two Brigades of the Division were still on the far side of the river, and, although a large number of men did manage to get across, nearly all the equipment was lost.

22ND Mountain Regiment (22ND Mountain Regiment, India)
12TH Frontier Force Regiment (12TH Frontier Force Regiment, Pakistan)

Yenangyaung, 1942 (Burma).

Yenangyaung was the location of a strategically and tactically important oil refinery in Burma. As a result of the speed and success of the Japanese advance up through Burma, the retreating Allied forces were forced to blow up the oil fields and refinery to prevent them falling into the hands of the Japanese. This difficult task was left to a small group of men who had experience with explosives and demolitions, some from serving with the Bombay Pioneers. The oil facilities were destroyed at 2200 hours on April 16TH, 1942. The Allied forces were too weak to hold the oil fields and had to retreat to the north. Part of this force had to fight its way out, with the loss of its guns.

22ND Mountain Regiment (22ND Mountain Regiment, India)
Bombay Engineers (Corps of Engineers, India)
1ST Punjab Regiment (1ST Punjab Regiment, Pakistan)

Monywa, 1942 (Burma).

The River Chindwin joins the Irrawaddy near to the fairly large town of Monywa. The Burma Divison had been made responsible for delaying the Japanese south of Monywa. On 30TH April, 1942, reinforcements arrived at Monywa where there had been a heavy air raid, and were employed clearing wreckage from the railway station. During that evening bursts of Light Machine Gun fire were heard and a great deal of confusion occurred among the people still in the town. Capt. Niblett deployed "D" Coy. covering the town on the riverfront, and "B" Coy. astride the road facing south. Active patrolling was carried out throughout the night. In the early hours of the next morning heavy mortar and artillery fire was brought down on the riverbank and town from the west side of the Chindwin River. The British had no guns or mortars with which to engage the enemy. A force of 200 Japanese crossed the river down-stream, out of range of small arms fire. And the Burma Division was once more cut off south of Monywa. Lt-Col. Thomas, who was commanding all troops in Monywa, ordered a withdrawal, and the force withdrew to Budalin, about 15 miles to the north, arriving on 2ND May.

1ST Punjab Regiment (1ST Punjab Regiment, Pakistan)
13TH Frontier Force Rifles (13TH Frontier Force Rifles, Pakistan)

Burma, 1942-1945. (Campaign Honour)

This Campaign Honour was awarded to all of the regiments that had served in Burma during 1942-1945. After severe fighting in January 1942, the Japanese offensive forced the British to retire across the River Chindwin into India. By the end of the year the Japanese had virtually occupied all of Burma. In 1943 and 1944 British offensives across the Chindwin led to the complete defeat and withdrawal of the Japanese from Imphal and Kohima. In January 1945 the advance reached Meiktila. Rangoon fell to British troops landed from the sea, and they joined up with the main Fourteenth Army advancing southwards. It was in this campaign that the newly raised Sikh Light Infantry first tasted blood and earned their first Battle Honour. Also in this Campaign the 1ST Battalion, the Sikh Regiment, earned eight Battle Honours besides the Campaign Honour.

11TH Sikh Regiment	(11TH Sikh Regiment, India)
Sikh Light Infantry	(The Sikh Light Infantry, India)
7TH Cavalry	(7TH Cavalry, India)
8TH Cavalry	(8TH Cavalry, India)
Deccan Horse	(9TH Horse, India)
Bengal Engineers	(Corps of Engineers, India)
Bombay Engineers	(Corps of Engineers, India)
1ST Punjab Regiment	(1ST Punjab Regiment, Pakistan)
2ND Punjab Regiment	(2ND Punjab Regiment, India)
8TH Punjab Regiment	(8TH Punjab Regiment, Pakistan)
12TH Frontier Force Regiment	(12TH Frontier Force Regiment, Pakistan)
13TH Frontier Force Rifles	(13TH Frontier Force Rifles, Pakistan)
14TH Punjab Regiment	(14TH Punjab Regiment, Pakistan)
15TH Punjab Regiment	(15TH Punjab Regiment, Pakistan)
16TH Punjab Regiment	(16TH Punjab Regiment, Pakistan)

Donbaik, 1943 (Burma).

This Battle Honour covers a series of operations in the vicinity of Donbaik over the period 8TH January–18TH March 1943. Four assaults on Donbaik itself by the 14TH Indian Division and the 2ND British Division were repulsed and the British were driven back by a Japanese counter-offensive.

1ST Punjab Regiment	(1ST Punjab Regiment, Pakistan)
8TH Punjab Regiment	(8TH Punjab Regiment, Pakistan)

Chronology of Sikh Battle Honours (cont.)

North Arakan, 1944 (Burma).

This Battle Honour covers the 1944 offensive into Arakan over the period 1ST January to 12TH June. The British made slow but steady progress against fanatical Japanese opposition, who were being materially assisted by air supply.

1ST Punjab Regiment — (1ST Punjab Regiment, Pakistan)
12TH Frontier Force Regiment — (12TH Frontier Force Regiment, Pakistan)
13TH Frontier Force Rifles — (13TH Frontier Force Rifles, Pakistan)
14TH Punjab Regiment — (14TH Punjab Regiment, Pakistan)
15TH Punjab Regiment — (15TH Punjab Regiment, Pakistan)
11TH Sikh Regiment — (11TH Sikh Regiment, India)

Buthidaung, 1944 (Burma).

This Battle Honour covers the fighting involving the 7TH Indian Division in the vicinity of Buthidaung during the earlier phases of the offensive in January and February 1944, and later fighting during March and April. The Japanese had attempted an invasion of India, beginning in the coastal strip of Arakan. There, a platoon of 1ST Battalion, Sikh Regiment was sent to observe a Japanese post and seize it if possible, which they did. They then fought off violent counter-attacks after which the position was surrounded, preventing re-supply. Asked by radio how long they could hold out, the platoon commander replied: 'Without food for 6 more days; without ammunition, as long as you like, we have bayonets.' It was no idle boast, as the Sikhs repeatedly proved.

11TH Sikh Regiment — (11TH Sikh Regiment, India)
19TH Lancers — (19TH Lancers, Pakistan)
2ND Punjab Regiment — (2ND Punjab Regiment, India)
12TH Frontier Force Regiment — (12TH Frontier Force Regiment, Pakistan)
14TH Punjab Regiment — (14TH Punjab Regiment, Pakistan)

Razabil, 1944 (Burma).

Razabil covers the fighting to secure and hold this strong bastion in the Mayu Hills during January and March. The first attacks in the latter part of January were repulsed by the Japanese, involving heavy casualties to the attackers, but the 5TH Indian Division captured Razabil in the mid-March.

1ST Punjab Regiment — (1ST Punjab Regiment, Pakistan)
14TH Punjab Regiment — (14TH Punjab Regiment, Pakistan)

Chronology of Sikh Battle Honours (cont.)

Kaladan, 1944 (Burma).

By the end of 1944, General Sir William Slim's 14TH Army was poised for a right-flank offensive against Lieutenant-General Sakurai Seizo's 28TH Japanese Army in the coastal strip between the Irrawaddy and the Bay of Bengal. General Sir Philip Christison's XV Corps of four divisions launched the offensive on 12TH December 1944, and every move forward was challenged by Japanese counter-attacks.

During this offensive the 33RD Mountain Battery, Indian Artillery, in which Havildar Umrao Singh was a field gun detachment commander, was subjected to a sustained bombardment from Japanese guns. Havildar (sergeant) Umrao Singh was the only non-commissioned officer of either the Royal Artillery or the Indian Artillery to be awarded the Victoria Cross in the Second World War. Umrao Singh won his award for valour in what all gunners regard as their near-sacred duty – the defence of their guns. Miraculously, after six hours of incessant fighting, the 24-year-old had managed to save his gun; it was pressed into action soon after and helped retain the critical sliver of territory, considerably delaying the Japanese advance further east into British-India.

33RD Mountain Battery (${33}^{RD}$ Mountain Battery, India)
16TH Punjab Regiment (16TH Punjab Regiment, Pakistan)

Mayu Tunnels, 1944 (Burma).

There were only two roads through the Arakan and one had been designed as a railway and ran through a series of tunnels from Maungdaw to Buthidaung on the Mayu River. The Japanese were in control of this road and so could pass men and supplies quickly from one side of the Mayu hills to the other. The first objective was the capture of the two tunnels used by the Japanese for storage and gun emplacements. The Japanese were subjected to three days of shelling and dive bombing. A determined attack by the British resulted in the taking of four enemy positions camouflaged in thick bamboo, which lay one after the other on a spur commanding the approach to the first tunnel. The battle developed into fierce hand-to-hand fighting, which drove back the enemy and the first tunnel was captured. The next day a Sherman tank was brought up to fire into the mouth of the second tunnel. Bodies and debris were blown out of the other end of the tunnel as ammunition stored inside exploded. The Japanese abandoned the tunnels without further fighting.

13TH Frontier Force Rifles (13TH Frontier Force Rifles, Pakistan)
1ST Punjab Regiment (1ST Punjab Regiment, Pakistan)

Maungdaw, 1944 (Burma).

Maungdaw covers a long series of operations from January to March, involving the 5TH and 25TH Indian Divisions and 3RD Special Service Brigade, which resulted in the capture of this town.

12TH Frontier Force Regiment (12TH Frontier Force Regiment, Pakistan)

Defence of Sinzweya, 1944 (Burma).

This Battle Honour covers the defence of the Corps Maintenance Centre, generally known as the "Battle of the Box", from the 5TH to the 29TH February 1944.

24TH Engineering Battalion (Corps of Engineers, India)

Point. 551, 1944 (Burma).

Point. 551 was captured by the Japanese a year earlier and was retaken in an action lasting from 3RD April to 22ND May 1944

2ND Punjab Regiment (2ND Punjab Regiment, India)
13TH Frontier Force Rifles (13TH Frontier Force Rifles, Pakistan)

Ramree, 1944 (Burma).

Ramree Island lies off the Burma coast and was captured along with the rest of Southern Burma, during the early stages of the Burma Campaign, by the rapidly advancing Imperial Japanese Army in 1942. In January 1945 the Allies were able to launch attacks to retake Ramree and its neighbour Cheduba, with the intention of building sea-supplied airbases on them. As the 4TH, 26TH, 36TH and 71ST Indian Brigades, with Royal Navy Marine units, landed and outflanked the Japanese stronghold; the nine hundred defenders abandoned it and began a march to join a larger battalion of Japanese soldiers across the island. The route forced the Japanese to cross 16 kilometres of fetid mangrove swamps, and as they struggled through the thick forests the British forces encircled the area. Trapped in the mud-filled swampland, tropical diseases soon started afflicting the Japanese, but worse was the presence of huge numbers of scorpions, thousands of mosquitoes, and saltwater crocodiles. Repeated calls by the British for the Japanese to surrender were ignored: the Marines holding the perimeter shot any Japanese attempting to escape, while within the swampland hundreds of soldiers died over the course of several days for lack of food or drinking water. When the British eventually moved in on the swamp, they found that of the nine hundred troops that originally fled into the swamp, only around twenty seriously wounded and weakened Japanese soldiers had survived.

12TH Frontier Force Regiment (12TH Frontier Force Regiment, Pakistan)
13TH Frontier Force Rifles (13TH Frontier Force Rifles, Pakistan)

Chronology of Sikh Battle Honours (cont.)

Ngakyedauk Pass, 1944 (Burma).

This Battle Honour commemorates the defeat of the Japanese counter-offensive in the Arakan. The brunt of the fighting fell upon the 7TH Indian Division. In the 'Battle of the Box' in February 1944, the Japanese attacked the XV Corps' Administrative Area, defended mainly by service troops, but they were unable to deal with tanks supporting the defenders. Troops from 5TH Division broke through the Ngakyedauk Pass to relieve the defenders of the box. Although battle casualties were approximately equal, the overall result was a heavy Japanese defeat. Their infiltration and encirclement tactics had failed to panic Allied troops.

Bengal Engineers (Corps of Engineers, India)
1ST Punjab Regiment (1ST Punjab Regiment, Pakistan)
2ND Punjab Regiment (2ND Punjab Regiment, India)
12TH Frontier Force Regiment (12TH Frontier Force Regiment, Pakistan)
13TH Frontier Force Rifles (13TH Frontier Force Rifles, Pakistan)

Bishenpur, 1944 (Burma).

Below Imphal at Bishenpur, the Japanese 33RD Division held out against the 17TH Indian Division (Black Cat) and the fighting was bitter with no side gaining any advantage. To rout the Japanese, the heaviest artillery bombarded the Japanese at Ningthoukhong Kha Khunou where the Japanese were at their strongest. It is said that not a single leaf was left on a tree after this action.

12TH Frontier Force Regiment (12TH Frontier Force Regiment, Pakistan)
14TH Punjab Regiment (14TH Punjab Regiment, Pakistan)

Tengnoupal, 1944 (Burma).

The British 37TH and 49TH brigades, attacking from the north, enabled the Allies to push aside the Japanese blocking positions. This opened up an escape route as well as enabling badly needed food, ammunition and medicine to get through to the retreating 17TH Division. With the Japanese still in pursuit, the British eventually reached the Imphal Plain. The British 20TH Division, under Maj. Gen. Douglas Gracey, guarded the road from Tamu. The Japanese force moved northwest up the valley to attack Gracey's right flank. Contact was made on March 14TH and in accordance with prearranged plans, the 20TH Division pulled back, barring the way to Imphal. Although the Japanese continued to advance, the British dug in along Tengnoupal Ridge and effectively blocked the road to the plain behind them.

1ST Patiala Infantry (15TH Battalion, Punjab Regiment, India)
2ND Punjab Regiment (2ND Punjab Regiment, India)

Chronology of Sikh Battle Honours (cont.)

Kennedy Peak, 1944 (Burma).

The advance of the 5TH Indian Division continued till Kennedy Peak was reached. At about 2,440 meters, it was the highest point along the road to Kalemyo. A strong Japanese rear guard position here was initially outflanked but later attacked and taken in the first week of November after a week-long battle.

1ST Punjab Regiment (1ST Punjab Regiment, Pakistan)
12TH Frontier Force Regiment (12TH Frontier Force Regiment, Pakistan)

Imphal, 1944 (Burma).

This Battle took place in the region around the city of Imphal, the capital of the state of Manipur in Northeast India from March until July 1944. Japanese armies attempted to destroy the Allied forces at Imphal and invade India, but were driven back into Burma with heavy losses. Together with the simultaneous Battle of Kohima in which the encircled Allied forces at Imphal were relieved, this battle was the turning point of the Burma Campaign.

7TH Light Cavalry (7TH Light Cavalry, India)
2ND Punjab Regiment (2ND Punjab Regiment, India)
12TH Frontier Force Regiment (12TH Frontier Force Regiment, Pakistan)
13TH Frontier Force Rifles (13TH Frontier Force Rifles, Pakistan)
14TH Punjab Regiment (14TH Punjab Regiment, Pakistan)
16TH Punjab Regiment (16TH Punjab Regiment, Pakistan)

Tamu Road, 1944 (Burma).

This battle honour covers the operations in which the Japanese were cleared along the Tamu Road from 12TH March to 25TH March.

16TH Punjab Regiment (16TH Punjab Regiment, Pakistan)
12TH Frontier Force Regiment (12TH Frontier Force Regiment, Pakistan)

Shenam Pass, 1944 (Burma).

The Japanese besieged Imphal for a number of months, with the Allied defenders stoutly resisting all attempts to dislodge them. The Imphal siege was eventually lifted after the victory at Kohima and Allied forces were soon launching their own offensive into Burma. During this particular time-period they fought intense, and numerous engagements with Japanese forces at Scraggy Hill and Shenam Pass.

12TH Frontier Force Regiment (12TH Frontier Force Regiment, Pakistan)

Chronology of Sikh Battle Honours (cont.)

Litan, 1944 (Burma).

Litan was taken by the Japanese during their advance to surround Imphal. The 1ST Patiala Infantry inflicted heavy casualties on the Japanese before withdrawing.

Field Marshal Slim had this to say about the Patialas: 'I want it conveyed to 1ST Patiala that if I were to pick one unit for any special task, it would be 1ST Patiala. I am sanctioning one month's leave to the whole unit at Shillong.'

1ST Patiala Infantry — (15TH Battalion, Punjab Regiment, India)
2ND Punjab Regiment — (2ND Punjab Regiment, India)
13TH Frontier Force Rifles — (13TH Frontier Force Rifles, Pakistan)
16TH Punjab Regiment — (16TH Punjab Regiment, Pakistan)

Kanglatongbi, 1944 (Burma).

The Japanese 15TH Division encircled Imphal from the north. Its 60TH Regiment, after desperate fighting, captured a British supply dump at Kanglatongbi on the main Imphal-Dimapur road a few miles north of Imphal, but the depot had been emptied of food and ammunition. The Japanese, after bitter fighting, were steadily pushed back and the Kohima-Imphal road re-opened. The operations lasted from 21ST April to 22ND June 1944.

1ST Battalion, 11TH Sikh Regiment — (1ST Battalion, 11TH Sikh Regiment, India)
2ND Punjab Regiment — (2ND Punjab Regiment, India)
14TH Punjab Regiment — (14TH Punjab Regiment, Pakistan)

Kohima, 1944 (Burma).

The Battle of Kohima (the "Stalingrad of the East") was the turning point of the Japanese U Go offensive into India in 1944. It was fought from April 4TH to June 22ND around the town of Kohima on the Indo–Burmese border. The battle took place in two stages. In early April the Japanese attempted to capture Kohima ridge, a feature that dominated the road by which the major British and Indian troops at Imphal were supplied. By mid-April, the small British force at Kohima was relieved, and from April 18TH to June 22ND, British and Indian reinforcements counter-attacked to drive the Japanese from the positions they had captured. The battle ended on June 22ND when British and Indian troops from Kohima and Imphal met at Milestone 109, ending the siege of Imphal.

1ST Punjab Regiment — (1ST Punjab Regiment, Pakistan)

An historic meeting - Jemadar Karnail Singh of The 7TH Cavalry welcomes the leading troops of 149TH Regiment on the Imphal-Kohima road.

Defence of Kohima, 1944 (Burma).

The siege of Kohima began on 6TH April. The garrison was continually shelled and mortared by the Japanese and was slowly driven into a small perimeter on Garrison Hill. The medical dressing stations were exposed to Japanese fire and wounded men were hit again as they waited for treatment. Some of the heaviest fighting took place at the north end of Kohima Ridge around the Deputy Commissioner's bungalow and tennis court, in what became known as the 'Battle of the Tennis Court'. The tennis court became a no man's land, with the Japanese and the defenders of Kohima dug in on opposite sides, so close to each other that grenades were thrown between the trenches. The defenders' situation was desperate until day broke, when troops of 161ST Indian Brigade arrived to relieve the garrison.

1ST Punjab Regiment (1ST Punjab Regiment, Pakistan)
Burma Regiment (Burma Regiment, Burma)

Relief of Kohima, 1944 (Burma).

The British 2ND Division had begun to arrive at Dimapur in early April, having moved from Southern India where they had been training for amphibious landings. Their leading troops relieved 161ST Brigade at Jotsoma on April 15TH, and 161ST Brigade, in turn, broke through to Kohima on April 18TH. By now Kohima resembled a battlefield from the First World War, with trees smashed and the ground covered in craters, but the relief was under way. After a day's heavy fighting, the leading troops of 161ST Brigade broke through and relieved the Kohima garrison.

1ST Punjab Regiment (1ST Punjab Regiment, Pakistan)
PAVO Cavalry (PAVO Cavalry, Pakistan)

Jail Hill, 1944 (Burma).

After the relief of Kohima, the 6TH Brigade pressed forward to take Jail Hill on 4TH May. Heavy fighting erupted along the length of Kohima Ridge between 4TH and 7TH May 1944. Regiments lost heavily attacking Jail Hill and further attacks ground to a halt, with the Japanese still retaining Jail Hill. The British were finally forced to abandon the foothold gained on the feature.

1ST Patiala Infantry (15TH Battalion, Punjab Regiment, India)
Bengal Engineers (Corps of Engineers, India)
15TH Punjab Regiment (15TH Punjab Regiment, Pakistan)

Chronology of Sikh Battle Honours (cont.)

Naga Village, 1944 (Burma).

The British 5TH Brigade entered Naga Village during the night of 4TH -5TH May. A counter-attack by the Japanese pushed them back to the western edge of the village, which they managed to hold. During four days of bitter fighting, the British and Japanese were hopelessly intermingled. One side would attack, the other counter-attack, neither would give way. During daylight they fought ferociously ten or fifteen yards apart and at night they crept even closer attacking with grenades and bayonets. It was on the 11TH May that, under the cover of dense smoke bombs, a British attack was launched, but this was only partially successful, as next day the enemy still held several bunkers. The only effective weapon was a tank, which the 'Sappers' had winched up through liquid mud to the high ground, and dug it in so that it was able to bombard each Japanese bunker below it, and so ended the Battle of Naga Village.

1ST Patiala Infantry	(15TH Battalion, Punjab Regiment, India)
14TH Punjab Regiment	(14TH Punjab Regiment, Pakistan)
15TH Punjab Regiment	(15TH Punjab Regiment, Pakistan)

Kangaw, 1945 (Burma).

In Burma during January 1945, following the capture of the Myebon Peninsula, 3RD Commando Brigade was given the task of making a further landing near the strongly defended village of Kangaw, with the intention of cutting the Japanese lines of withdrawal down the coast. The Commandos landed and occupied positions in the mangrove swamp. Subsequently they were ordered to capture a heavily wooded ridge known as Hill 170. Two days of hand-to-hand fighting were necessary before the Japanese could be driven from the ridge and no sooner were they dislodged than they subjected it to heavy artillery fire. After a lull of several days, the Japanese counter-attacked repeatedly at dawn on 31ST January. Sustaining heavy casualties the Japanese were finally beaten off, leaving their dead and dying among the forward positions.

2ND Punjab Regiment	(2ND Punjab Regiment, India)
19TH Lancers	(19TH Lancers, Pakistan)

Ru–Ywa, 1945 (Burma).

Tanks of the 19TH Lancers, the first Indian tanks to take part in a sea landing, did great work in the Kangaw area, where they cut the Japanese main escape route from the Arakan. On 16TH February a formation of 25TH Division landed across the bay at Ru-Ywa. The landing was another shattering surprise to the Japanese. Heavy counter attacks by the Japanese were repulsed and the bridgehead consolidated.

19TH Lancers	(19TH Lancers, Pakistan)

Taungup, 1945 (Burma).

In the coastal belt of Southern Arakan, the Japanese were able to hold the two main passes across the Arakan Range of hills, the An Pass and Taungup Pass. The enemy had to be cleared, particularly from the Taungup Pass on the road to Prome. Taungup was captured by 29TH April 1945 and Arakan operations came to an end.

12TH Frontier Force Regiment (12TH Frontier Force Regiment, Pakistan)

Tongzang, 1945 (Burma).

This Battle Honour commemorates the re-conquest of Tongzang. In March 1945 the Japanese had started their advance into India from Tongzang, when they attacked a detachment defending the bridge over the Manipur River. The 5TH India Division re-took the position in the third week of September and crossed the raging river.

2ND Punjab Regiment (2ND Punjab Regiment, India)

Gangaw, 1945 (Burma).

On 22ND January, 3RD Commando Brigade landed on the beaches at Daingbon Chaung. Having secured the beaches, they moved inland and became involved in very heavy fighting with the Japanese. The following night a brigade of the 25TH Division was landed in support. The fighting around the beachhead involved hand-to-hand fighting, as the Japanese realised the danger of encirclement and threw all their available troops into the fight. The Commandos and Indian troops managed to turn the tide of the battle and take the village of Gangaw on 29TH January. Meanwhile the forces on the Myebon Peninsula linked up with the 82ND Division fighting its way overland towards Gangaw. Caught between the 82ND Division and the forces already in Kangaw, the Japanese were forced to scatter, leaving behind thousands of dead and most of their heavy equipment.

19TH Lancers (19TH Lancers, Pakistan)
2ND Punjab Regiment (2ND Punjab Regiment, India)

Kyaukmyaung Bridgehead, 1945 (Burma).

This Battle Honour commemorates the establishing of a bridgehead over the Irrawaddy by the 19TH Indian Division, and its defence against the Japanese counter-attacks.

1ST Patiala Infantry (15TH Battalion, Punjab Regiment, India)
7TH Light Cavalry (7TH Light Cavalry, India)
12TH Frontier Force Regiment (12TH Frontier Force Regiment, Pakistan)
15TH Punjab Regiment (15TH Punjab Regiment, Pakistan)

Chronology of Sikh Battle Honours (cont.)

Minmu Bridgehead, 1945 (Burma).

This Battle Honour commemorates the establishing of a bridgehead over the Irrawaddy by the 20TH Indian Division and its defence against the Japanese counter-attacks. The Japanese suffered heavy casualties in their counter attacks, which were repulsed.

Bombay Engineers	(Corps of Engineers, India)
PAVO Cavalry	(PAVO Cavalry, Pakistan)

Nyaungu Bridgehead, 1945 (Burma).

Following the victory at Kohima, the Sikhs and the Punjabis were in the vanguard of the forces driving the Japanese out of Burma. On February 14TH 1945, they were required, at short notice, to establish a bridgehead over the Irrawaddy at Nyaungu, after the original assault force had been repulsed from the landing beach. Immediately on arrival, the battalions mounted an attack which cleared the beaches and ensured the success of this, the longest opposed river crossing of the war, which was held against counter attacks.

1ST Patiala Infantry	(15TH Battalion, Punjab Regiment, India)
1ST Battalion, 11TH Sikh Regiment	(1ST Battalion, 11TH Sikh Regiment, India)
14TH Punjab Regiment	(14TH Punjab Regiment, Pakistan)
15TH Punjab Regiment	(15TH Punjab Regiment, Pakistan)
13TH Frontier Force Rifles	(13TH Frontier Force Rifles, Pakistan)
12TH Frontier Force Regiment	(12TH Frontier Force Regiment, Pakistan)

Taungtha, 1945 (Burma).

17TH Indian Division and 255TH Tank Brigade commenced an advance from the Nyaungu Bridgehead towards Meiktila, and after heavy fighting they captured Taungtha on 25TH February and swept on towards Meiktila.

1ST Patiala Infantry	(15TH Battalion, Punjab Regiment, India)
1ST Punjab Regiment	(1ST Punjab Regiment, Pakistan)
5TH Lancers	(5TH Lancers, Pakistan)
13TH Frontier Force Rifles	(13TH Frontier Force Rifles, Pakistan)
15TH Punjab Regiment	(15TH Punjab Regiment, Pakistan)

Sikh Scout in Burma 1943

Meiktila, 1945 (Burma).

The British recapture of Burma hinged on a successful crossing of the Irrawaddy and the subsequent destruction of the Japanese forces on the east bank of the river. Mandalay was the obvious target and was assigned to the XXXIII Corps on the 14th Army's northern flank. The IV Corps were on the left flank and their initial goal was to seize Meiktila, an important communications centre astride the Japanese lines of communication and a location for which they would be certain to fight. The 17TH Division, with attached Armour from the 255TH Indian Tank Brigade, was to cross the Irrawaddy River through a bridgehead established by the 7TH Indian Division and to capture Meiktila. The 99TH Brigade was left at Palel, to be flown in to Meiktila when captured. The two infantry brigades, together with their supporting tanks, drove down the Gangaw Valley behind the 7th Division and were concentrated at Pauk, 40 miles or so west of the Irrawaddy by February 12TH.

Bengal Engineers	(Corps of Engineers, India)
7TH Light Cavalry	(7TH Light Cavalry, India)
1ST Punjab Regiment	(1ST Punjab Regiment, Pakistan)
5TH Lancers	(5TH Lancers, Pakistan)
9TH Horse	(9TH Horse, India)
12TH Frontier Force Regiment	(12TH Frontier Force Regiment, Pakistan)
13TH Frontier Force Rifles	(13TH Frontier Force Rifles, Pakistan)

Capture of Meiktila, 1945 (Burma).

17TH Division launched a four-pronged attack on Meiktila on February 28TH 1945. A large part of the Japanese 168TH Regiment from the 49TH Division, and miscellaneous anti-aircraft and line of communication troops, defended it, in all about 4,000 strong. The 255TH Tank Brigade undertook a flanking movement to the north and east of Meiktila to attack from the east; the 4TH Brigade came in from the north and the 63RD Brigade came in from the west, largely on foot over difficult terrain. By the day's end the town was largely surrounded and it took three further days of close quarter fighting before the town was captured.

9TH Horse	(9TH Horse, India)
5TH Lancers	(5TH Lancers, Pakistan)
12TH Frontier Force Regiment	(5TH Lancers, Pakistan)
PAVO Cavalry	(PAVO Cavalry, Pakistan)
13TH Frontier Force Rifles	(13TH Frontier Force Rifles, Pakistan)

Chronology of Sikh Battle Honours (cont.)

Defence of Meiktila, 1945 (Burma).

As anticipated the Japanese reacted strongly and a large force was assembled to retake Meiktila. However the Japanese units were already in a weakened state and were to prove unable to co-ordinate their actions effectively. The British, taking advantage of their mobility and Armour, sent five columns out on sweeps on March 5TH, and a second series began on March 9TH with the 63RD Brigade heading towards Pyawbwe and the 48TH Brigade towards Mahlaing. A third series followed between March 13TH and 14TH which prevented concentration of Japanese forces.

The Sikh Light Infantry	(The Sikh Light Infantry, India)
9TH Horse	(9TH Horse, India)
Bombay Engineers	(Corps of Engineers, India)
5TH Lancers	(5TH Lancers, Pakistan)
12TH Frontier Force Regiment	(12TH Frontier Force Regiment, Pakistan)

Fort Dufferin, 1945 (Burma).

Fort Dufferin commemorates eleven days of hard fighting from 20TH March in which the Japanese garrison fought to the death to defend Mandalay against 19TH Indian Division.

12TH Frontier Force Regiment	(12TH Frontier Force Regiment, Pakistan)
15TH Punjab Regiment	(15TH Punjab Regiment, Pakistan)

Mandalay, 1945 (Burma).

This Battle Honour commemorates the capture of Mandalay by the 2ND British Division and 19TH Indian Division after severe hand-to-hand fighting. The battles of Mandalay and Meiktila had cost the Japanese around a third of their already weakened numbers, against some 10,000 British casualties. The Japanese 15TH Army retreated to the south, and central Burma was now in British hands. The Japanese retreat opened the road to Rangoon and with it, the reconquest of Burma.

1ST Patiala Infantry	(15TH Battalion, Punjab Regiment, India)
7TH Light Cavalry	(7TH Light Cavalry, India)
PAVO Cavalry	(PAVO Cavalry, Pakistan)
15TH Punjab Regiment	(15TH Punjab Regiment, Pakistan)
12TH Frontier Force Regiment	(12TH Frontier Force Regiment, Pakistan)

Chronology of Sikh Battle Honours (cont.)

Kyaukse, 1945 (Burma).

The 20TH Indian Division captured the big Japanese railway depot at Kyaukse. The British forces now held most of the important positions on the road between Mandalay and Meiktila. The Japanese forces in central Burma were brought to battle and defeated. They were not able to slip away largely intact as they intended and instead had been compelled to fight the main action with improvised forces, against the carefully organised British defence around Meiktila.

12TH Frontier Force Regiment	(12TH Frontier Force Regiment, Pakistan)
14TH Punjab Regiment	(14TH Punjab Regiment, Pakistan)

Letse, 1945 (Burma).

Throughout the month of April, the allies continued to engage the Japanese and this led to the capture of Letse and Seikpyu. On the morning of the 24TH of April, leading troops were pinned down with heavy fire from a ridge with a prominent Golden Pagoda and a monastery. The objective was captured, supported by heavy artillery concentration. Thirty-nine Japanese bodies were recovered.

14TH Punjab Regiment	(14TH Punjab Regiment, Pakistan)
2ND Field Regiment	(2ND Field Regiment, India)

Rangoon Road, 1945 (Burma).

This Battle Honour covers the final drive south to capture Rangoon in co-operation with the sea-borne landings over the period 1ST April to 6TH May 1945. The 5TH Indian Division formed the spearhead of the Fourteenth Army's advance.

The Sikh Light Infantry	(The Sikh Light Infantry, India)
7TH Light Cavalry	(7TH Light Cavalry, India)
9TH Horse	(9TH Horse, India)
5TH Lancers	(5TH Lancers, Pakistan)
PAVO Cavalry	(PAVO Cavalry, Pakistan)
19TH Lancers	(19TH Lancers, Pakistan)
1ST Punjab Regiment	(1ST Punjab Regiment, Pakistan)
14TH Punjab Regiment	(14TH Punjab Regiment, Pakistan)

Pyawbwe, 1945 (Burma).

The British began by striking at the delaying position held by the remnants of the Japanese Thirty-Third Army at Pyawbwe. The Indian 17TH Division and 255TH Armoured Brigade were initially halted by a strong defensive position behind a dry chaung, but a flanking move by tanks and mechanized infantry struck the Japanese from the rear and shattered them. From this point, the advance down the main road to Rangoon faced little organised opposition.

Pyawbwe, 1945 (Burma). (cont.)

The Sikh Light Infantry	(The Sikh Light Infantry, India)
9TH Horse	(9TH Horse, India)
5TH Lancers	(5TH Lancers, Pakistan)
PAVO Cavalry	(PAVO Cavalry, Pakistan)
12TH Frontier Force Regiment	(12TH Frontier Force Regiment, Pakistan)

Pyinmana, 1945 (Burma).

This Battle Honour commemorates the capture of a strongly held Japanese stronghold of Pyinmana. The town and the bridge were seized before the Japanese could organise their defence. Japanese Thirty-Third Army HQ was attacked here and although Lieutenant-General Honda and his staff escaped, they had little means of controlling the remnants of their formations.

5TH Lancers	(5TH Lancers, Pakistan)
15TH Punjab Regiment	(15TH Punjab Regiment, Pakistan)
2ND Punjab Regiment	(2ND Punjab Regiment, India)

Taungoo, 1945 (Burma).

The Japanese Fifteenth Army had reorganised in the Shan States and was reinforced by the Japanese 56TH Division. They were ordered to move to Toungoo to block the road to Rangoon, but a general uprising by Karen forces, who had been organised and equipped by Force 136, delayed them long enough for the Indian 5TH Infantry Division, now leading IV Corps, to reach the town first. The Indian 19TH Division followed up the lead units of IV Corps and drove the Japanese back from Toungoo after two weeks fighting.

5TH Lancers	(5TH Lancers, Pakistan)
12TH Frontier Force Regiment	(12TH Frontier Force Regiment, Pakistan)

Pegu, 1945 (Burma).

The Indian 17TH Division resumed the lead of the advance and met Japanese rearguards north of Pegu, 40 miles north of Rangoon, on 25TH April. General Kimura had formed the various lines of communication troops, naval personnel and even Japanese civilians in Rangoon into the Japanese 105TH Independent Mixed Brigade. This scratch formation used buried aircraft bombs, anti-aircraft guns and suicide attacks with pole charges to delay the British advance until 30TH April, when the Japanese withdrew into the hills west of Pegu.

5TH Lancers	(5TH Lancers, Pakistan)
12TH Frontier Force Regiment	(12TH Frontier Force Regiment, Pakistan)

Chronology of Sikh Battle Honours (cont.)

Shandatgyi, 1945 (Burma).

This Battle Honour commemorates the destruction of the Japanese forces at Shandatgyi. The 7TH Indian Division destroyed a Japanese rearguard at Shandatgyi in the second week of May 1945. "The forward platoon having now rejoined from Shandatgyi, the company put in a full-scale attack under cover of the Battalion mortars, which arrived just in time to get into action. The company set fire to the village with smoke grenades, but in spite of this the enemy resisted stubbornly and they were driven out only after some fierce and bitter fighting. Subadar Bachan Singh again displayed great gallantry in this attack and personally led the leading troops forward in the assault. It was largely due to his initiative and example that the Sikhs managed to rout the enemy in their strong position. Some thirty-three bodies and a mass of equipment were recovered at the end of the day".

1ST Battalion, 11TH Sikh Regiment	(1ST Battalion, 11TH Sikh Regiment, India)

The Irrawaddy, 1945 (Burma).

This Battle Honour commemorates the destruction of the remnants of the Japanese 28TH Army. Japanese forces in Burma were split into three groups: one division from the 28TH Army still remained west of the Irrawaddy; the rest of the 28TH Army was in the hills between the Irrawaddy and Sittang Rivers and a third group, composed of remnants of the 15TH and 33RD Armies, was generally east of the Sittang River. The remaining months of the war saw repeated and violent attacks by the Japanese in the two pockets west of the Sittang, to open an escape route to the east. By 18TH June, the Japanese pockets had shrunk and by August, the Japanese 28TH Army had ceased to exist. During the fifteen-month period of the Japanese Imphal campaign and the Allied counter offensive, 97,000 enemy dead had been counted.

1ST Battalion, 11TH Sikh Regiment	(1ST Battalion, 11TH Sikh Regiment, India)
PAVO Cavalry	(PAVO Cavalry, Pakistan)
15TH Punjab Regiment	(15TH Punjab Regiment, Pakistan)
13TH Frontier Force Rifles	(13TH Frontier Force Rifles, Pakistan)
12TH Frontier Force Regiment	(12TH Frontier Force Regiment, Pakistan)

Kama, 1945 (Burma).

This Battle Honour commemorates the severe fighting at Kama. The Japanese forces still remaining on the Irrawaddy route put up strong resistance at Kama and suffered heavy casualties.

8TH Punjab Regiment	(8TH Punjab Regiment, Pakistan)
1ST Battalion, 11TH Sikh Regiment	(1ST Battalion, 11TH Sikh Regiment, India)

Chronology of Sikh Battle Honours (cont.)

Arakan Beaches, 1945 (Burma).

Arakan Beaches covers the final stages of the Arakan campaign over the period 12TH January to 29TH April 1945. The operations were mainly along the coast, but those based on Kaladan Valley were also included.

1ST Punjab Regiment	(1ST Punjab Regiment, Pakistan)
12TH Frontier Force Regiment	(12TH Frontier Force Regiment, Pakistan)
13TH Frontier Force Rifles	(13TH Frontier Force Rifles, Pakistan)
16TH Punjab Regiment	(16TH Punjab Regiment, Pakistan)

Sittang, 1945 (Burma).

This Battle Honour covers the successful operations over the period 10TH May to 15TH August 1945. The final campaign for clearing Japanese invaders from Burma was well under way, with a desperate enemy grudgingly giving ground before a more powerful Allied force, composed of units the majority of which were Indian veterans. Their Japanese opponent, still a formidable challenge, was a ruthless and bold soldier who obediently fought and marched until he died or killed himself. The British prevented the Japanese Army from breaking out of Pegu Yomas intact and crossing the River Sittang, and defeated the Japanese 33RD Army, which was trying to attack westwards across the river to assist it. These operations mainly involved 5TH and 17TH Indian Divisions. Japan surrendered on 16TH August 1945. Burma had been re-occupied but it was not long before it became an Independent Republic.

The Sikh Light Infantry	(The Sikh Light Infantry, India)
11TH Sikh Regiment	(11TH Sikh Regiment, India)
8TH Cavalry	(8TH Cavalry, India)
16TH Cavalry	(16TH Cavalry, Pakistan)
14TH Punjab Regiment	(14TH Punjab Regiment, Pakistan)

A Sikh Patrol in Burma 1945

Chronology of Sikh Battle Honours (cont.)

INDIA 1947-1971

After partition in 1947 the Indian units contained Sikhs and other classes.

Jammu and Kashmir, 1947-1948 (India). (Campaign Honour)

This Campaign Honour was awarded to all the regiments that had served in Jammu and Kashmir during 1947-1948. In August 1947, the Indian subcontinent was partitioned into the Dominions of India and Pakistan. While most of the Princely States had joined one or the other of the Dominions, the Maharajah of Jammu and Kashmir remained undecided and entered into a Standstill Agreement with both India and Pakistan. In October 1947 Pakistan decided to force the Maharajah to accede to union with Pakistan. The Pakistani Major General Akbar Khan was entrusted with the task of invading the Kashmir Valley. With well-armed men from the North West Frontier Province, machine-guns, mortars, and backed by regular army units, he descended on the Valley. The Maharajah, after making a desperate appeal and signing an Instrument of Accession with India, fled the Valley. The Government of India took steps to defend the Valley and rushed troops to Srinagar and Jammu. The Indian Army, with a fistful of soldiers, defended and liberated one strategic point after another until the Pakistanis were expelled. The war lasted 14 months and ended on 1ST January 1949 when the UN sponsored ceasefire came into effect.

1ST Battalion, The Sikh Regiment
5TH Battalion, The Sikh Regiment
15TH Battalion (Patiala), Punjab Regiment
7TH Cavalry
Central India Horse
1ST Battalion, Parachute Regiment
2ND Battalion, Parachute Regiment
3RD Battalion, Parachute Regiment
1^{ST,} Battalion, Brigade of Guards
2ND Battalion, Brigade of Guards
4TH Battalion, Brigade of Guards

Srinagar, 1947 (Kashmir).

As the Pakistani raiders at Baramula indulged themselves in looting, pillaging, burning and raping, the Indian Army rushed the 1ST Battalion, The Sikh Regiment to nearby Srinagar by air. This very strong battalion of nearly 1,200 men had been especially reinforced by attaching two independent Rifle Companies. One was a Sikh Company from a battalion of the 12TH Frontier Force Regiment (that Regiment having been allotted to Pakistan), and the other was a Rifle Company formed from the Sikh personnel of the Mountain Artillery. The orders to the Sikhs were to deny the airfield and the civil aviation radio at Srinagar to the Pakistani raiders. On arrival at the airfield, the Commanding Officer deployed troops at strategic points to safeguard the airfield, and they were soon in contact with the raiders. The raiders opened mortar and Medium Machine Gun fire on the Company positions, and, seeing that they might be cut off, it was decided to withdraw to Sangram. Lt. Col. Ranjit Rai was among the last to withdraw and during the process he was hit and killed. Command of the battalion then fell on Major Harwant Singh MC, who deployed it around Pattan. Here the battalion checked the raiders progress towards Srinagar and held them off for three days, thus enabling troops to be inducted into the theatre through the Srinagar airfield.

Indian Air Force
1ST Battalion, The Sikh Regiment
3RD Battalion, Parachute Regiment
Patiala Mountain Battery
7TH Cavalry

Naushera, 1947 (India).

This Battle Honour commemorates the capture and occupation of Naushera, thus securing the route which led into the Kashmir Valley. The enemy was holding the bridge on the River Bains, supported by mortars and machine guns. This opposition was cleared on November 26TH and 27TH. It was decided to abandon Kotliand and take defences in the Jhangar-Naushera area. Jhangar, which was an important communication centre and considered a gateway to Naushera, was Pakistan's prime target. There were several thrusts and counter thrusts and the Jhangar defences changed hands twice. Eventually the Indian troops holding Jhangar had to fall back on Naushera on December 24, 1947. The enemy followed closely and occupied some important heights around Naushera. The final battle of Naushera was fought in February 1948, when the enemy attacked in great strength, but was repulsed with heavy loss.

7TH Cavalry
1ST Battalion, Brigade of Guards
2ND Battalion, Brigade of Guards
2ND Battalion, Parachute Regiment

Chronology of Sikh Battle Honours (cont.)

Jhangar, 1948 (Kashmir).

This Battle Honour commemorates the recapture of Jhangar on 13TH March 1948. The capture of Jhangar was of special significance for 50TH Parachute Brigade to avenge the setback they had suffered in December 1947. The operation commenced in the last week of February 1948. 19TH Infantry Brigade advanced along the Northern ridge, while 50TH Para brigade cleared the hills dominating the Naushera-Jhangar road in the south. Many fierce battles were fought during this twin thrust toward Jhangar in which the enemy fled in panic, leaving behind much equipment including vehicles, arms, ammunition and stores. They were eventually driven from this area and Jhangar recaptured. Pakistan brought its regular forces into the fray in May 1948. Jhangar was once again subjected to heavy artillery bombardment and determined Infantry attacks. Brigadier Usman, the hero of Naushera and Jhangar, however, frustrated all enemy attempts to recapture Jhangar.

In this theatre the Patialas earned a number of Honours and awards. Sepoy Hari Singh was awarded the Maha Vir Chakra. One officer and two NCOs also earned VrCs, namely, Major Joginder Singh, Naik Mehar Singh and Lance Naik Naurang Singh, the latter posthumously.

7TH Cavalry
2ND Battalion, Parachute Regiment
15TH Battalion (Patiala), Punjab Regiment

Rajauri, 1948 (Kashmir).

This Battle Honour commemorates the capture of Rajauri by the 19TH Brigade on 12TH April. The tanks performed an outstanding feat of arms by advancing along the riverbed. They first engaged the enemy in the town and the fort and then fired at enemy defences on the surrounding hills. Indian soldiers earned seven major gallantry awards for their actions in taking Rajauri.

Bombay Engineers
Central India Horse

Tithwal, 1948 (Kashmir).

This Battle Honour covers the capture of Tithwal in January 1948. The 1ST Battalion, The Sikh Regiment took Chowkibal and charged on through Chamkot and captured Tithwal. The enemy fled in all directions abandoning everything. The attack had ejected the enemy from its main supply base and recovered 15,000 square kilometres of the state territory.

This area was the scene of fighting again from July to October during which Lance Naik Karam Singh of 1ST Battalion, The Sikh Regiment earned the highest gallantry award the Param Vir Chakra.

Tithwal, 1948 (Kashmir). (cont.)

"The enemy made numerous attempts to recapture Richmar Gali, and thence Tithwal. On 13TH October 1948, coinciding with Id, the enemy decided to launch a brigade attack to retake Richmar Gali, and bypassing Tithwal, advance into the Srinagar Valley. Lance Naik Karam Singh was commanding a section at Richmar Gali. The enemy commenced its attack with heavy shelling of guns and mortars. The fire was so accurate that not a single bunker in the platoon locality was left unscathed. Communication trenches caved in. Bravely, Lance Naik Karam Singh went from bunker to bunker, giving succor to the wounded and urging the men to fight. The enemy launched eight separate attacks that day. In one such attack, the enemy managed to obtain a foothold in the platoon locality. Immediately, Lance Naik Karam Singh, who was severely wounded by then, with a few men, hurled himself in a counter-attack and evicted the enemy after a close quarter encounter which accounted for many enemy dead, having been dispatched by the bayonet. Lance Naik Karam Singh proved himself to be a dauntless leader of men in crisis. Nothing could subdue him and no amount of fire or hardship could break his spirit."

1ST Battalion, The Sikh Regiment
1ST Madras Regiment

Uri, 1948 (Kashmir).

Uri commemorates fighting in the Uri sector between 19TH May and 19TH June 1948. The Sikhs retook Baramula on November 8TH. The battalion then moved towards Uri and retook it from the raiders. A piquet, known as Nalwa piquet, was established across the Jhelum River overlooking Uri. The Pakistanis made a number of attempts to capture this piquet but were foiled. In the defence of one of the attempts, Naik Nand Singh earned a posthumous MVC. On December 12TH, a strong patrol was sent out of Uri and on the way back a large Pakistani force near the village of Bhatgiran ambushed it. There was a fierce fight in which the Sikhs suffered heavy casualties (62 killed and 60 wounded). Among the casualties were officers and several senior JCO's and NCO's. Among the dead was Jemadar Nand Singh, who had earlier won a Victoria Cross in Burma. On later interrogations of Pakistani prisoners it was found that the enemy suffered more than 500 casualties in this encounter. The Sikhs won two posthumous Maha Vir Chakras (Sub. Bishan Singh OBI, MC and Jemadar Nand Singh VC) and two Vir Chakras (Sub. Gurcharan Singh MC & Bar and Jemadar Mal Singh MC) during this battle. Thus the threat to Kashmir Valley was averted.

1ST Battalion, The Sikh Regiment
One Mountain Battery
One Troop Field Artillery

Chronology of Sikh Battle Honours (cont.)

Shalateng, 1948 (Kashmir).

This Battle Honour commemorates the battle of Shalateng. A massive Pakistani raiding force was attacked and dispersed, leaving 618 dead on the battlefield. The Pakistanis abandoned 138 lorries and buses, large quantities of arms including medium machine-guns, ammunition, rations and baggage.

1ST Battalion, The Sikh Regiment
15TH Battalion (Patiala), Punjab Regiment

Punch, 1948 (Kashmir).

This Battle Honour commemorates the relief of the garrison at Punch, which had been besieged by Pakistani soldiers disguised as tribal raiders.
A Column under Brigadier Pritam Singh went forward from Punch to meet the link -up column for the relief of the garrison at Punch, but they were delayed by a stiff encounter with the enemy at Potha, a dominating position enroute. By now Mendhar, another enemy stronghold, had been breached and the way to Punch was cleared. On arrival of the relief columns there was great jubilation in Punch, but as Rajouri and some other key areas were still in enemy hands, the siege of Punch was still not over. It was decided to use 19TH Infantry Brigade to clear the axis for good. This was achieved in September 1948. This operation resulted in the capture of nearly 5,000 square kms of territory in Rajouri, Mendhar and Punch areas, and three brigades of the enemy deployed were driven out, with heavy casualties. The long siege of Punch was at last broken. The defence of Punch against great odds was another outstanding example of the heroic effort of the troops and their patriotic fervour in most unfavourable circumstances.

1ST Battalion, Parachute Regiment
3RD Battalion, Parachute Regiment
4TH Mountain Battery

Gurais, 1948 (Kashmir).

The Gurais village due north of Srinagar was a position of great potential both for defensive and offensive operations. Gurais and Kargil had fallen to the enemy in May. The Indian troops entered Gurais on 29TH June and the raiders were pursued across the river. With the capture of Gurais, Kashmir Valley had been secured and the enemy attempts to take it were repulsed.

2ND Battalion, Brigade of Guards

Chronology of Sikh Battle Honours (cont.)

Zoji La, 1948 (India).

This Battle Honour commemorates the capture of the Zoji La Pass. The Zoji La Pass is about three kilometres long and is flanked by massive features and was covered with deep snow. About 500 Pakistani soldiers, supported by mortars and medium machine-guns, held the area. The importance of Zoji La lay in the fact that it commanded entry to Leh. The Indus Valley provided a direct all-weather approach to Leh and Kargil from Giligit and Skardu. Once Zoji La closed in winter, there was no direct route available to Srinagar and Leh. After December 1947, when the Pakistanis had occupied Skardu, Zoji La, Dras and Kargil in strength, the Indus Valley route to Leh was clear and the capture of Leh would only be a matter of time. Between Kargil and Leh only two state Forces platoons - guarding the bridge at Khaltse - stood in the way of the enemy. The Indian Commander, General Thimayya, decided to clear Zoji La, Dras and Kargil. 77TH (Para) Brigade was given the task of capturing Zoji La in September 1948. This brigade included 1ST Patiala, which was located at Baltal after clearing the Sonamarg valley, and was put under the command of the Brigade for this mission. So strong was the enemy position that the battalion attacking Zoji La frontally could make no headway, despite adequate artillery support and strafing of enemy positions by Tempest aircraft. It was decided to use light Armour to dislodge the enemy from Zoji La, and then make a dash for Drass and Kargil. Full credit must be given to the CO of 7TH Cavalry, Lt. Col. (Later Major General) Rajinder Singh 'Sparrow', who did not hesitate for a moment to accept this seemingly impossible mission. During the assault, determined infantry soldiers with bared bayonets closely followed tanks. Troops fought without winter clothing and equipment at temperatures 20 degrees below freezing point and tanks operated for the first time ever at a height of 3,529 meters. 15TH Battalion (Patiala) Punjab Regiment had to capture the high ground, which they achieved after a bayonet charge and hand-to-hand fighting lasting about six hours, driving out the quilted enemy that were not already bayoneted. In this theatre the following Patialas were awarded gallantry awards. Mahavir Chakra awardees were: Jemadar Sampuran Singh, Jemadar Hardev Singh (posthumously), and Sepoy Amar Singh. Among the Vir Chakra awardees were: Subedar Sant Singh (posthumously), Naib Subedar Balwant Singh, Havildar Mukand Singh, Lance Naik Sajjan Singh and Lance Naik Chand Singh (both posthumously) Sepoys Gajjan Singh, Hazura Singh, Zaila Singh, Teja Singh and Bachan Singh (all posthumously).

Lt Col (Later Major General) Rajinder Singh 'Sparrow' was awarded the Mahavir Chakra for his gallantry, determination and leadership in this theatre. (He was later awarded a Bar to his MVC in 1965.)

A UN cease-fire was arranged on the 31 December 1948, and came into effect on January 5TH, 1949.

7TH Cavalry
15TH Battalion (Patiala), Punjab Regiment

Chronology of Sikh Battle Honours (cont.)

Indo-Pak War, 1965. (Campaign Honour)

The Indo-Pakistani War of 1965 was a culmination of skirmishes that took place between April 1965 and September 1965. This conflict became known as the Second Kashmir War, fought over the disputed region of Kashmir, the first having been fought in 1947. The war began following Pakistan's Operation Gibraltar, which was designed to infiltrate forces into Jammu and Kashmir to precipitate an insurgency against rule by India. The five-week war caused thousands of casualties on both sides. It ended in a United Nations (UN) mandated ceasefire and the subsequent issuance of the Tashkent Declaration. Much of the war was fought by the countries' land forces in Kashmir and along the International Border between India and Pakistan. This war saw the largest amassing of troops in Kashmir since the Partition of India in 1947, a number that was overshadowed only during the 2001-2002 military standoff between India and Pakistan. Most of the battles were fought by opposing infantry and armored units, with substantial backing from air forces.

Jammu and Kashmir, 1965 (India). (Campaign Honour)

This Campaign Honour was awarded to all the regiments that had served in Jammu and Kashmir during 1965. The conflict was initiated by Pakistan with a large-scale infiltration in August 1965, and escalated by a massive attack in the Chhamb sector on 1ST September. Indian authorities took prompt action to find and round up the intruders. They sent out patrols and armoured cars to clear the valley and a large number of the enemy were killed or captured. They engaged the Pakistani regular troops and went on to occupy the areas across the cease-fire line, which had been used for infiltration. The Campaign Honour 'Jammu and Kashmir 1965' was awarded for the period 5TH August to 3RD November 1965.

2ND Battalion, The Sikh Regiment
7TH Battalion, The Sikh Regiment
5TH Battalion, The Sikh Light Infantry
6TH Battalion, The Sikh Light Infantry
9TH Battalion, Punjab Regiment
19TH Battalion, Punjab Regiment
18TH Cavalry
20TH Lancers
Bengal Engineers
Bombay Engineers
1ST Battalion, Parachute Regiment

Lieutenant General Harbaksh Singh, Padma Bhushan, VrC, was the GOC-in-C Western Army Command during the 1965 Indo-Pak War. Much of the success of the ground war was attributed to his brilliant military tactics.

Chronology of Sikh Battle Honours (cont.)

Haji Pir, 1965 (India).

This Battle Honour covers the destruction of the Pakistani guerrillas. The Haji Pir Bulge was the main infiltration route for the guerrillas into Srinagar Valley. Offensive operations were mounted to seal off the infiltration routes and destroy the guerrillas' administrative bases. To secure the Haji Pir Bulge, it was necessary to capture the Haji Pir Pass dominating the area. The 1ST Para, after scaling 1,220 meters of steep, slippery hillside at night, secured the pass. The enemy, being surprised, fled in panic. "Major Ranjit Singh Dayal led his men to a glorious victory in a battle which was a race against time. He and his men pushed forward towards the Haji Pir Pass, unmindful of a relentless shelling by the enemy". The 19TH Punjab went in and captured Bedori, no doubt helped by the capture of the Pass. Strong enemy counter attacks were repulsed and Sank, Ledi Wali, Bedori Kahuta and Gitian were captured.

1ST Battalion, Parachute Regiment
19TH Battalion, Punjab Regiment

Raja Chand Tekri, 1965 (India).

This Battle Honour covers the severe fighting at Raja Chand Tekri. The enemy had established two strongly held piquets at Raja Chand Tekri and used them as a base for many operations. Sikhs who were active in the Chhamb area in August were asked to capture Rani feature on the Uri-Hajipir axis in early September. In the initial plans 2ND Battalion, The Sikh Regiment was to capture Rani after 3RD Dogra had captured the Raja feature. The 3RD Dogra attack on Raja failed miserably and Commanding Office of 2ND Battalion, The Sikh Regiment, volunteered to capture Raja. The Raja feature was at a height of 7,700 feet and strongly defended. The enemy had fortified bunkers and had laid a deep minefield and wire obstacles around the feature. On the night of September 5TH /6TH the 2ND Sikhs moved in to attack. When they reached the forward location they came under heavy machinegun fire. A company-strength attack was launched, but it came under heavy fire. Naib Sub. Darshan Singh valiantly led one platoon up the hill, despite heavy machinegun fire, till he fell down wounded. The Company commander then moved up to lead but he too was seriously wounded. The attack seemed to stall and as daylight was fast approaching something had to be done, so waves of Sikh soldiers leapt over wire obstacles and swarmed over the enemy position. A group of them even charged through a minefield. This time the Sikhs fought their way to the top of the feature and captured it after hand-to-hand fighting lasting two hours. The enemy fought to the last man. The battalion suffered 162 casualties (42 killed) and received one Vir Chakra (Naik Chand Singh). It also received the battle honour 'Raja Picquet' in this action.

2ND Battalion, The Sikh Regiment

Chronology of Sikh Battle Honours (cont.)

Kalidhar, 1965 (India).

This Battle Honour covers the military actions in the Kalidhar area. After the Indian offensive towards Lahore and Sialkot, the enemy continued to exert pressure in Kalidhar area by large infiltrations. The infiltrators were checked and the raiders hunted down.

"On October 1965, a company of Sikh Light Infantry Regiment, in which Sepoy Dharam Singh was serving, was ordered to clear an encroachment on a feature near Kalidhar in Jammu and Kashmir, which had been made by Pakistani forces notwithstanding the cease–fire. When its advance was held up due to a minefield, which was covered by enemy medium machine gun fire and shelling, Sepoy Dharam Singh volunteered and crossed the minefield to give a lead to the others. His gallant act inspired them in achieving the objective in time. Subsequently, during the counter–attack launched by the enemy, he killed two enemy soldiers who closed in on him. In this action Sepoy Dharam Singh displayed commendable courage and devotion to duty."

6TH Battalion, Sikh Light Infantry
9TH Battalion, Punjab Regiment

Op Hill, 1965 (India).

This Battle Honour covers the severe fighting at Op Hill. The enemy occupying Op Hill continued shelling the base at Balnoi well after the cease-fire. It took two days of severe fighting to evict the enemy. Sikhs were part of a three-battalion attack to clear the Pakistanis from OP Hill feature. In the first phase 2ND Battalion, Dogra Regiment cleared a number of heights but the going was slow as all the heights were held in strength and the Dogras suffered heavily. The enemy still held portions of OP Hill and as daylight was approaching, time was becoming critical. 7TH Battalion, The Sikh Regiment was ordered to rush up a feature called Jungle Hill. There was fierce fighting but in the end the enemy was ejected. The leading company of 7TH Battalion suffered 80 casualties (21 killed). Capt. Sansar Singh of the 7TH Battalion, The Sikh Regiment was awarded the Vir Chakra for this operation.

5TH Battalion, The Sikh Light Infantry
7TH Battalion, The Sikh Regiment
23RD Mountain Regiment
169TH Mountain Regiment

Chronology of Sikh Battle Honours (cont.)

Punjab, 1965. (Campaign Honour)

This Campaign Honour was awarded to all the regiments that had served in the Punjab during 1965. The conflict was initiated by Pakistan with a large-scale infiltration in August 1965, and escalated by a massive attack in the Chhamb sector in Jammu and Kashmir. In order to relieve pressure in the Chhamb sector, India's 4TH Army Division crossed the international border from the Indian Punjab into Pakistan, aimed at threatening Lahore. The tank battles of 1965, in the annals of military history, are the most intense ever since World War Two. Close to a thousand tanks, on both sides, took part in the pitched battles and offensives. India had its largest haul of Pakistani tanks when the offensive of Pakistan's 1ST Armoured Division was blunted at the Battle of Assal Uttar on September 10TH. The battle was so fierce and intense that at the end of the war, the 4TH Indian Division (aka "The Fighting Fourth") had accounted for about 97 tanks, either destroyed or captured in a damaged or intact condition. Indian losses in the Khem Karan sector were 32 tanks. Around 15 of them were captured by the Pakistan Army, mostly Sherman tanks. India had its 1ST Armoured Division on the offensive in this area. Equipped with four armoured regiments, this division faced stiff opposition from the Pakistani 6TH Armoured Division. Some of the fiercest tank battles were fought at Phillora and then at Chawinda. At the end of the fighting, India had claimed more than 170 tanks, of which 42 were captured in the 1ST Corps area. India's own losses in the area were 29 tanks destroyed and another 41 damaged. This is substantiated by the Pakistani Official History of the 6TH Armoured Division "*Men of Steel*".

A galaxy of Sikh generals took part in this war: Lieutenant General Harbaksh Singh, Lieutenant General Joginder Singh Dhillon, Major General Rajinder Singh, Major General Gurbaksh Singh, Major General Amrik Singh and Major General Mohinder Singh. When the cease-fire came into effect on 23RD September, neither side could claim achievement of their strategic aims. Both sides suffered heavy loss of life and equipment, particularly tanks - Pakistan more than India.

2ND Lancers
3RD Cavalry
4TH Horse
8TH Cavalry
18TH Cavalry
Poona Horse
Deccan Horse
Scinde Horse
1ST Battalion, The Sikh Light Infantry
4TH Battalion, The Sikh Regiment
5TH Battalion, Brigade of Guards
7TH Battalion, Punjab Regiment
13TH Battalion, Punjab Regiment
16TH Battalion, Punjab Regiment
Central India Horse
Bengal Engineers

Chronology of Sikh Battle Honours (cont.)

Burki, 1965 (India).

This Battle Honour commemorates the capture of this heavily defended fortress. On 10TH September, the Sikhs were given the task of capturing Burki, which is located on the east bank of Ichhogil Canal. The enemy positions around this village were very formidable, containing a chain of over a dozen concrete pillboxes. The walls of these pillboxes were about 4 feet thick and each of them had a Browing machine-gun, a light machine gun, a rocket launcher and a few riflemen. Behind the village was the height of the bank of the Ichhogio Canal on which the enemy had sited its Bren machine-guns to cover the front of the village and thicken the fire from the pillboxes. The Sikhs formed up about 1,000 yards away from the outskirts of Burki and launched an attack, supported by artillery. At half way they came under heavy enemy small arms fire, near the outposts of the Burki village. The opposition was eliminated and the enemy ran back to their main defences at Burki. The Sikhs, shouting their war cry of "Sat Siri Akal" pressed forward against the enemy, despite heavy shelling and well co-ordinated fire from the pillboxes. The pillboxes were eliminated one by one and the valiant Sikhs displayed many acts of outstanding courage and bravery. The enemy fired more than 2,000 shells in 30 minutes, and then fled from their formidable positions, leaving behind their equipment and their dead.

4TH Battalion, The Sikh Regiment
5TH Battalion, Brigade of Guards
16TH Battalion, Punjab Regiment

Dograi, 1965 (India).

This Battle Honour commemorates the capture Dograi. In the first phase the 13TH Battalion, Punjab Regiment, supported by tanks, only partially captured Pakistani defences east of Dograi. In the second phase the troops swept through the village, captured several tanks and killed about 200 enemy soldiers. The tanks advanced to the objective and destroyed several bunkers and enabled the 13TH Punjab to close in on Dograi. The defenders at Dograi put up strong resistance. After severe hand-to-hand fighting for each pillbox, the village was captured a day before the cease-fire, and a fierce counter-attack launched by Pakistani tanks and infantry was repulsed. Both sides suffered heavy casualties. The enemy left 300 dead and 100 were taken prisoner. The Indian casualties were 200 dead and wounded.

7TH Battalion, Punjab Regiment
13TH Battalion, Punjab Regiment
Scinde Horse

Chronology of Sikh Battle Honours (cont.)

Asal Uttar, 1965 (India).

The Battle of Asal Uttar was the largest tank combat in the period between World War Two and the Arab-Israeli Six Day War. On September 10TH, 1965, three Indian armoured regiments with 45 old American M4 Sherman tanks, 45 light French built AMX-13 tanks and 45 British-built Centurion tanks were deployed outside the village of Asal Uttar in the western Punjab province of India. These tanks had set up defensive positions in a "U" formation and were superbly camouflaged by tall un-harvested sugarcane stalks. The Indian force was assembled to attempt to stop the invading Pakistani armoured drive. The Pakistani force contained no less than 300 of the new American M47 Patton tanks along with a few M24 Chaffee Tanks. The 46-ton Patton was considered one of the best and most modern designs of the time and included a 90mm main gun that outranged the Indian tanks. The Indian tanks were largely outgunned, as well as grossly outnumbered by a factor of no less than 2:1. Advancing into an Indian artillery barrage, the Pakistani Armour fell into the Indian trap. Much like the Americans at the Battle of Bunker Hill, the Indian gunners held fast until they could "see the whites of their enemy's eyes". Opening fire from their camouflaged hiding places, at ranges of as short as five hundred meters, the smaller Indian tanks were able to penetrate the Pakistani Pattons from all angles and shortly set dozens on fire. The Pakistanis left the field in disarray, leaving almost a hundred tanks behind. The Indians lost 32 tanks but gained a powerful victory, offsetting their defeat the day before at Taroah. This led to stalemate and a ceasefire that ended the 1965 Indo-Pakistan War on September 22ND.

Deccan Horse
3RD Cavalry
91ST Mountain Regiment
40TH Medium Regiment

Phillora, 1965 (India).

The Indian 1ST Armoured Brigade was hurled against Phillora. A Pakistani counterattack at Phillora was repulsed with heavy damage and the Pakistanis settled in defensive positions. However, the Pakistani situation improved as reinforcements arrived. For the next several days, Pakistani forces repulsed Indian attacks on Chawinda. A large Indian assault on 18TH September involving India's 1ST Armoured and 6TH Mountain Divisions was repelled, with the 1ST Armoured Division being mauled and being taken out of action, while the 6TH Indian mountain division lay disintegrated in front of the Pakistani defences. The Indians withdrew back to a defensive position near their original bridgehead. The Pakistanis followed up by launching Operation Windup, which forced the Indians back across the international border for the most part, though the coming of the ceasefire meant that the Indians still managed to retain some territory.

4TH Horse
Poona Horse

East Pakistan, 1971. (Campaign Honour)

This Campaign Honour was awarded to all the regiments that had served in East Pakistan during 1971. The operations from 3RD to 20TH December gave India her first decisive and conclusive victory over Pakistan since 1947. The enemy had been outmanoeuvred and out generaled by Lt. Gen. Jagjit Singh Aurora. The conflict ended in the birth of Bangla Desh.

4TH Battalion, The Sikh Regiment
2ND Battalion, The Sikh Light Infantry
4TH Battalion, The Sikh Light Infantry
Bengal Engineers
Bombay Engineers
4TH Battalion, Brigade of Guards
5TH Battalion, Brigade of Guards
8TH Battalion, Brigade of Guards
7TH Battalion, Punjab Regiment
7TH Cavalry
45TH Cavalry
63RD Cavalry
69TH Cavalry
2ND Battalion, Parachute Regiment

Darsana, 1971 (East Pakistan).

This Battle Honour commemorates the capture of Darsana, an important railway communication centre, after a hard fought action.

45TH Cavalry

Siramani, 1971 (East Pakistan).

This Battle Honour commemorates the attack of 4TH Battalion, The Sikh Regiment, in the Eastern sector on the Jessore front. The battalion cleared the village of Burinda, which then opened the road to Jessore. The battalion then continued the advance to Khulna and on December 16TH attacked Shyamganj and established a roadblock south of Siramani, and went on to capture the village. Next day the enemy Brigade Commander together, with his troops, surrendered. Naik Mohinder Singh won a posthumous Vir Chakra.

4TH Battalion, The Sikh Regiment

Bogra, 1971 (East Pakistan).

This Battle Honour commemorates the capture of Bogra, an important military communication centre, against stiff Pakistani resistance. Bogra was surrounded on all sides by superior numbers of Indian Army and Mukti Bahini forces. Pakistani Brig. Malik's resistance continued even after the Pakistani Eastern Command surrendered in Dacca on 16TH December. The battle involved great personal valour on both sides, highlighted by the fact that soldiers on either side won their nation's highest military Honours.

63RD Cavalry
69TH Armoured Regiment

Chronology of Sikh Battle Honours (cont

Hilli, 1971 (East Pakistan).

The main objective of the Indian Army was to control Bogra, thereby cutting off Pakistani forces in the north from the rest of East Pakistan. The best way of getting to Bogra was through Hilli. The frontal assault on the Pakistan fortifications took a huge toll on both sides, the Indian Army suffering the greater number of casualties. The Indian forces finally broke through, forcing the Pakistani 4TH Frontier Force Battalion to withdraw for the defence of Bogra. The Indian side consisted of the 20TH Indian Mountain Division, led by Major General Lachhman Singh. On the Pakistan side there was the 205TH Brigade of the Pakistan Army, led by Brigadier Tajammul Hussain Malik. He put up a stiff resistance that earned praise from many quarters. He had placed defences along the railway line and at the Railway Station. The defensive positions were sited in depth to cover all routes leading into East Pakistan. They fought the entire Indian division and the Mukti Bahini soldiers, untill the Indians decided to bypass Hilli. Brigadier Malik then withdrew the forces in Hilli to avoid being cut off.

8TH Battalion, Brigade of Guards

Sylhet, 1971 (East Pakistan).

This Battle Honour commemorates the Indian Army's capture of the fortress at Sylhet, on 16TH December. The surrender of the entire Sylhet Garrison, included 3 Brigadiers, 1 Colonel, 107 officers, 219 JCO's and 6,190 Pakistani soldiers and 39 non-combatants.

During the battle at Sylhet between 7TH and 16TH December, the Indians had 1 officer, 2 JCO's and 11 other ranks killed, and 3 officers and 36 other ranks wounded.

9TH Battalion, Brigade of Guards
99TH Field Regiment
Bombay Engineers

Lieutenant General Jagjit Singh Arora, the liberator of Bangla Desh.
1971 Indo – Pak war.

Akhaura, 1971 (East Pakistan).

This Battle Honour commemorates the capture of Akhaura, an important rail junction. On the very first day of this 14-day war, 4TH Battalion, Brigade of Guards was ordered to capture a Pakistani position at Gangasagar, near Akhaura, on the border between the Indian state of Tripura and present-day Bangladesh. It was a well-fortified position, held in good strength by the enemy. The capture of this position was necessary, as it was the key to the capture of Akhaura. The 4TH Guards launched an attack on enemy positions at 0400 hours on 4TH December 1971. The Indian troops came under intense shelling and heavy small-arms fire, but they pushed on regardless and were soon engaged in hand-to-hand combat. The Guards cut a swath through the enemy lines, clearing bunker after bunker for a distance of 1.5 km. As a result of the fall of Gangasagar, the southern and southwestern flanks of Akhaura were exposed and the enemy rear was threatened. As a result, the enemy was forced to vacate Akhaura.

4TH Battalion, Brigade of Guards

Mian Bazaar, 1971 (East Pakistan).

7TH Cavalry squadron linked up with the 21ST Mountain Division on December $4^{TH.}$. The 1ST Squadron supported the 301ST Mountain Brigade's advance on the Lalgarh-Bangalmuri-Mian Bazar area. This was defended by elements of the 25TH Pakistani Field Force Regiment. When the infantry got delayed by the Pakistani defences at Lalgarh, 1ST Squadron was ordered to take Mian Bazar, which was held by a rifle company and the 25TH Frontier Force Headquarters. Despite shelling and direct fire from 500 meters, the Pakistani troops maintained their position. Then the 7TH Cavalry squadron rushed the defences at 1130 hours and by 1200 hours the Pakistanis had been overwhelmed. As a result of the squadron's actions, the Pakistanis retreated into a roadblock that had been set up by the 11TH Gurkhas, and surrendered.

7TH Cavalry has the rare distinction of being the only armoured regiment to have earned honours in two theatres - the Campaign honour ‘Punjab 1971’ and, of course, ‘East Pakistan 1971’.

7TH Cavalry

Chronology of Sikh Battle Honours (cont

Jammu and Kashmir, 1971. (Campaign Honour)

This Campaign Honour was awarded to all the regiments that had served in Jammu and Kashmir during 1971. On 3RD December the Pakistani Army launched a well-planned, massive attack directed at Chhamb and Punch in the hope of capturing large chunks of Jammu and Kashmir. The 26TH Indian Division cleared the Chicken's Neck salient east of Akhnur, thus safeguarding the rear of the Chhamb garrison. The Pakistani offensive in Punch was repulsed with heavy casualties. In the rest of Jammu and Kashmir, the Indian Army took the initiative and captured several dominating features to seal infiltration routes. In the Kargil sector, 15 enemy posts were captured.

5TH Battalion, The Sikh Regiment
5TH Battalion, The Sikh Regiment
18TH Battalion, Punjab Regiment
21ST Battalion, Punjab Regiment
9TH Battalion, Para (Commando)
72ND Armoured Regiment
Bengal Engineers
Bombay Engineers
7TH Battalion, Brigade of Guards
11TH Battalion, Brigade of Guards
12TH Battalion, Brigade of Guards

Chhamb, 1971 (Kashmir).

In the Jammu and Kashmir theatre, Pakistan had near parity with India in Armour and Artillery, while India had more infantry divisions. Pakistan's most successful thrust was in Chhamb where the 23RD Pakistani Division (along with two additional infantry brigades, one extra armoured brigade and Corps artillery units) under the able leadership of Major General Iftikhar Khan, completely overwhelmed the forward defensive positions of the Indian 10TH Division, commanded by Major General Jaswant Singh. Chhamb village was taken and the Pakistanis threatened to advance towards Jammu, the summer capital of the state of Jammu & Kashmir. Heavy fighting continued in this sector for a week until the indecisiveness of the Indian Divisional commander forced the Indian Corps Commander to intervene personally and launch heavy attacks to push the Pakistanis back to a non-threatening position.

72ND Armoured Regiment
151ST Air Defence Regiment

Shingo River Valley, 1971 (Kashmir).

This Battle Honour commemorates the ejection of the enemy and capture of the strategic army posts of Brachil Pass, Trishul feature, Wali, Hathi Matha, Malik, and Sherquila, thus gaining the command of both banks of River Shingo.

7TH Battalion, Brigade of Guards
871ST LT Regiment

Chronology of Sikh Battle Honours (cont

Defence of Punch, 1971 (Kashmir).

This Battle Honour commemorates the defence of Punch territory by the Indian Army. The Pakistani Army had occupied Thanpir, Chandak and Mandi. An Indian assault brigade ejected the enemy forces from Thanpir and Chandak and compelled them to withdraw from Mandi. 6TH Battalion, The Sikh Regiment, was in Punch and were holding piquet's 405 and 406, situated on hills northeast of the town. These piquets were key to the defence of Punch, as they dominated the town. The Pakistanis were also well aware that the success or failure of their plan to capture Punch depended on their ability to wrench control of the piquets from 6TH Sikhs. The Pakistanis gave the task of capturing the piquet's to 2ND POK Brigade composing 5TH Frontier Force Rifles, 7TH POK Battalion and 51ST Battalion, Punjab Regiment On the evening of 3RD December, the enemy subjected the piquets to heavy shelling and under this covering fire attacked with 5TH Frontier Force Rifles and 7TH POK Battalions. The Sikhs were ready for it, as they had shored up their defences and their machinegun fire, along with concentrated artillery fire, took a heavy toll of the enemy. The enemy then attacked the helipad, but was repulsed. On the 4TH morning they again shelled the Sikh positions and attacked with all the three battalions. Again the Indian artillery and the Sikh machine-guns took a heavy toll, but the enemy managed to capture the helipad. After this the enemy tried to establish a block between piquets 405 and 406 but the Sikhs did not allow this to happen. Throughout the day and night the enemy made repeated and determined attacks on piquets 405 and 406 but were repulsed, with heavy casualties. On 6TH December, 6TH Sikhs, following bitter fighting, evicted the Pakistanis from the helipad. After this the enemy made no major attack on the two piquets or Punch.

6TH Battalion, The Sikh Regiment
9TH Parachute Regiment

Nangi Tekri, 1971 (Kashmir).

This Battle Honour commemorates the capture of Nangi Tekri by the Indian Army. The Pakistanis were a strong presence in Nangi Tekri and other adjoining areas overlooking the Punch River. This made any Indian advance difficult. The 21ST Battalion, Punjab Regiment was given the daunting task of capturing the well-fortified position. On 10TH December, the Punjab Regiment began an attack on Nangi Tekri. There was heavy shelling from the Pakistani side. The assault almost failed. Many soldiers lost their lives. Undaunted the commanding officer continued the attack, remaining at the forefront and spurring his men into action. Inching their way through the enemy position, they finally beat the enemy in fierce hand-to-hand combat.

21ST Battalion, Punjab Regiment

Brachil Pass and **Wali Malik, 1971 (Kashmir).**

The Kargil sector in the north overlooks the critically vital Srinagar-Leh highway. In December 1971, the 21ST Battalion, Punjab Regiment, including Subedar Mohinder Singh, was deployed here to prevent Pakistani encroachments. Closeby lay the heavily fortified enemy position at Hathi Matha, from where, it was believed, further Pakistani offensives would commence. To prevent this, the 21ST Battalion, Punjab Regiment was asked to capture Brachil Pass, as it was an important vantage point. The attack commenced early on 7TH December and in a short while the Indians had reached the left shoulder of the pass. There they were held up by heavy enemy fire. Subedar Mohinder Singh, commanding a platoon, charged forward and engaged the enemy in close combat. His men, inspired by his daring, fought ferociously and forced the Pakistanis to retreat. This victory was a morale-booster and led to many other successes in this area. Subedar Singh was a worthy winner of the Mahavir Chakra bestowed upon him for his daring valour.

21ST Battalion, Punjab Regiment

Punjab, 1971 (India). (Campaign Honour)

This Campaign Honour was awarded to all of the regiments that had served in the Punjab during 1971. India's striking force of three infantry divisions, two armoured brigades, two independent artillery brigades and two engineer regiments fought local actions initiated by the enemy. The Theatre Honour 'Punjab 1971' covers fighting in both Pakistani and Indian Punjab.

2ND Battalion, The Sikh Regiment.
8TH Battalion, The Sikh Light Infantry
9TH Battalion, Punjab Regiment
15TH Battalion (Patiala), Punjab Regiment
22ND Battalion, Punjab Regiment

3RD Cavalry
4TH Horse
7TH Cavalry
Poona Horse
Scinde Horse

Lt. Gen. Niazi (right) signing the documents of surrender after the 1971 Indo-Pakistan war, December 16, 1971 to Lt. Gen. Jagjit Singh Arora.

Harar Kalan, 1971 (India).

Skinner's Horse moved to the Punjab theatre on October 16TH, 1971 as a part of 2ND Armoured Brigade, which was placed under HQ 39TH Infantry Division. 1ST Battalion, Dogra Regiment, supported by 'A' Squadron, launched an attack on Harar Kalan on December 8TH. Due to heavy resistance and well-coordinated defensive positions, the attack did not succeed. On the same day, the regiment was ordered to turn the flank of the enemy at Harar Kalan, Harar Khurd and Munian by breaching a lane in the defensive minefield at Shahbazpur. There were two routes to Shahbazpur. 'B' Squadron tried to make headway through the indirect route via Bhopalpur Majla. 'C' Squadron finally pushed through the other route and contacted the minefield at 4.25 am. A tank versus tank engagement took place in which three enemy tanks were destroyed. A minefield lane was created and a troop of 'C' Squadron was pushed through. Due to poor visibility, the tanks strayed and damaged their tracks. While the tanks were moving into the minefield lane, the regiment destroyed three more enemy tanks. The enemy withdrew at night and the villages of Khaira and Shahbazpur were cleared. The next day the regiment consolidated its position and 'A' Squadron destroyed three enemy tanks. The squadron relentlessly pressed on and cleared Harar Khurd of the enemy. Harar Kalan was finally captured by dusk on December 10TH.

1ST Horse (Skinner's Horse)
101ST Field Regiment

Basmantar River, 1971 (Punjab).

This Battle Honour commemorates the battle of Basantar River. Invading Shakargarh bulge was one of the most crucial components of Pakistan's war strategy in the western sector. Pakistan hoped that by occupying the bulge, the main link between Indian Army positions in Kashmir and Pathankot would be cut-off, following which, it could easily invade Jammu and Kashmir. Pakistani military forces stationed in Sialkot base would keep Pathankot at bay, thwarting any Indian attempts to recapture Shakargarh. However, Pakistan's battle plans were jeopardized because of the ingenuity of a bold attack by the Indians. The Indian Army attacked Pakistani positions in the region within four days of the declaration of the state of war, catching the Pakistanis by complete surprise. After a few days of intense fighting, the Indians had not only pushed the Pakistanis back, but had also come close to capturing Sialkot. This was not only the biggest tank battle of the 1971 conflict and the biggest battle in the Western Theatre, but also the only battle for which all the four arms were honoured for the first time in the history of the Indian Army.

Poona Horse
4TH Horse
161ST Field Regiment
75TH Medium Regiment

Chronology of Sikh Battle Honours (cont.)

Fatehpur, 1971 (India).

11TH December 1971, is a red letter day in the history of 8TH Battalion, The Sikh Light Infantry. Pak Fatehpur post, fortified on all four sides with high bunds, was a virtual fortress with innumerable automatic and anti-tank weapons deployed for its defence. Its diamond-like shape made it equally difficult to tackle from all sides. On the night of 11TH December, the men of 8TH Sikh Light Infantry discounted all difficulties and rushed forward on to this coveted objective, in the face of deadly small arms fire and devastating artillery shelling. Many a gallant soldier fell but others moved on undaunted. Before long the enemy was either destroyed or in desperate flight, leaving behind a large quantity of arms and ammunition. Apparently, the enemy had not accepted final defeat yet. He continued to plaster this position with accurate artillery and mortar fire from several directions. Two counter attacks attempted by the previously fleeing soldiers were disorganized and defeated. In this battle, three officers, one JCO and 32 other ranks sacrificed their lives and approximately 100 others were wounded. A young battalion, within five years of its raising, had fought its maiden battle in masterly style and had come of age. The number of officers killed and wounded is tribute to the quality of leadership provided by them.

8TH Battalion, The Sikh Light Infantry

Longanwala, 1971 (India).

The Battle of Longewala, (December 4^{TH,} 1971 - December 5TH, 1971) was one of the first major engagements in the Western Sector during the Indo-Pakistani War of 1971, fought between assaulting Pakistani forces and Indian defenders at the Indian border post of Longewala, in the Thar Desert of the Rajasthan state in India. The Indian infantry company was left with the choice of either attempting to hold out until reinforced, or fleeing on foot from a mechanised Pakistani infantry force. They chose the former. The isolated company kept the enemy at bay with heavy fire from machine-guns and two recoilless guns, which had been rushed in by the battalion commander. The company officer commanding ensured that all his assets were correctly employed and made the most use of a strong defensive position and weaknesses created by errors in enemy tactics. The Air Force was called in and shot up 17 tanks and 23 other vehicles. "All through the operations the Major kept up his men's morale, moving from bunker to bunker, urging them to hold on and fight back. His dynamic leadership and gallantry won Major Kuldip Singh the Mahavir Chakra".

23RD Battalion, Punjab Regiment
168TH Field Regiment

Parbat Ali, 1971 (India).

A Battalion of The Sikh Regiment carved a niche for itself during the Indo-Pak conflict of 1971, when it captured a well-fortified feature called 'Parbat Ali', approximately 65 kms deep inside Pakistani territory in the Barmer Sector. The Regiment was asked to spearhead the advance on a bridge along the Munabag-Gari-Khokhrapar-Naya Chor axis. It captured the enemy post 'Bop Gazi' on December 5TH, followed by another feature on the night of December 10TH - 11TH on its way to the town of Naya Chor. Between this enemy position and the township of Naya Chor stood the mighty Parbat Ali, held by the Pakistani 21ST Frontier Force Regiment and heavily fortified with bunkers and a high-density mine field. The battalion launched its attack on the night of December 12TH - 13TH simultaneously with two other companies, and had captured its objective by 4:30 am. As the third company began to attack the feature, it collided with the enemy's counter-attack force, which fled in disorder. Due to the strategic domination of the feature, the enemy launched two more fierce counter-attacks, which were successfully repulsed by the Sikhs. For this unparalleled bravery and valour, the battalion was awarded six Vir Chakras, three Sena Medals, one Vishisht Sewa Medal, and six Mention-in-Dispatches.

10TH Battalion, The Sikh Regiment
10TH Battalion, The Sikh Light Infantry
68TH Field Regiment
164TH Field Regiment

THE SIACHEN CONFLICT, 1984.

The Siachen Conflict sometimes referred to, as The Siachen War is a military conflict between India and Pakistan over the disputed Siachen Glacier region in Kashmir. India launched Operation Meghdoot on 13TH April 1984 when the Indian Army and the Indian Air Force went into the glacier region. Pakistan quickly responded with troop deployments and what followed was literally a race to the top. Within a few days, the Indians were in control of the area, as Pakistan was beaten to the Saltoro Ridge high ground by about a week. The two northern passes - Sia La and Bilafond La - were quickly secured by India. The contentious area is about 900 square miles (2,300 km2) to nearly 1,000 square miles (2,600 km2). Since 1984 Pakistan has launched several attempts to displace the Indian forces, but with little success. The most well known was in 1987, when an attempt was made by Pakistan to dislodge India from the area. The attack was masterminded by Pervez Musharraf (later President of Pakistan) heading a newly raised elite SSG commando unit, raised with United States Special Operations Forces help in the area. A special garrison with eight thousand troops was built at Khapalu. The immediate aim was to capture Bilafond La but after bitter fighting that included hand to hand combat, the Pakistanis were thrown back and the positions remained the same. The only Param Vir Chakra - India's highest gallantry award - to be awarded for combat in the Siachen area went to Naib Subedar Bana Singh (retired as Subedar Major/Honorary Captain), who in a daring daylight raid assaulted and captured a Pakistani post atop a 22,000 foot (6,700 m) peak, now named Bana Post. A cease-fire went into effect in 2003. Even before then, every year more soldiers were killed due to of severe weather rather than enemy firing. By 2003 the two sides had lost an estimated 2,000 personnel primarily due to frostbite, avalanches and other complications. Together, the nations have about 150 manned outposts along the glacier, with some 3,000 troops each. India has built the world's highest helipad on this glacier at a place called Sonam, which is at 21,000 feet (6,400 m) above the sea level, to serve the area. India also installed the world's highest telephone booth on the glacier.

A Sikh Soldier at Siachen war memorial

THE KARGIL WAR, 1999.

The Kargil War, also known as the Kargil conflict, was an armed conflict between India and Pakistan that took place between May and July 1999 in the Kargil district of Kashmir. The cause of the war was the infiltration of Pakistani soldiers and Kashmiri militants into positions on the Indian side of the Line of Control (LOC), which serves as the de facto border between the two states. The Indian Army, supported by the Indian Air Force, attacked the Pakistani positions and, with international diplomatic support, eventually forced withdrawal of the Pakistani forces across the LOC.

During the Kargil Conflict of 1999, two battalions, 8TH Battalion, Sikh Regiment and 14TH Battalion, Sikh Regiment were inducted into operations. 8TH Sikh was tasked to capture Tiger Hill. By 21ST May, the 8TH Sikh had isolated Tiger Hill from three directions, east, north and south. In order to inflict casualties, the enemy positions on Tiger Hill were subjected to artillery and mortar fire. On the night of 5TH July a group of 8TH Sikh comprising of 2 officers, 4 JCO's and 52 OR's, under heavy rain and fog, attacked and captured the Pakistani positions on the western spur. The enemy made a number of attempts to dislodge the Sikhs from these positions but failed to do so. Among the group of Sikh soldiers who attacked the western spur, both officers were injured and three out of the four JCO's were killed. The 14TH Sikh was air lifted to Leh from New Delhi on May 2ND, where they secured the Handangbrok heights in the Chorbatla area. They also captured points 5620, 5512, 5232, 5310 and 6041. Naik Subadar Jasbir Singh established a section post at a height of approx. 19,000 ft. This secured the eastern flank of Chorbatla.

The Chief of Army Staff (COAS) made a special instant award of "Unit Citation" to 8TH Battalion, The Sikh Regiment for their meritorious and gallant performance during the isolation of Tiger Hill, which facilitated the capture of Tiger Hill top, and battles of Helmet and India Gate (features to the West of Tiger Hill top), on the night of 7TH - 8TH July 1999, in Dras Sector.

India has signalled its desire to end its nearly 20-year-old military standoff with Pakistan on the forbidding Siachen glacier, with Prime Minister Manmohan Singh making it clear the time has come to consider options to demilitarise the world's highest battlefield. In fact, Manmohan Singh, who visited Siachen, became not only the first Prime Minister to go there but also to publicly speak about the need to end the deployment of troops on the 76-km glacier where temperatures can dip as low as minus 70 degrees Celsius. "The time has now come for us to try and transform this battlefield into a peace mountain," he told troops at Partapur, the Indian Army's base camp for operations on Siachen.

ABOUT THIS BOOK

In the British Army the medieval Standards, their rallying point on the battlefield, developed into Regimental Colours. As time passed the regiments were awarded Battle Honours, an official acknowledgement of their achievements in specific wars or operations of a military campaign. They are usually presented in the form of a name of a country, a region or a city where the regiment's distinguished act took place, together with the year when it occurred.

These Battle Honours can normally be found engraved, painted or embroidered on the Regimental Colours, which became the heart of the regiment, in which all of its history was woven.

The Sikh soldier has earned a galaxy of Battle Honours in his long service in all the arms of the British Indian Army, and the Indian Army since the Independence. This is a complete collection of the Regimental Battle Honours won by the Sikh soldier.

The front cover has two examples of historic Regimental Colours, showing their Battle Honours of the time. The Ferozepore Sikhs displayed Honours for Lucknow, Afghanistan 1878–79, Ali Masjid, Defence of Chitral and China 1900. The Ludhaiana Sikhs displayed Honours for China 60–62, Ahmad Khel, Kandahar 80 and Afghanistan 1878–80. The centre panel has Honours for the Anglo-Sikh Wars. The back cover has just some of the Battle Honours won by the Sikh soldier.

Narindar Singh Dhesi was born in 1940 at Eldoret in Kenya, where his father, Waryam Singh, an Akali freedom fighter, had migrated from the Punjab. He moved to England in 1957 and joined the British Army. After leaving the armed forces in 1964 he went into the building and construction industry. He is married with four children and is living in retirement at Southend on Sea, England.

A companion volume by the same author, *Sikh Soldier Gallantry Awards* is also available.

www.ingramcontent.com/pod-product-compliance
Lightning Source LLC
Chambersburg PA
CBHW081204170426
43197CB00018B/2916

* 9 7 8 1 8 4 5 7 4 8 9 1 3 *